Things Change

a reflection on the 70s, now and tomorrow thru images of Boston

Alanna Reilly
Gerald Reilly

The Raleigh Press, Publisher

To Kathy, for giving us the opportunity.

The Raleigh Press
Falmouth, Massachusetts

publisher@theraleighpress.com

ISBN: 978-0-9892753-0-9

Printed in USA

CONTENTS

The book is set up as one might walk, albeit erratically, from The Fens through the city to the North End. The table of contents refers in a general way to sections of downtown.

INTRODUCTION

Time is constant. Yet, it can pass in a flash, or seem endless. A span of forty years is geologically infinitesimal but, in human terms, it is generational. In a city, it can be transformative.

In the wider society, the past forty years have brought incredible changes in culture and technology. Cousin Eddie films your same sex marriage on his smartphone and catches your new mother-in-law, in the bushes, puffing a medi-blunt with your ex. Eddie immediately posts the video online.

Embarrassing? Maybe. But conceivable. Not in 1972.

This book contains photographs of Boston forty years ago and the same situations recreated from similar angles today. The black and white photographs were taken by me with a 35 mm Minolta SR-1 camera when I was twenty-something and living in Boston in the early seventies. The color pictures were taken by my twenty-something daughter, Alanna, while living in Boston and using the camera in her Apple iPhone 4s.

The iPhone camera has few adjustable settings but it does have an 8 mega pixel lens and takes decent color. The lens tends to skew some images, but not disagreeably. We accepted this and worked with it. However, trying to replicate identical shots from these two different cameras was not practical.

The color in the iPhone images was edited in Adobe Camera Raw. The editing process causes some lines to blur which creates an imaginative effect that emphasizes the brevity of the time span and the incredible, but so near, promise of tomorrow. No other editing was done.

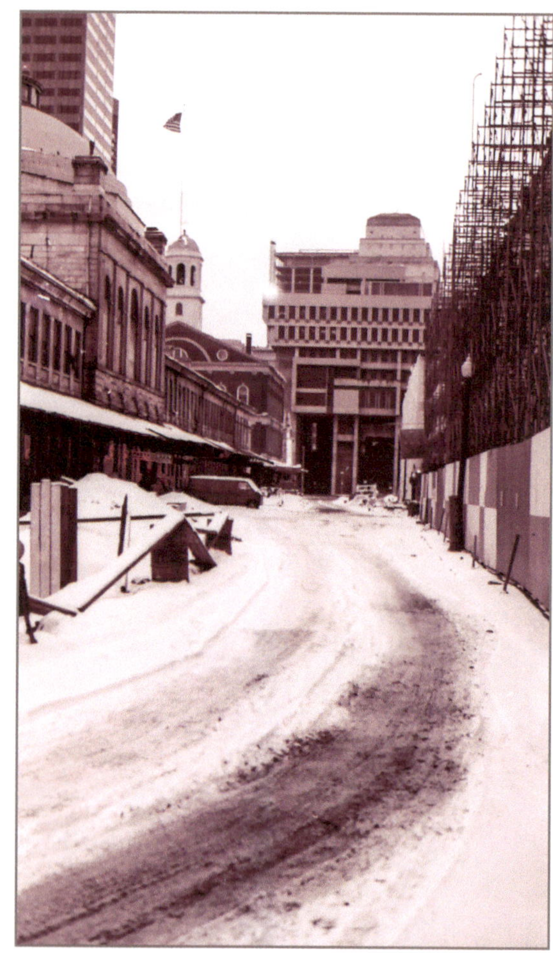

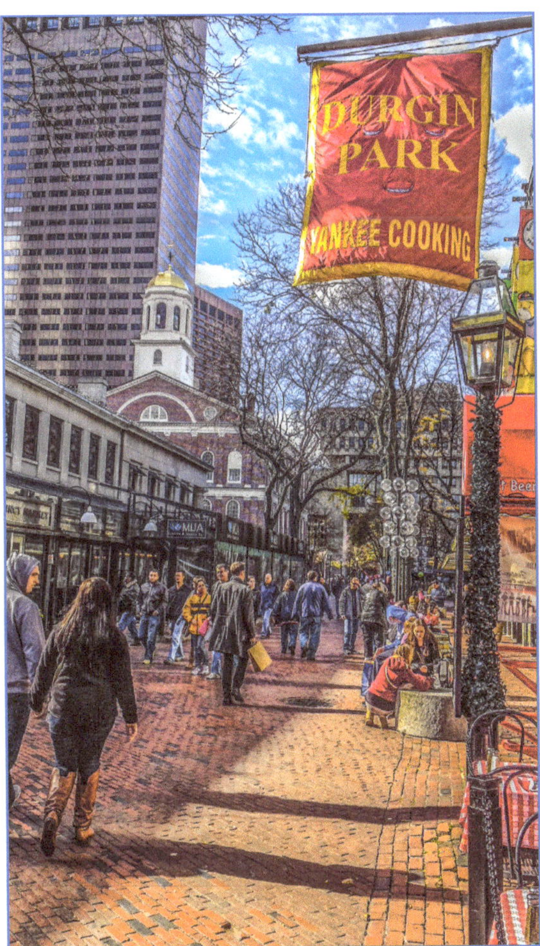

The pictures record changes in architecture and buildings in Boston, as well as scenes that appear not to have changed. All this can easily be photographed, cataloged and described in terms of bricks, concrete, steel and glass.

But, the book is also an attempt to highlight other important and dramatic changes that have happened, and are happening now in the digitized, multicultural, oil-fueled world that we share. These changes are extraordinary and they affect each of our lives.

Technology advances are astounding. Flat screen tv's no longer impress. Tablets and smart phones are not old enough to go to kindergarten yet but we can't remember not having them and we can't live without them. And changes that are even more exciting are just around the corner.

Genetic medicine, nanotechnology, 3D printers, e-publishing and online education are getting ready to really rock our world. We spotlight some of these important products and ventures and consider their hope and promise for tomorrow.

All of the research for this self-published book was done online in the new world of information that is available to anyone and growing everyday. The book is laid out as a person might walk from the Fens to Copley Square and then downtown to Faneuil Hall and Quincy Market, the Waterfront and the North End.

Things Change is not a comprehensive history or an in depth analysis. It is an anecdotal document of changes in Boston, and the larger society, in the past forty years and a look at new ideas that will impact the future.

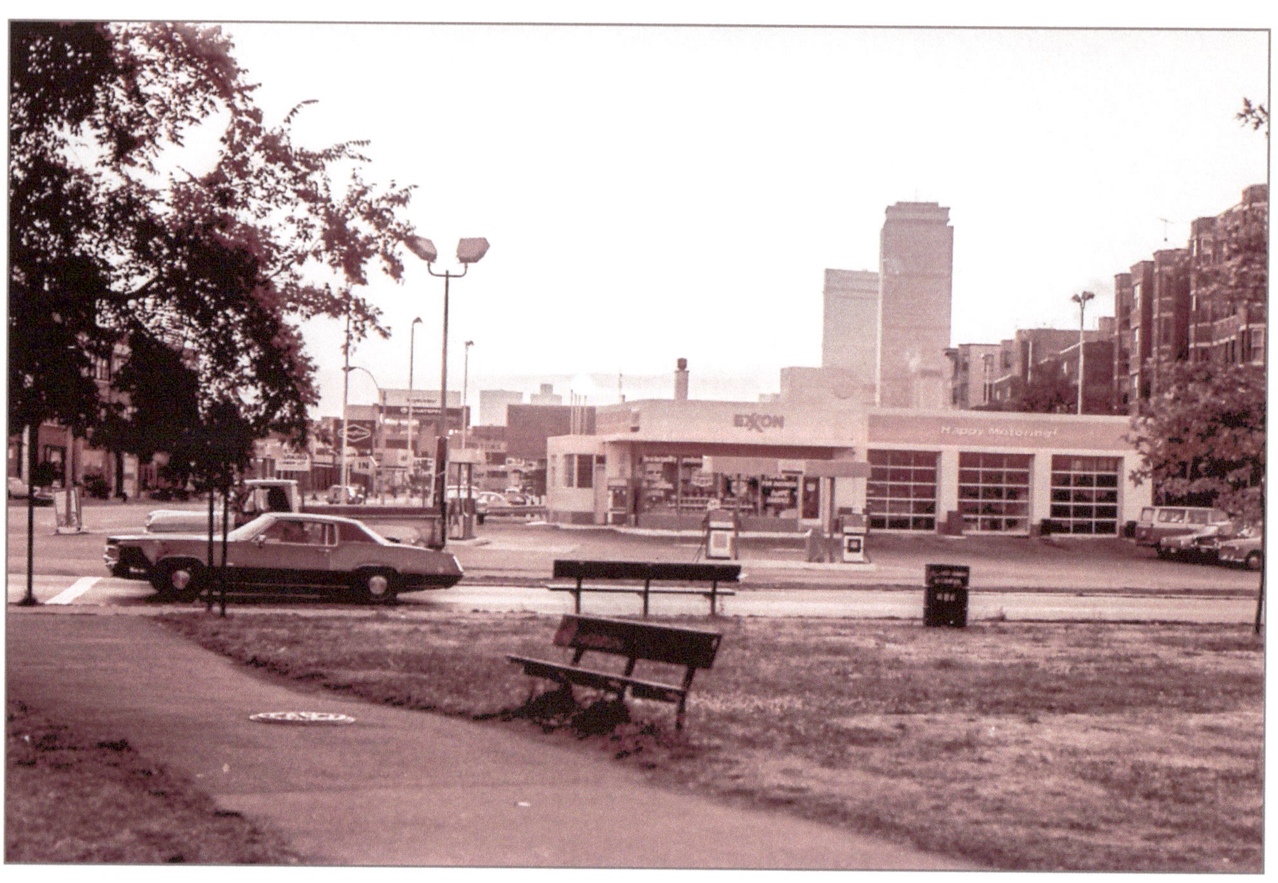
EXXON
Happy Motoring!

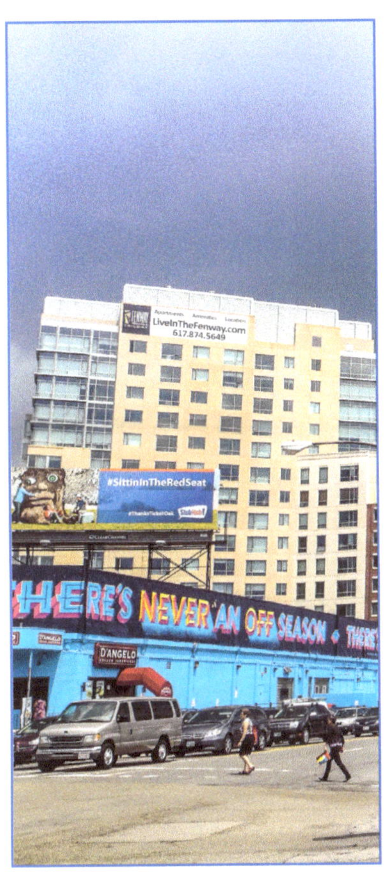

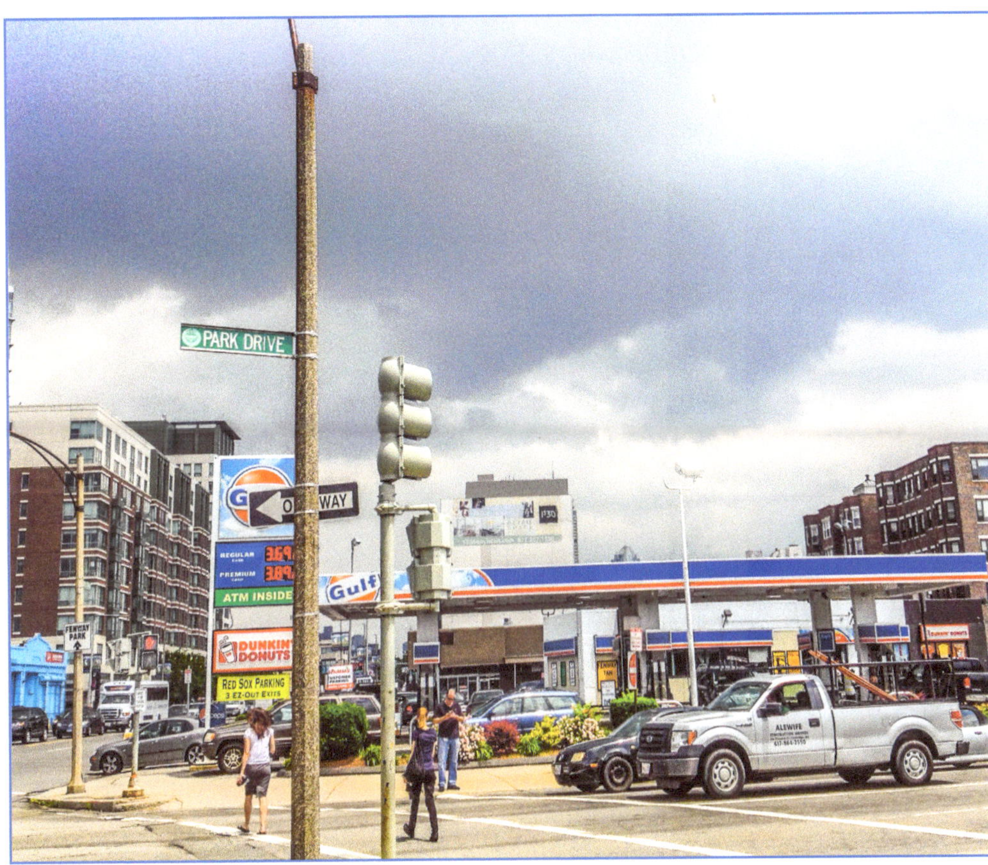

Boylston Street from Park Drive to the Fens is rapidly changing. Recently completed developments are thriving. And major new projects are either coming out of the ground or maneuvering through the approval process.

Above, the view of the Pru is blocked by new construction.

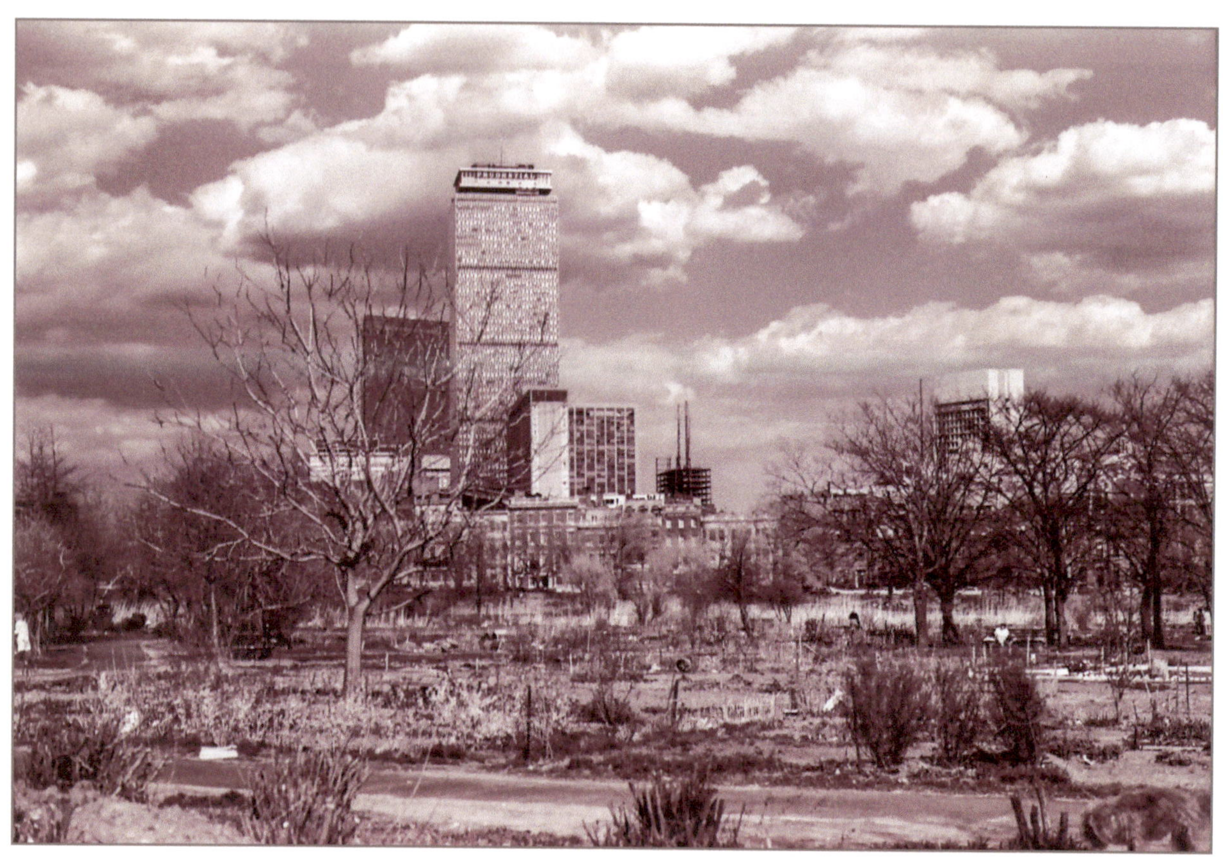

The Pru stands tall across
the Fens while, at right,
the vicissitudes of forty
summers impede the view.

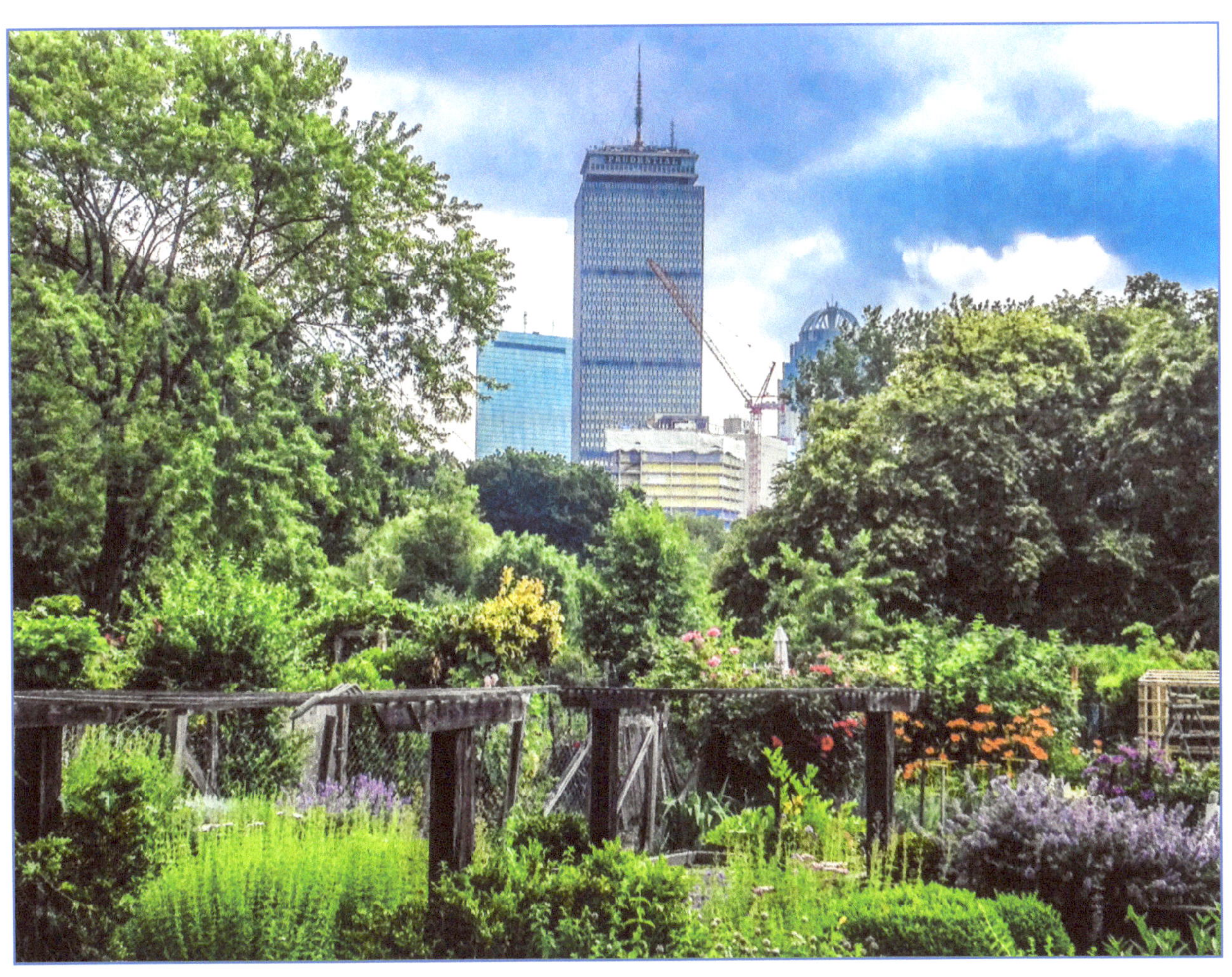

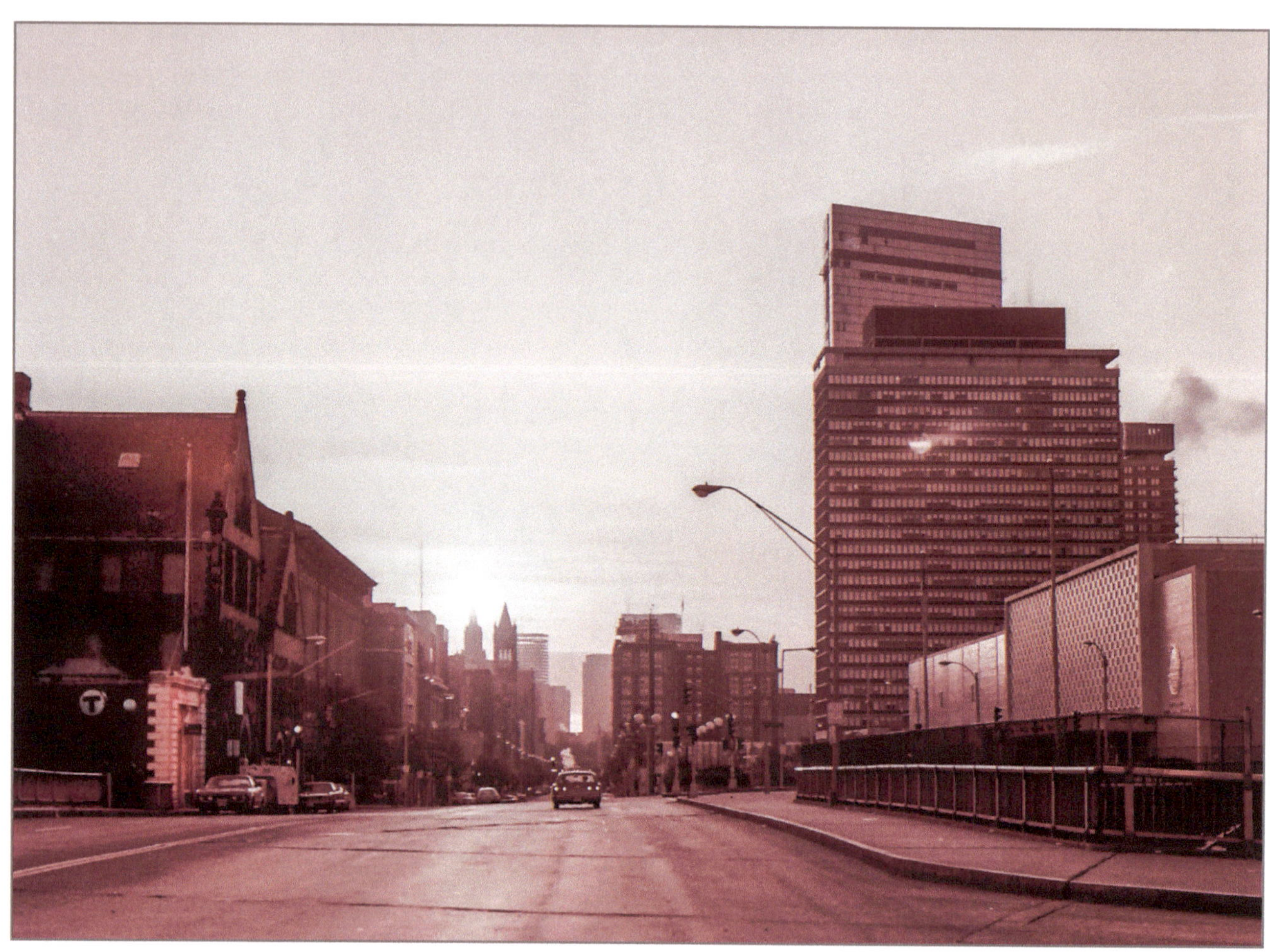

Boylston Street

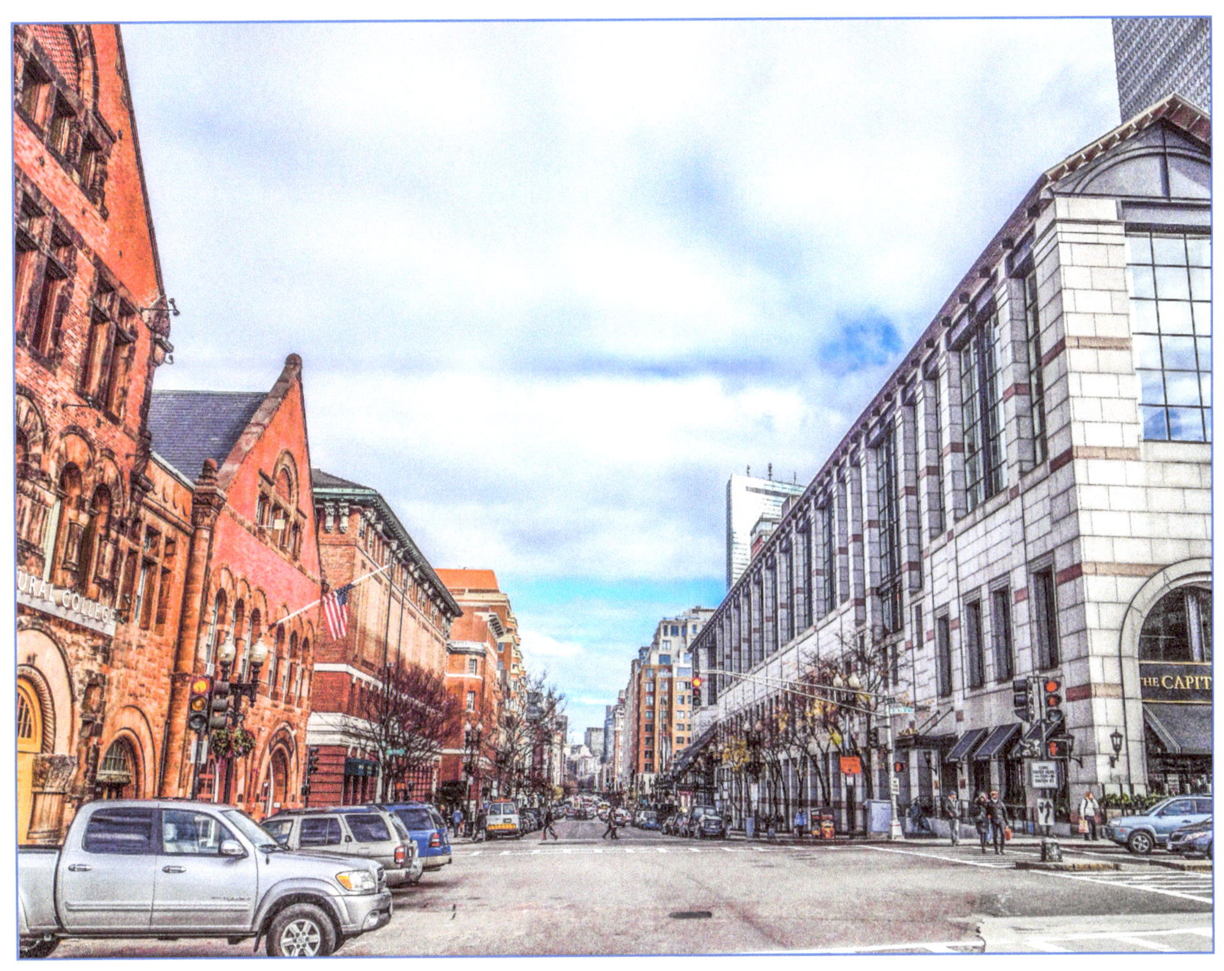
THE CAPIT

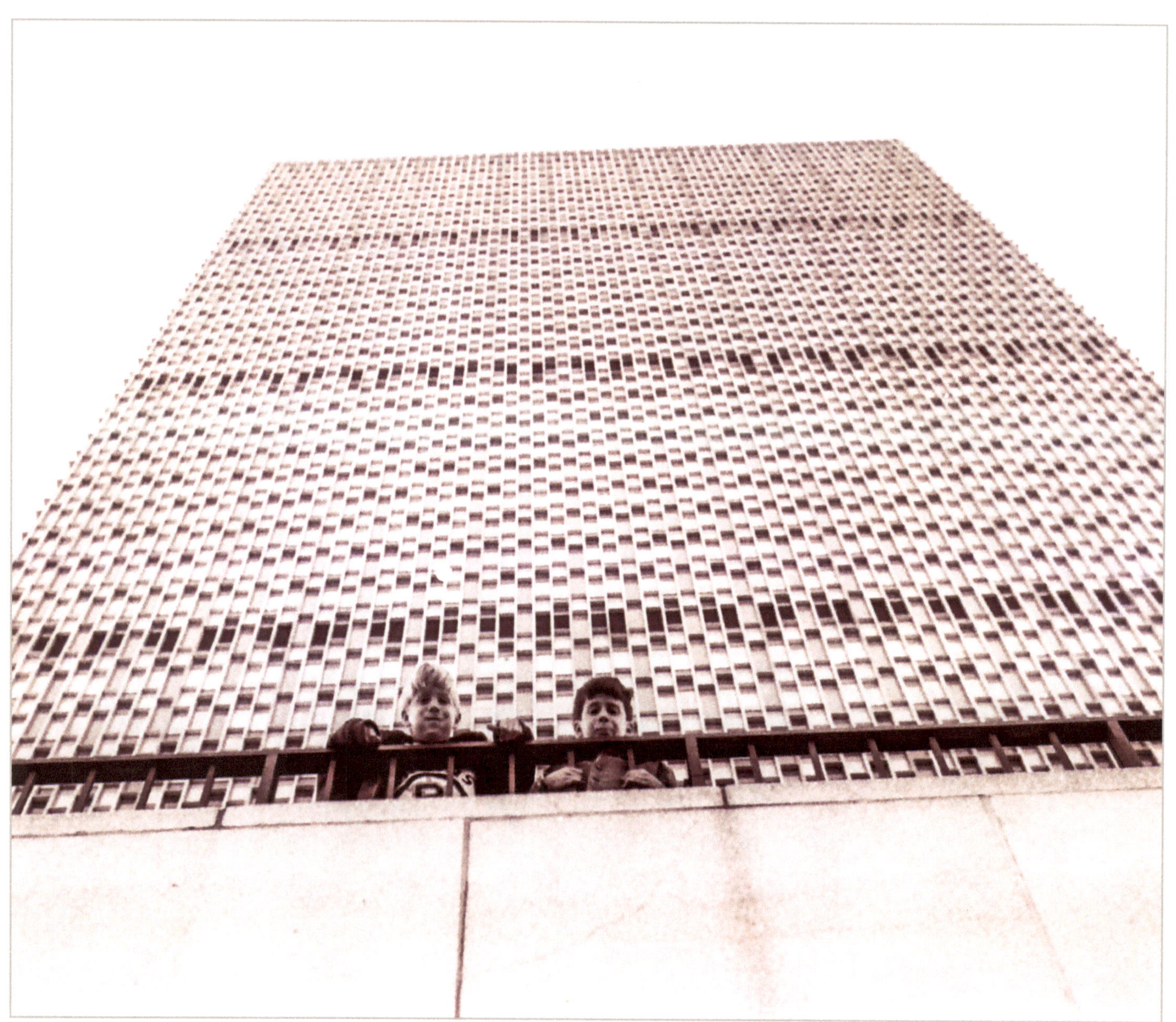

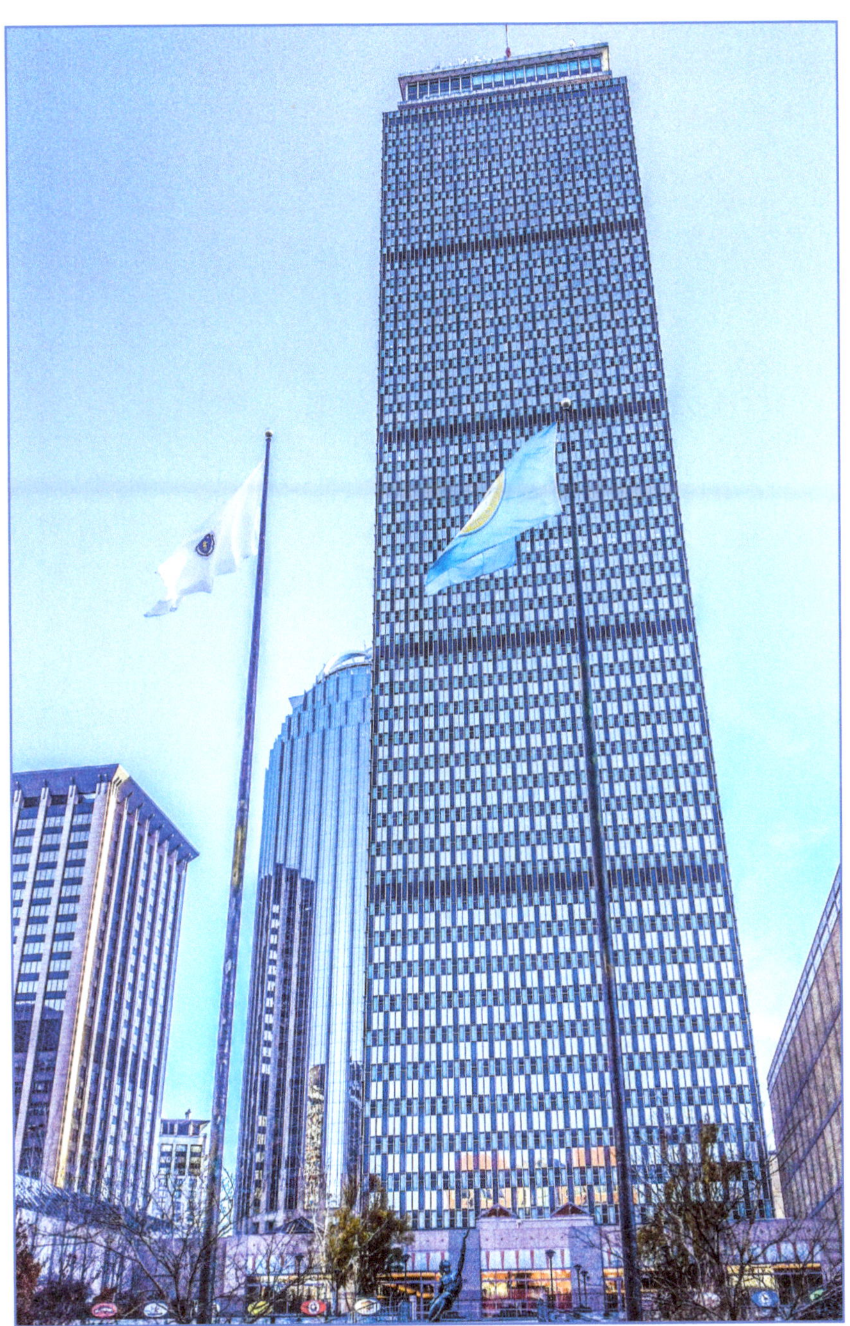

At the Prudential Center, 52 floors of offices, and the first tower of the new Sheraton Boston Hotel, were buzzing. Retailers did brisk business on the covered, sunless, open-air plaza opposite the moat that surrounded the tower. Shopping convenience depended on the direction of the wind.

Busy stores on the plaza were the dry cleaner, the store selling film and greeting cards and the stationery store, which stocked plenty of carbon paper.

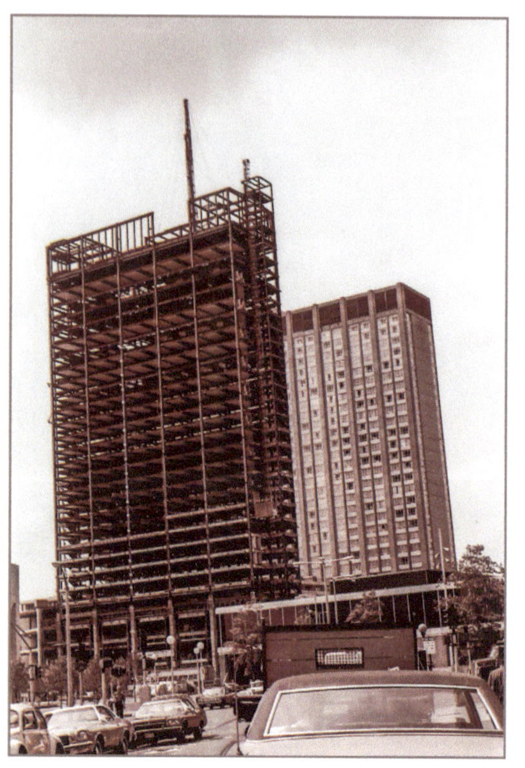

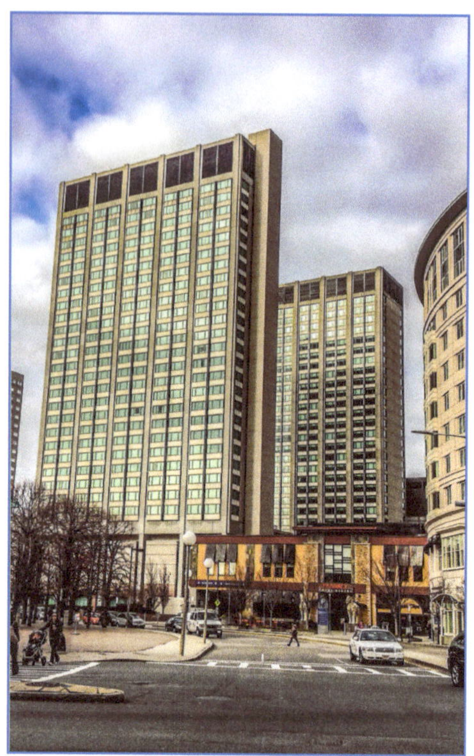

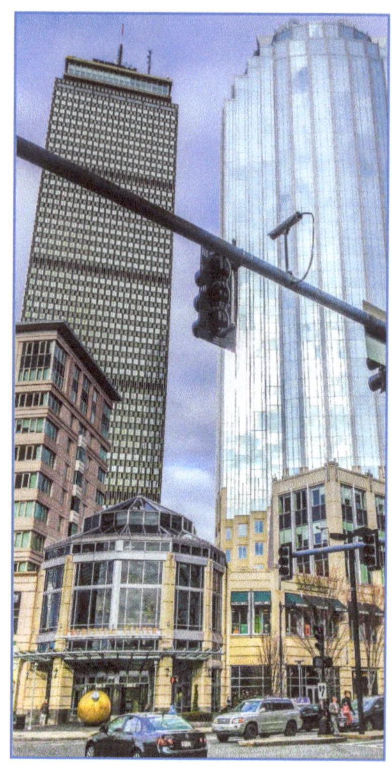

Video surveillance has exploded since New York City introduced cctv cameras in Times Square in 1973. Millions of these cameras now prevent and solve crime, by watching us 24/7.

They also produce real revenue for cities, and lawyers, across the country by issuing tickets for speeding or running a red light, with no police present.

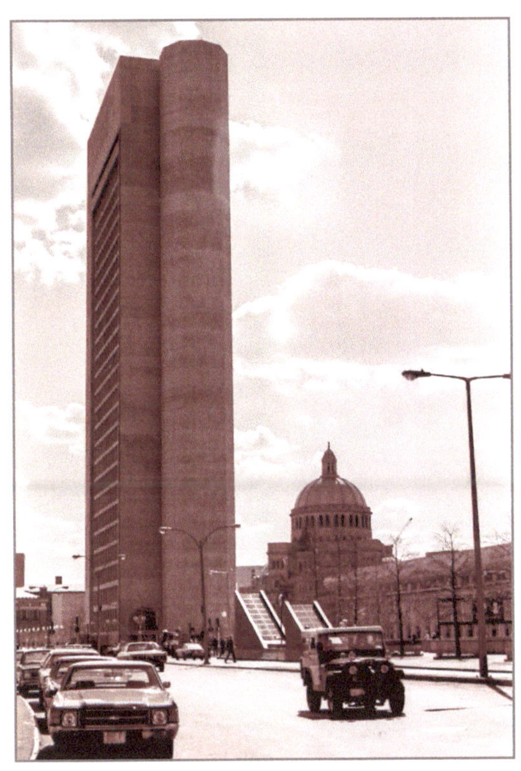

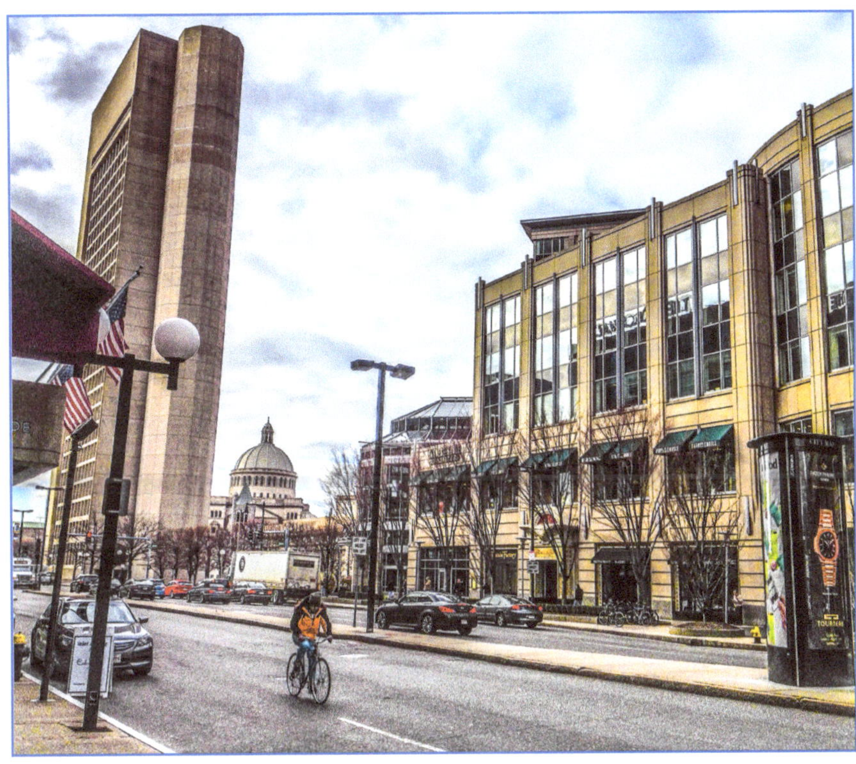

Above, The Mother Church, The First Church of Christ, Scientist, is pictured just past the Prudential Center on Huntington Avenue.

At far left, the second tower of the Sheraton Boston Hotel is under construction.

Windows started popping out of the John Hancock building before it was finished. The first was a fluke. The next was a problem. Then it started raining windows. Streets were closed off and wind tunnels were constructed at MIT.

A pause of concern tarnished the optimism that the beautiful blue glass building had brought to the Back Bay. Plywood temporarily replaced enthusiasm.

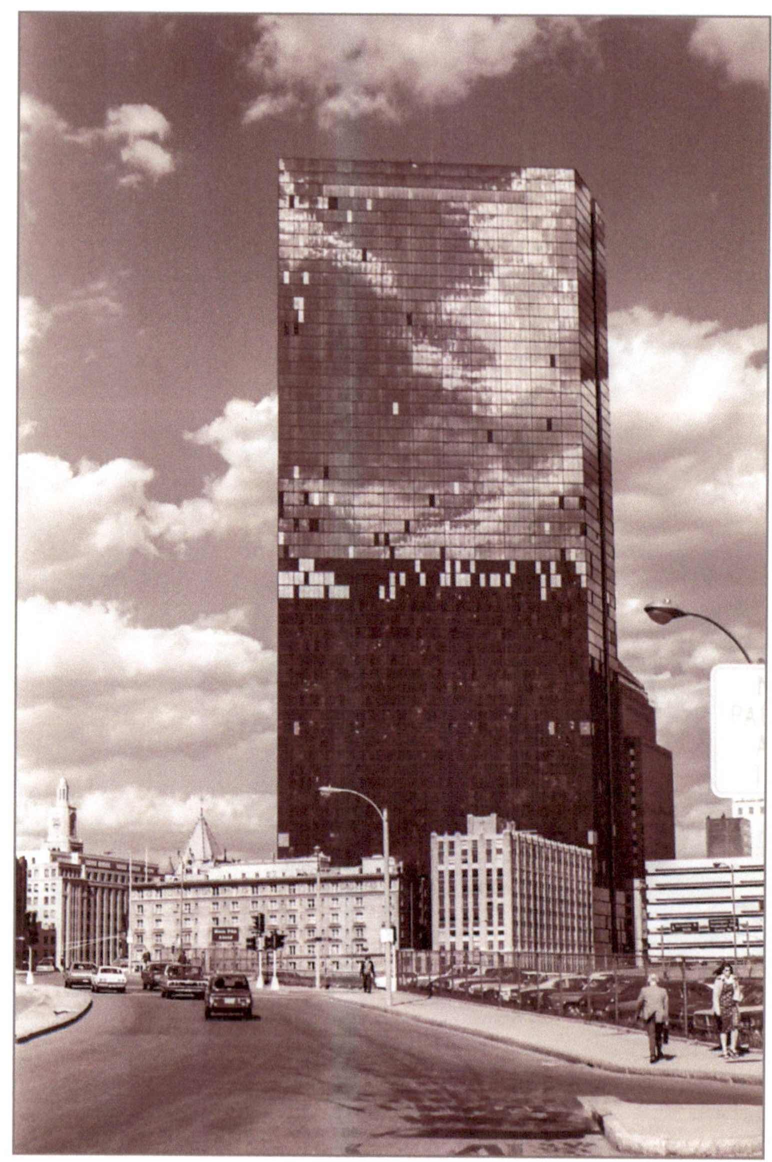

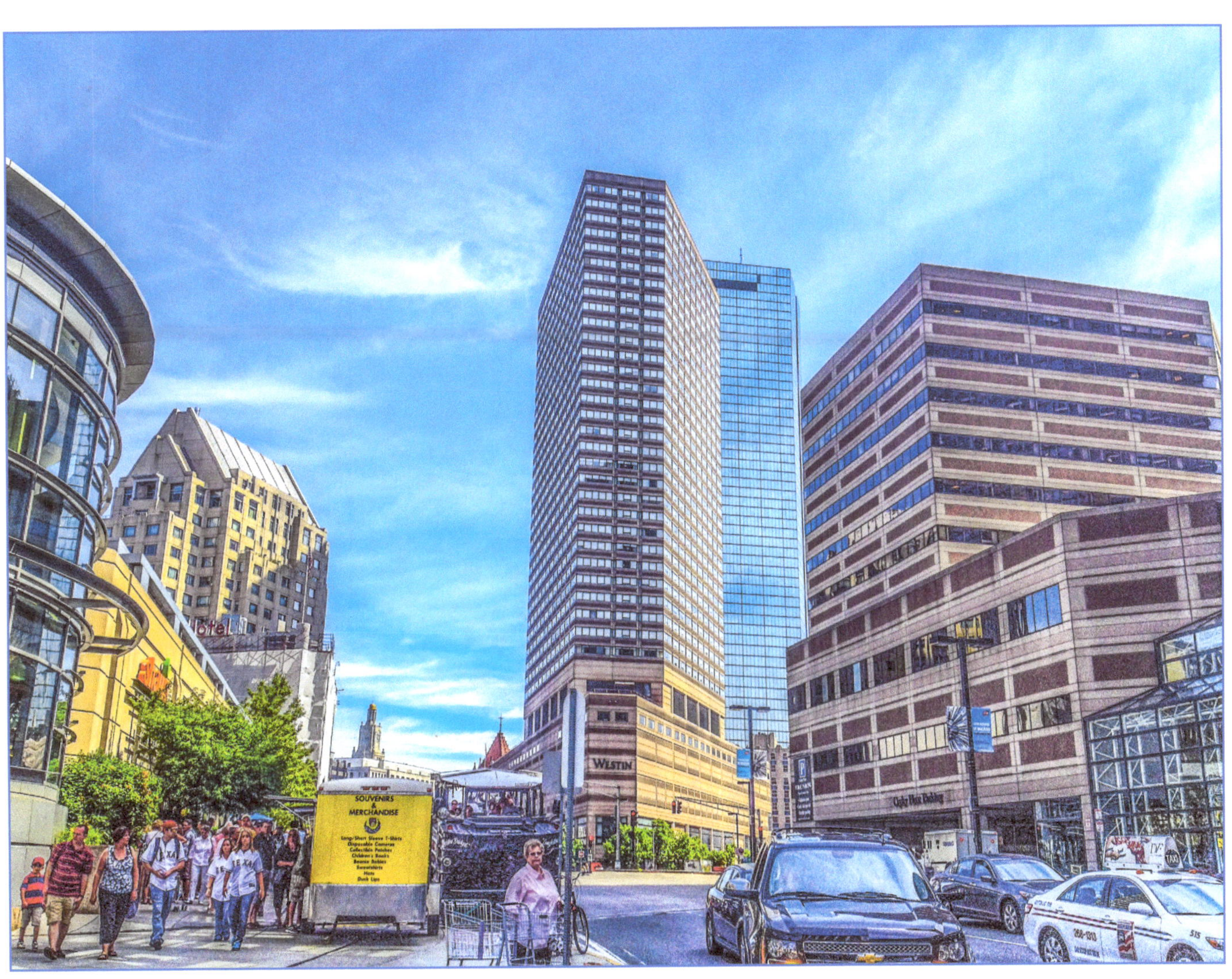
SOUVENIRS
&
MERCHANDISE
WESTIN
TAXI

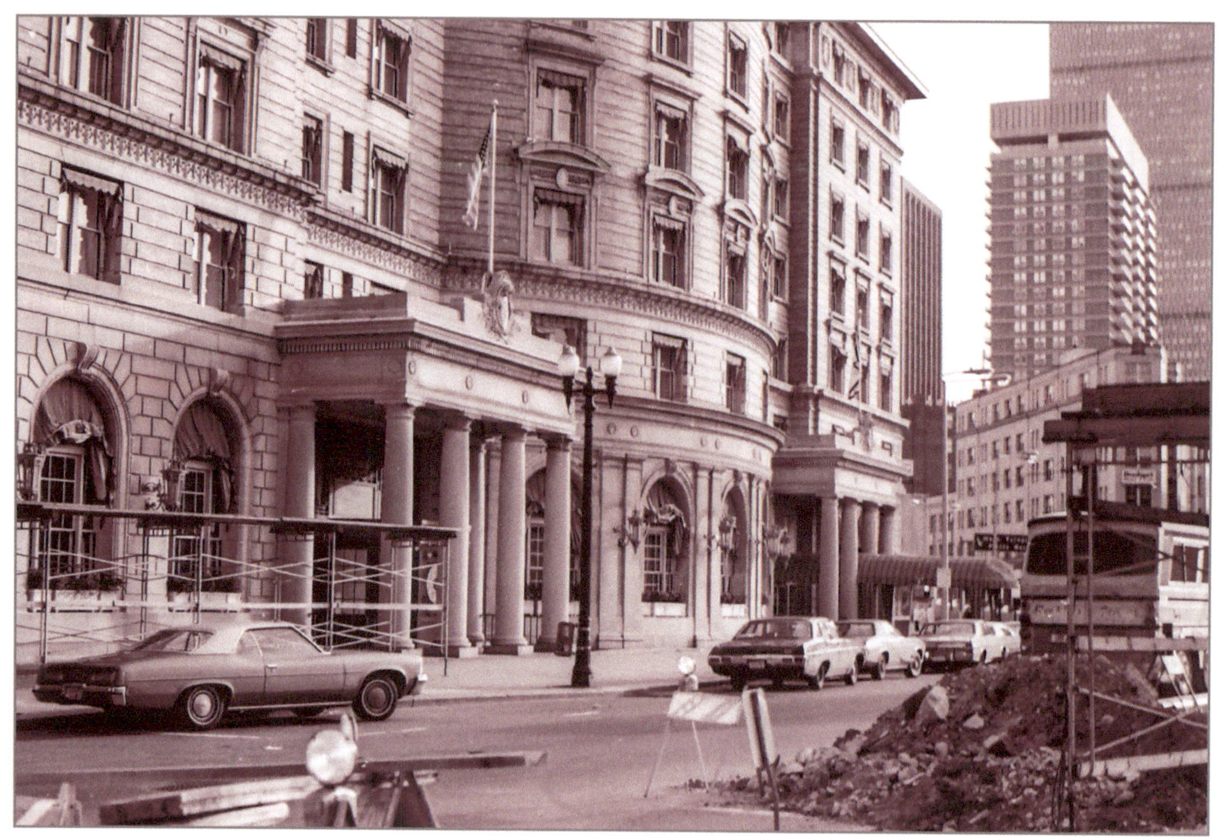

Copley Plaza Hotel

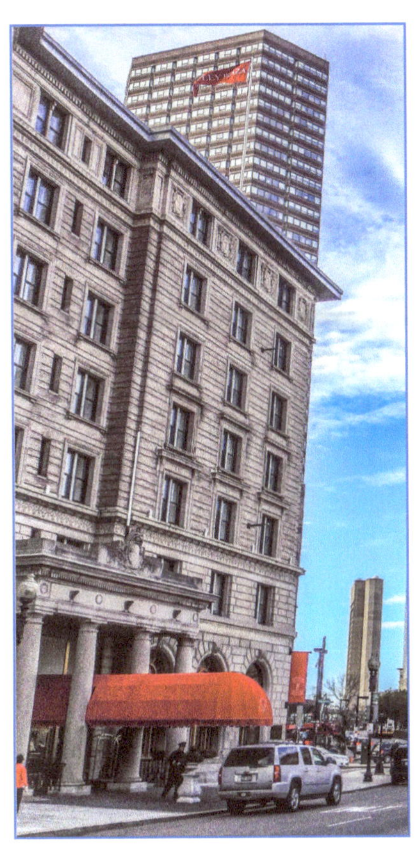

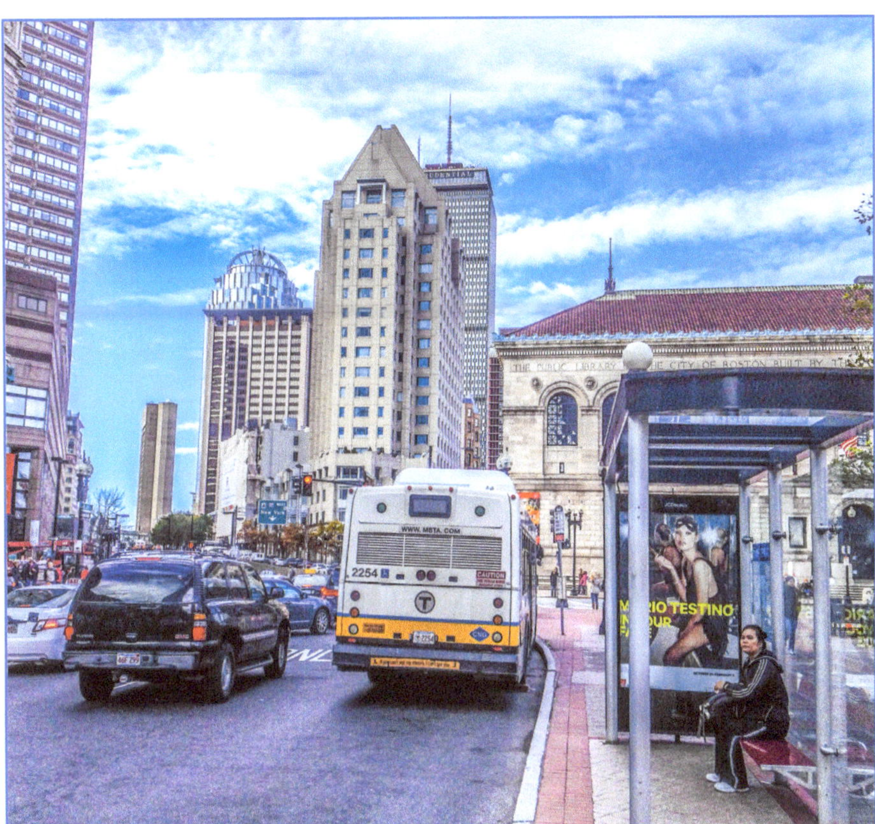
WWW.MBTA.COM
2254
CAUTION

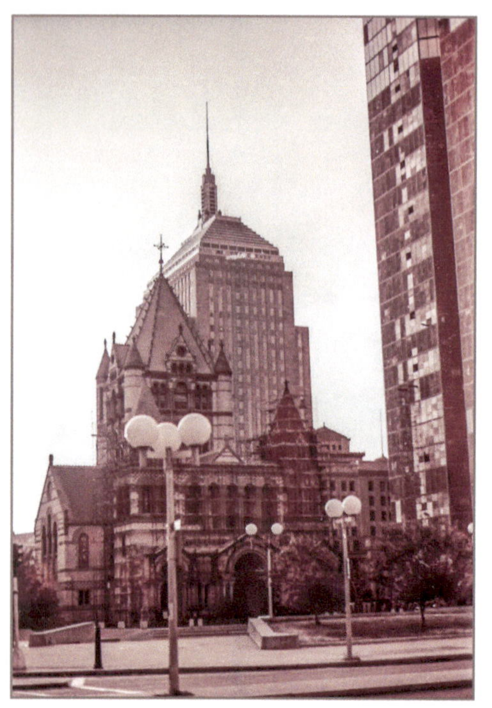

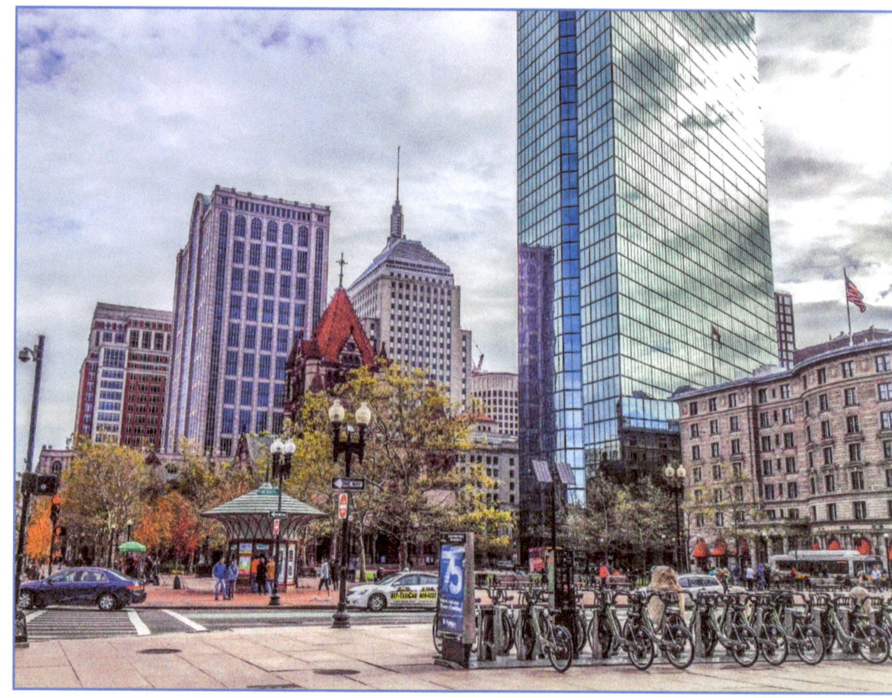

Copley Square was redesigned in the late sixties and in 1969 it was sunken and cemented. At that time, the Boston Redevelopment Authority's design process did not provide for public input.

It soon had the feel of a prison yard. What had been designed to offer a respite from the noise of street life became a haven for the unseemly.

Although, in fairness to the planners, the characters that made the new square unwelcoming were not part of the scene when the project was developed. Drugs and skateboards were just coming into vogue.

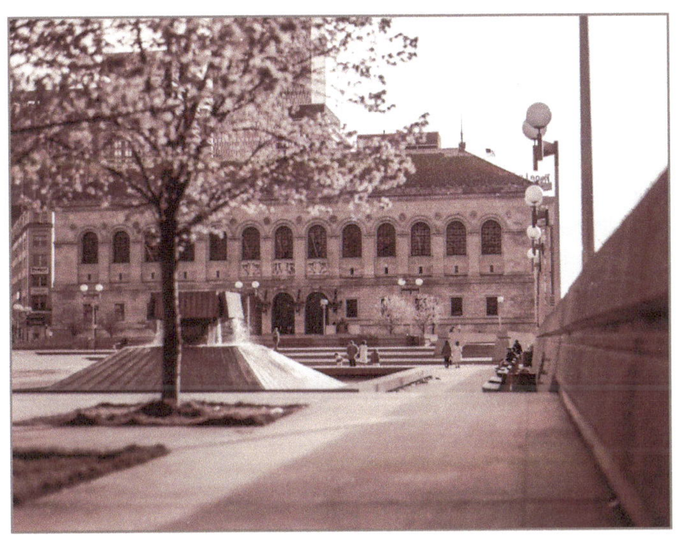

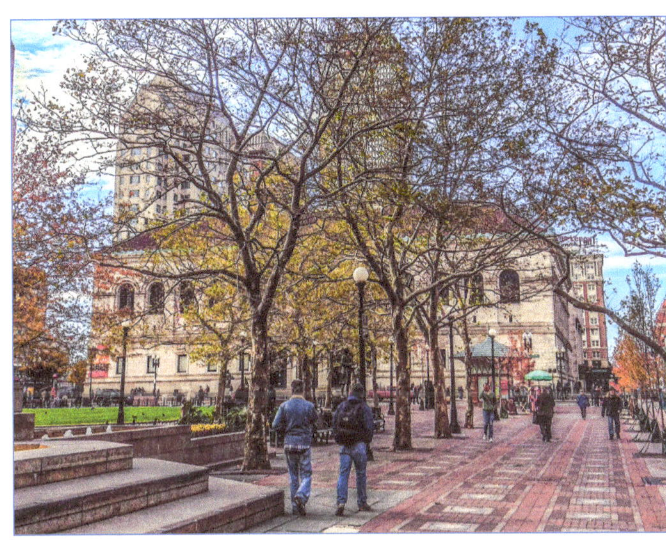

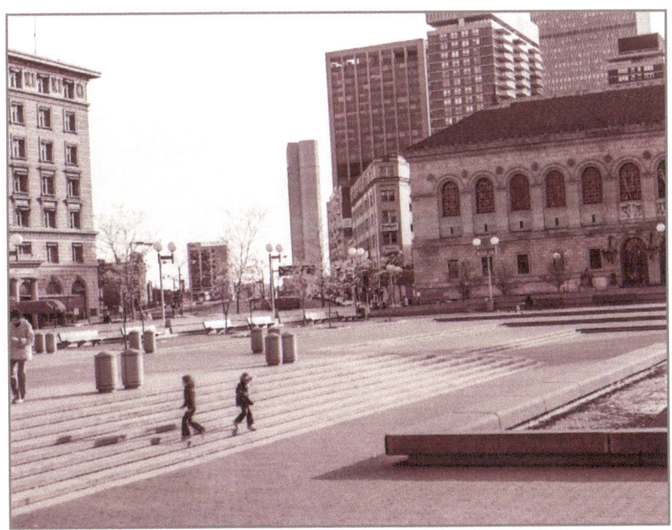

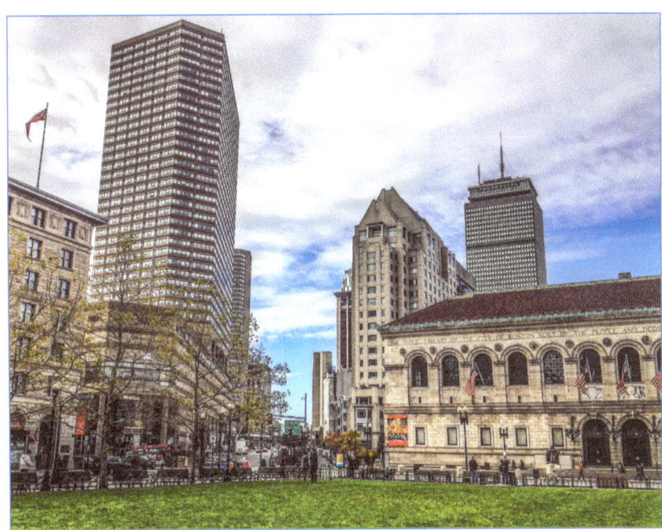

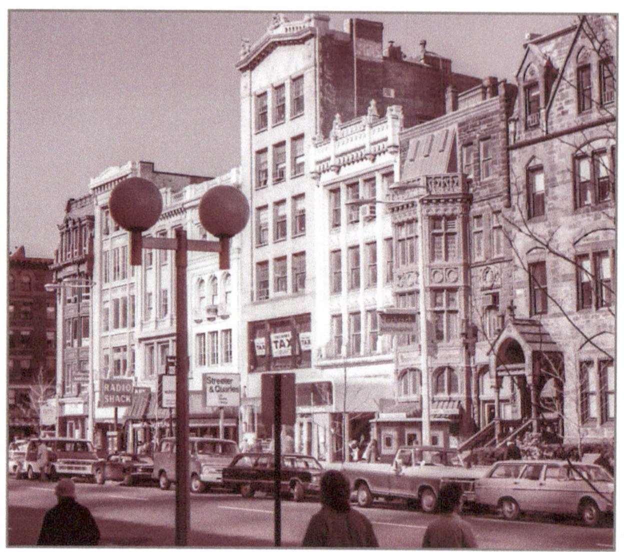

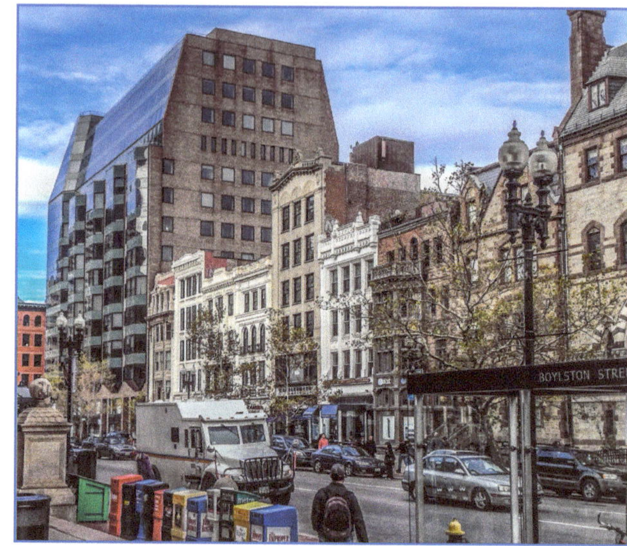

The Boston Marathon did not allow women to run officially until 1972. There had been unofficial women runners for a few years but they encountered formidable obstructions.

In 1967, twenty year old K.V. Switzer had to be physically defended by her Syracuse University teammates when the race director and another official attempted to rip her number from her clothing while she was running.

Race officials defended themselves by expressing their real belief that women were not physically capable of running 26 miles. 8,966 women officially completed the 2012 Boston Marathon.

The argument has changed. The photos above show the area of the finish line of the Boston Marathon where, in 2013, Islamic terrorists exploded the first of two bombs that killed three innocent people and injured hundreds.

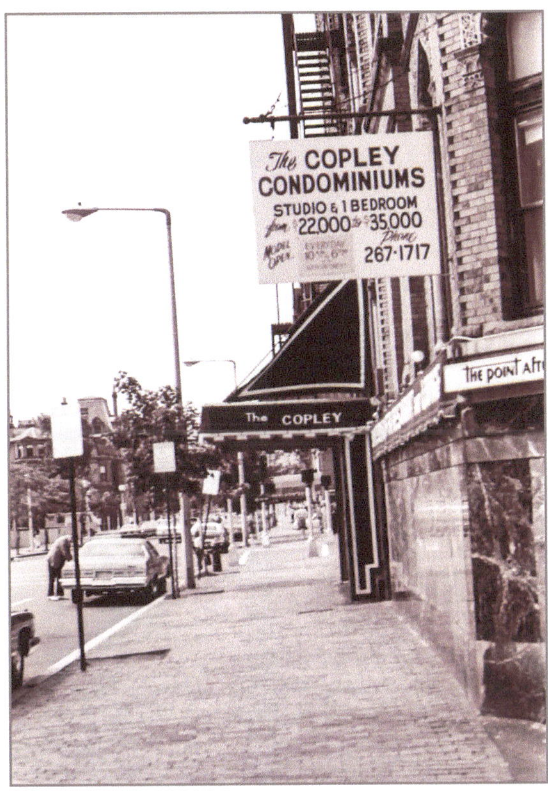

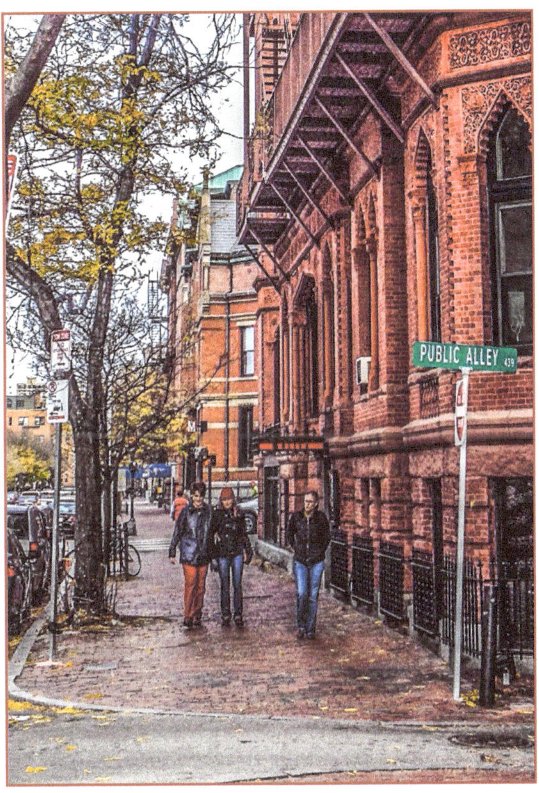

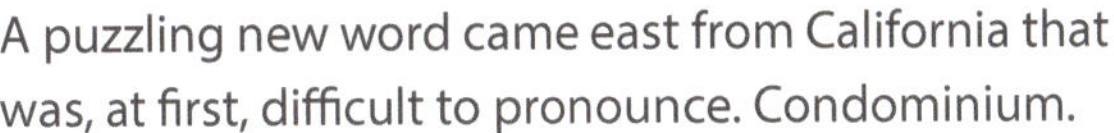

A puzzling new word came east from California that was, at first, difficult to pronounce. Condominium.

The Back Bay was a natural for condos. Tired apartment buildings in need of renovation were snapped up. Renters were stunned by the outrageous asking prices for their units.

Buyers at The Copley on Dartmouth Street could drink and dine in style downstairs at The Point After, owned by Boston Patriot, Gino Cappelletti. Cappelletti was a receiver and kicker who led the American Football League in scoring five times. He played in all of the first 153 Patriots' games before retiring in 1970.

Gino retired again in 2012, when, after 32 years in the broadcast booth as the Patriots' radio color man, he finished a storied career during which he had been a familiar and trusted voice of the team.

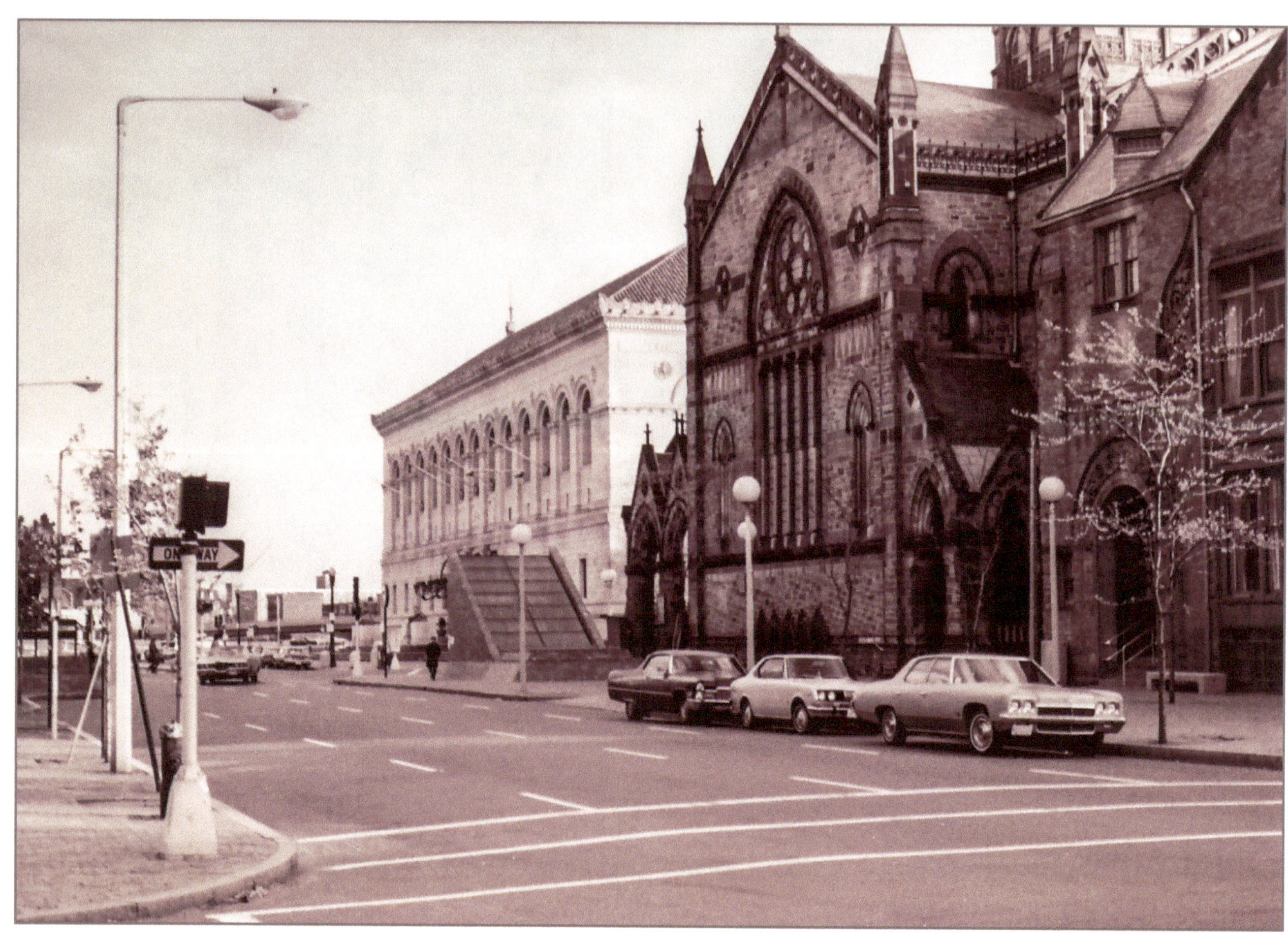

The Back Bay ends at Huntington Avenue on the other side of the Boston Public Library. A vacant triangular lot and then the train tracks disconnected the more upscale section of the city from the South End. Copley Place now seamlessly blends these neighborhoods.

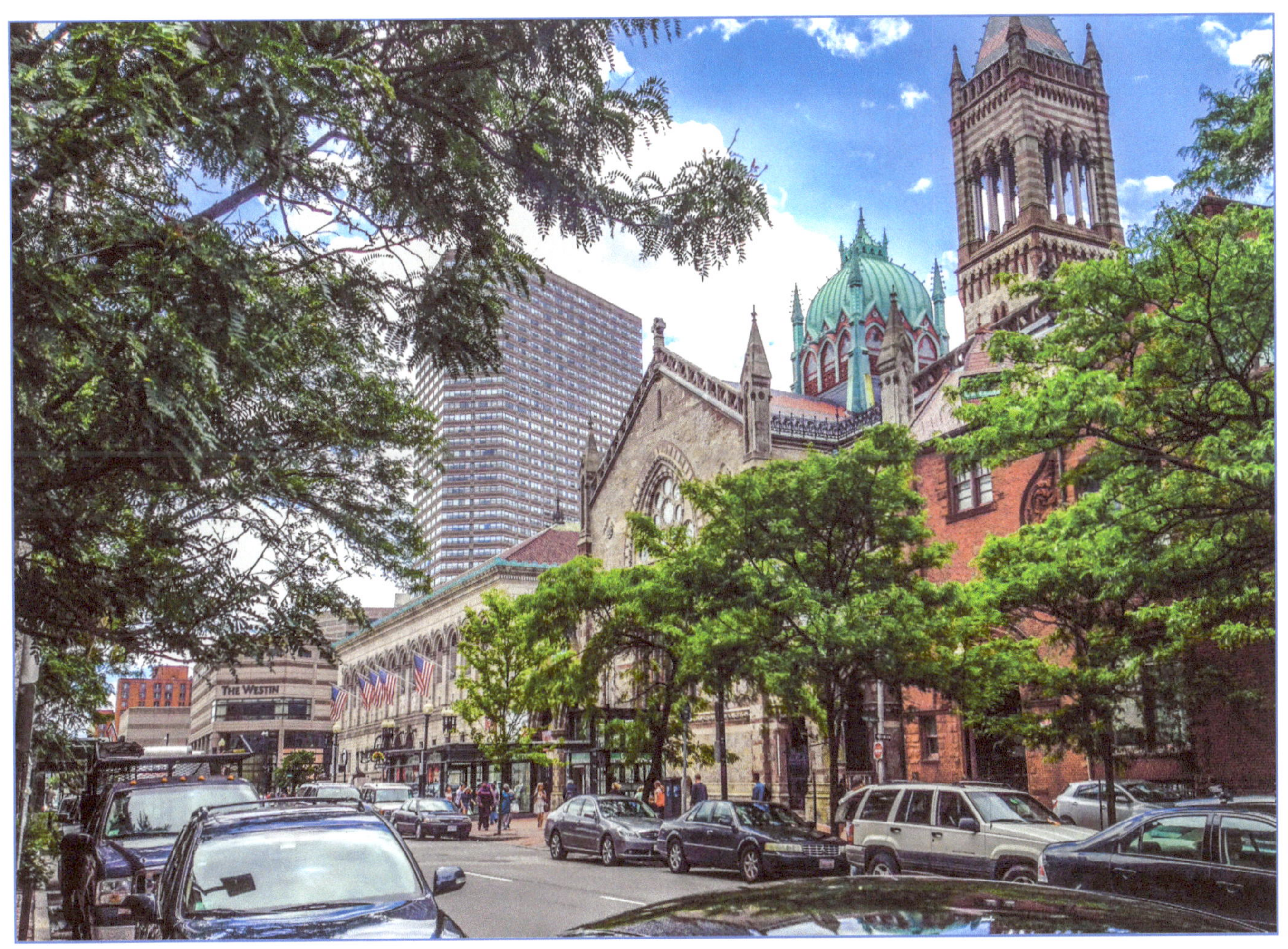
THE WESTIN

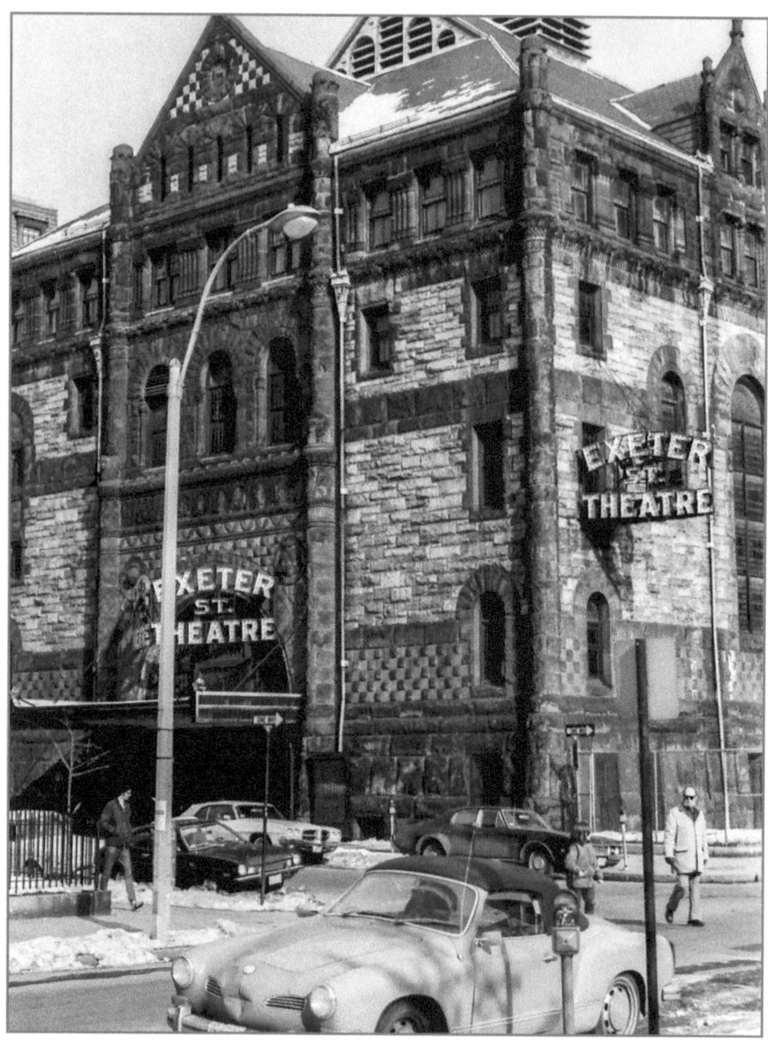

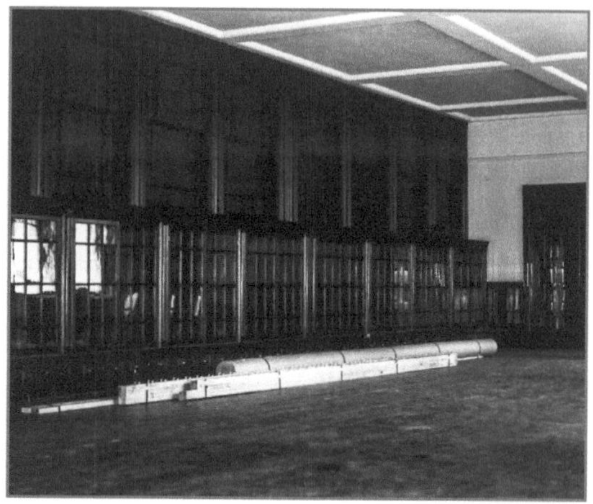

The First Spiritual Temple was built at the corner of Exeter and Newbury Streets in 1885. For the next ninety years, The Spiritual Fraternity hosted leading mediums who lectured and conducted seances there. The building was sold in 1975 when the church moved to Brookline.

At the time the church was consecrated it claimed nearly 1000 congregants. The group functioned independently until 1914 when it became necessary to convert the main auditorium into a movie theater to finance the work of the church.

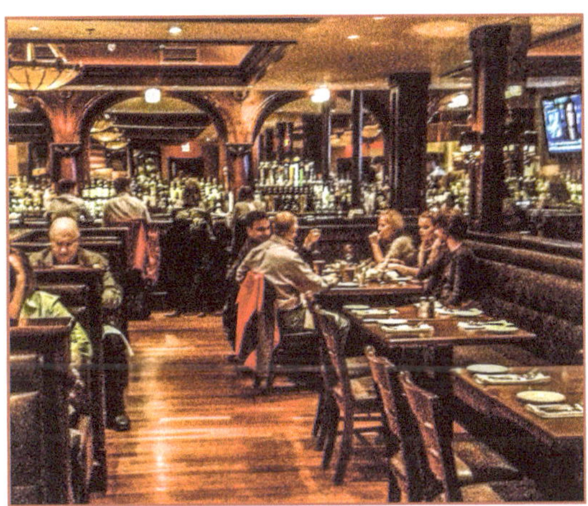

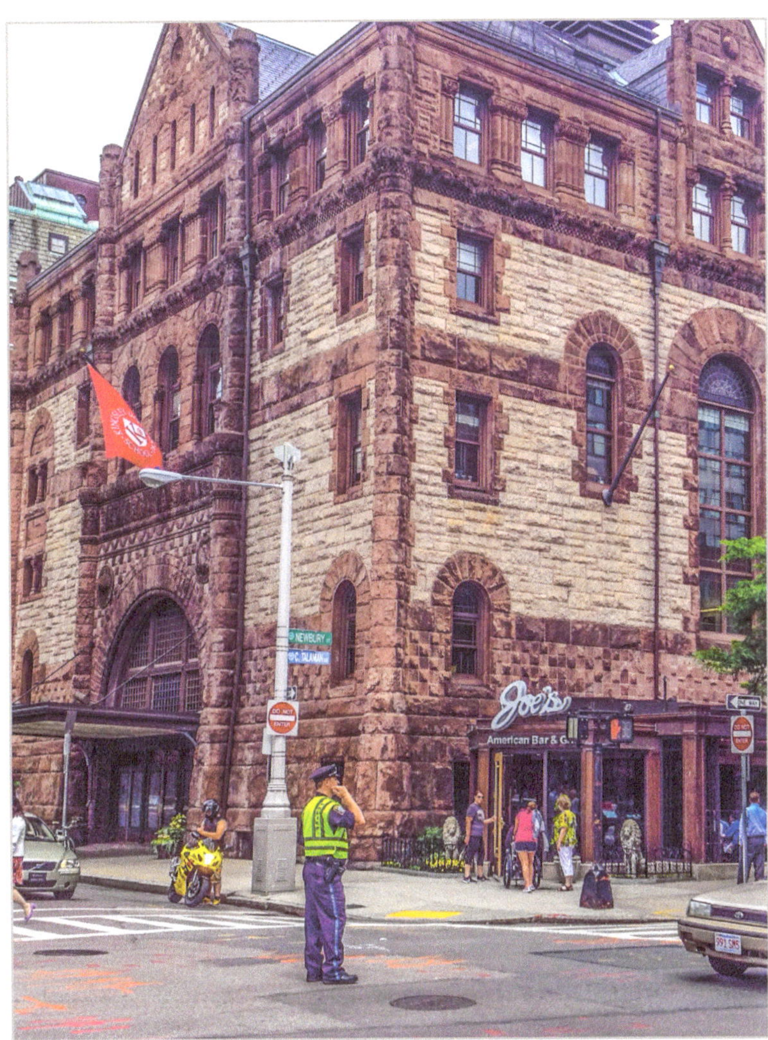

The Exeter St. Theatre operated for fifty-eight years supporting the church and, when it closed in October, 1973, it was a critically regarded art cinema.

The building now houses offices, a Montessori School and Joe's American Bar and Grill. The bar and dining room at Joe's occupy the former location of the spiritualist library where mediums regularly conducted seances for nearly 100 years.

Above, the library before the building was sold, in 1975, and the room as it is now.

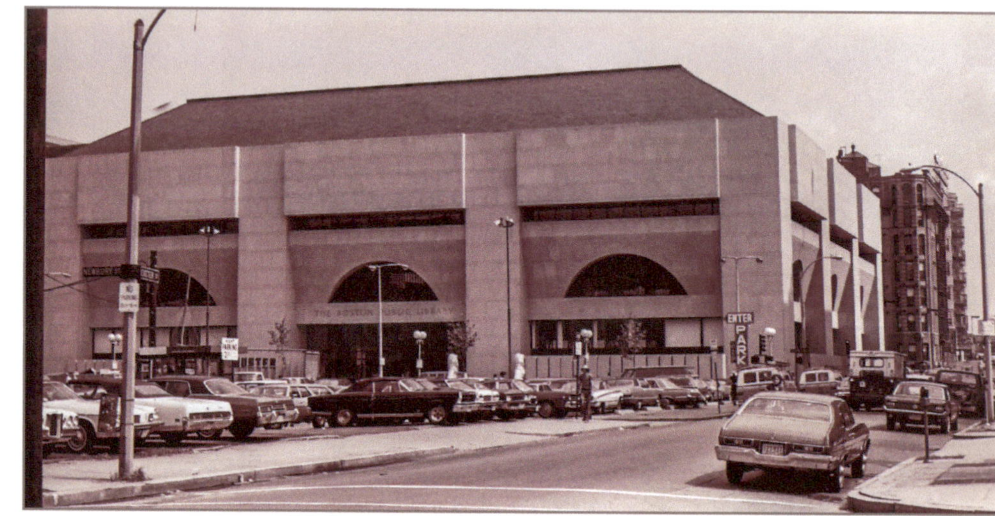

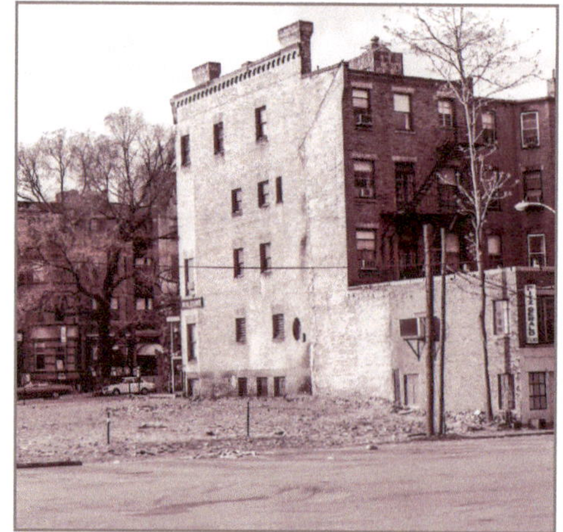

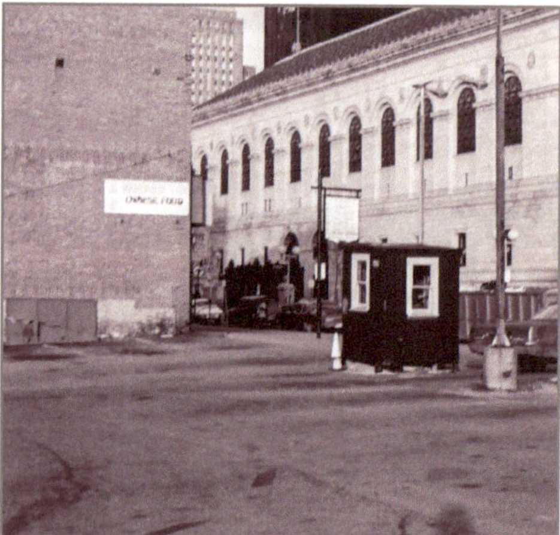

The new Boston Public Library, in all its modernist glory, cast a lonely stare across parking lots when it opened in 1972. Parking on city streets was not a problem and scofflaws were plentiful as unpaid tickets were difficult to collect before computers and the boot.

At far right, the lots have been developed and imposing edifices complement a transformed neighborhood.

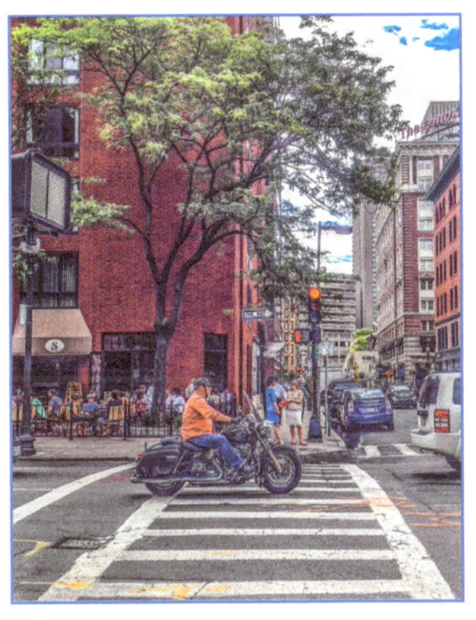
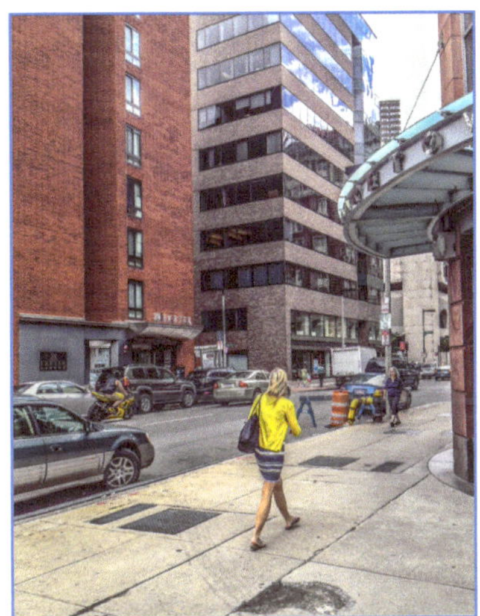
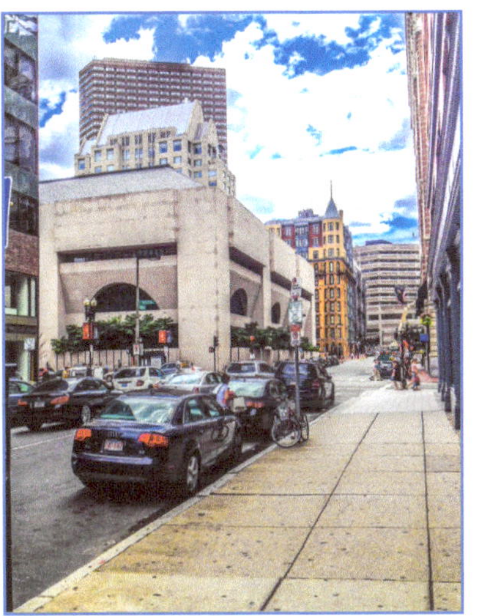
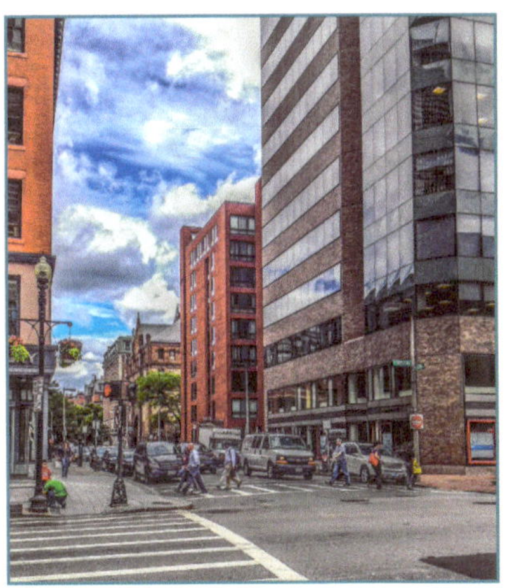
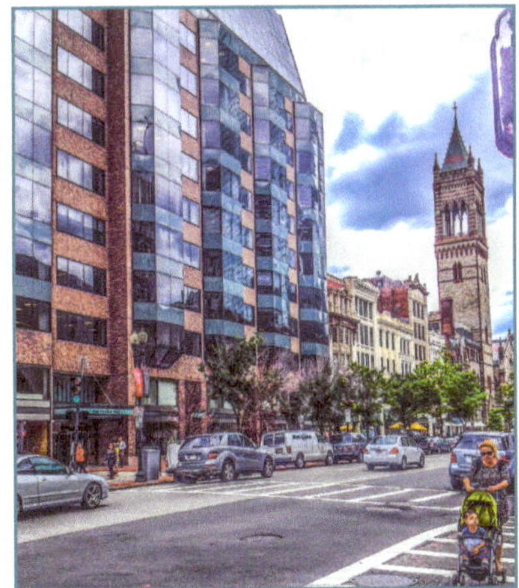
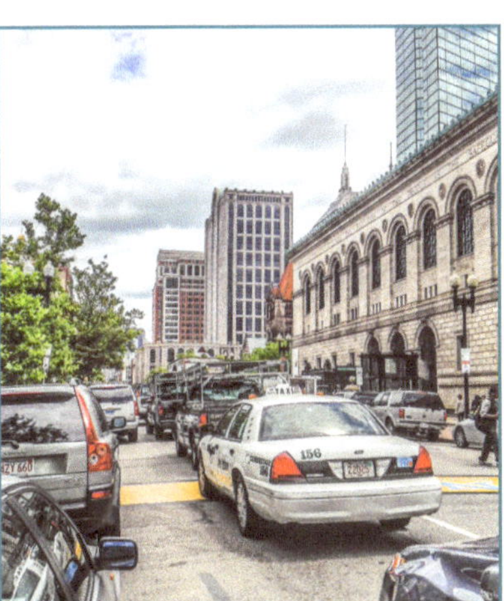

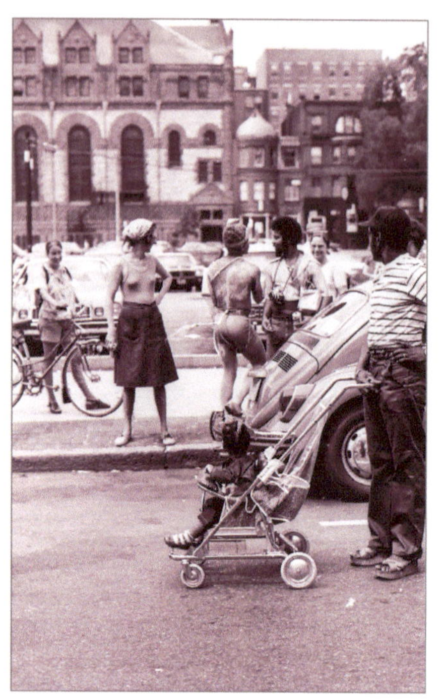

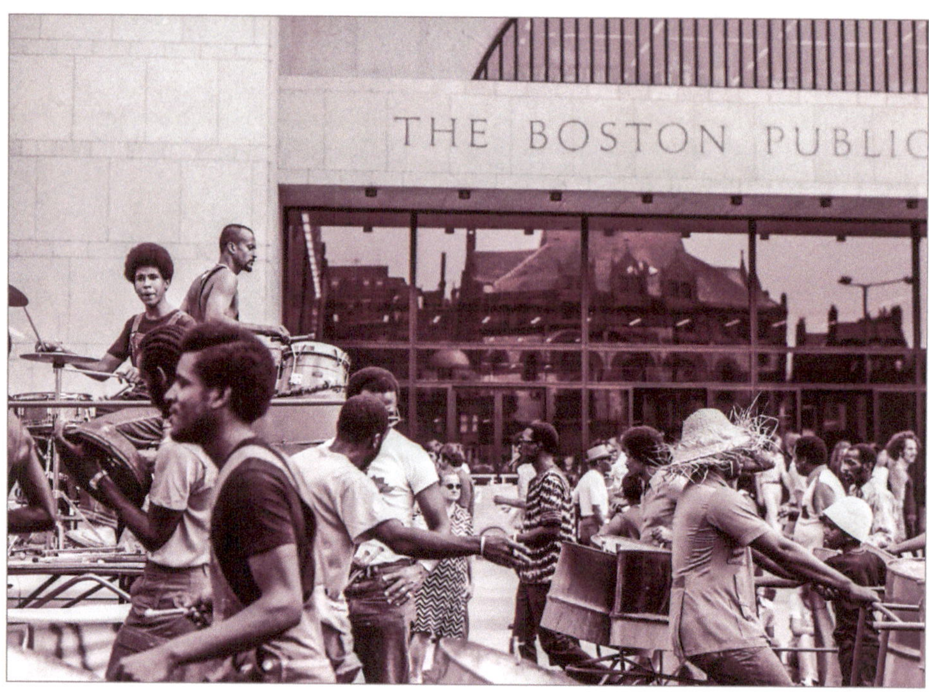

Burn your bra and party like it was the seventies.

The Exeter St. Theatre stands across the empty lots and is mirrored in the BPL's window.

Hippies advocated their version of free love. Although, love was not free for all. The American Psychiatric Association declassified homosexuality as a mental disorder in 1973. The American Psychological Society waited until 1975 to do likewise.

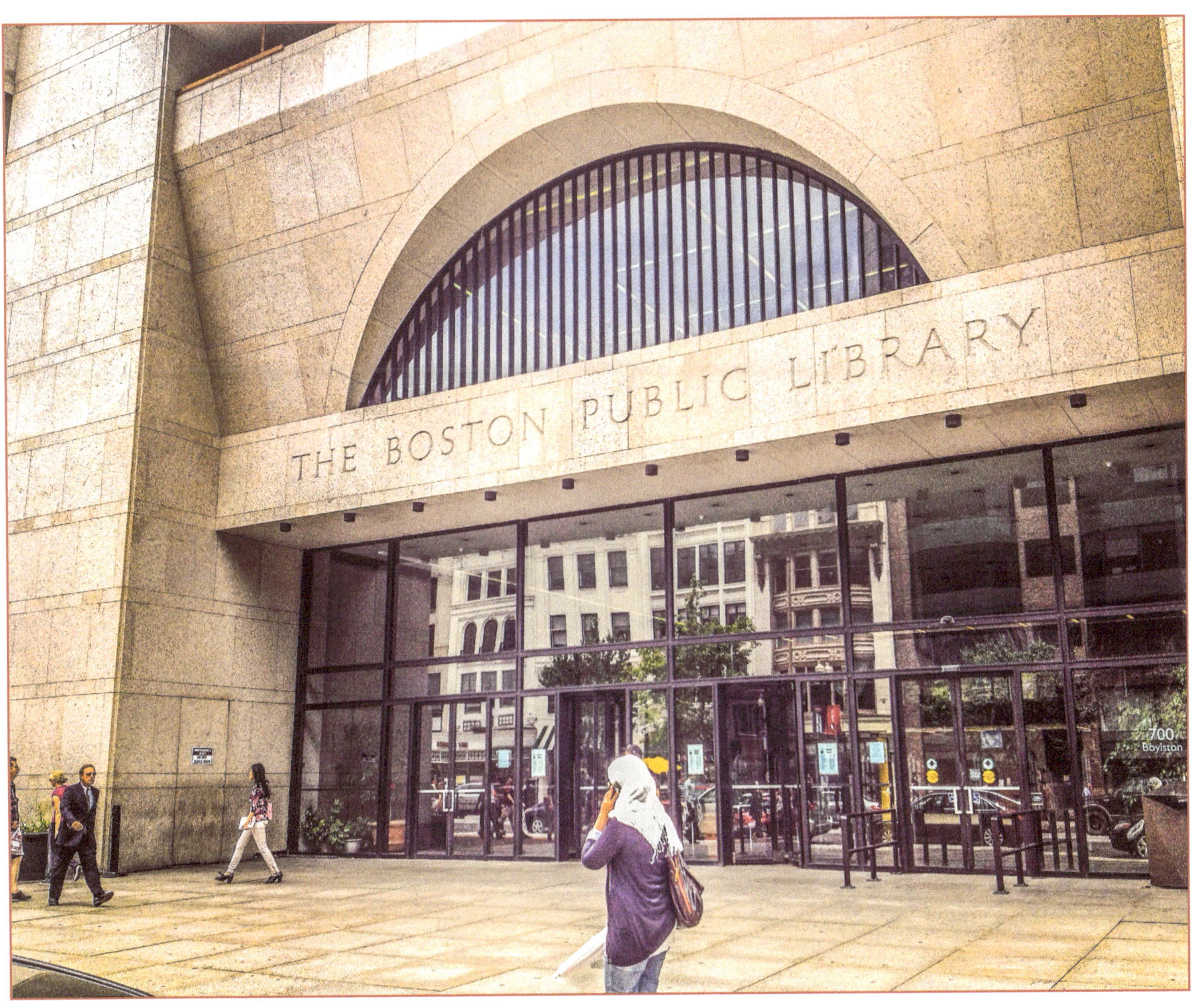
THE BOSTON PUBLIC LIBRARY
700
Boylston

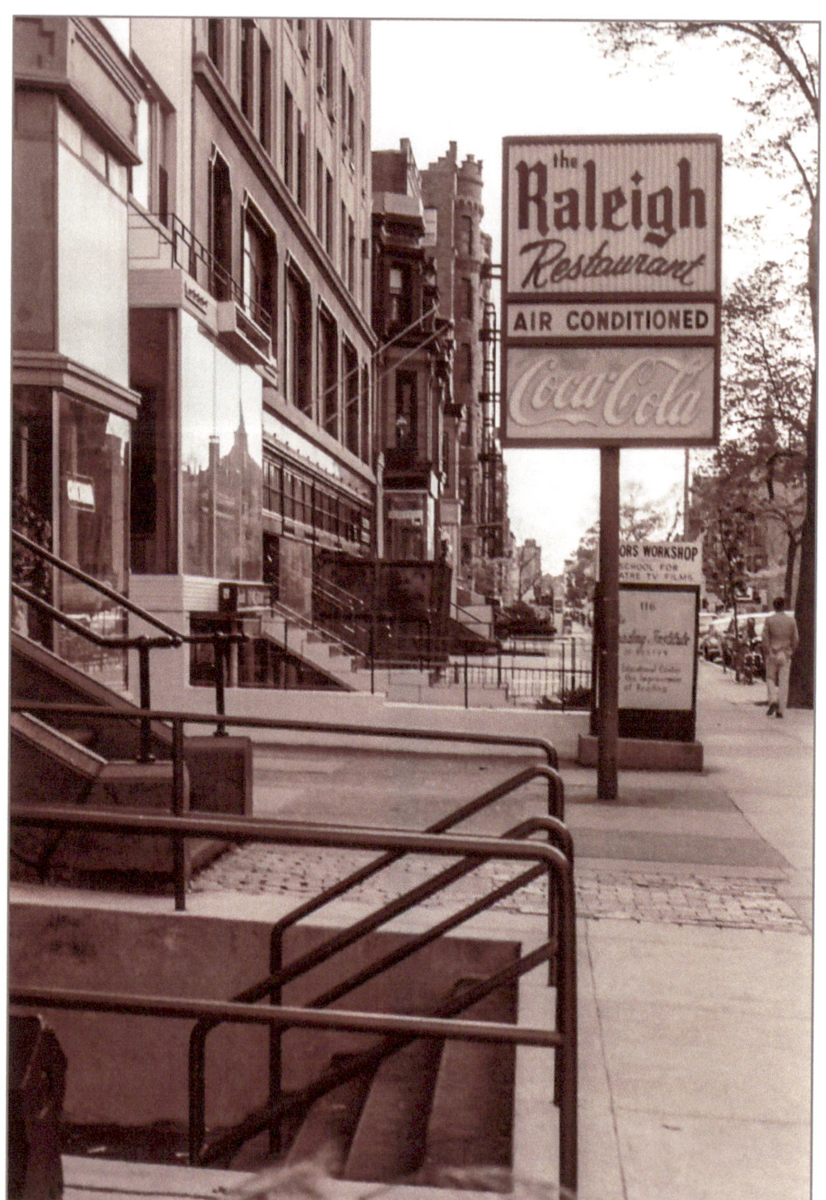

These pictures were taken on Newbury Street looking toward Dartmouth Street and, far right, turning around in the direction of Clarendon Street.

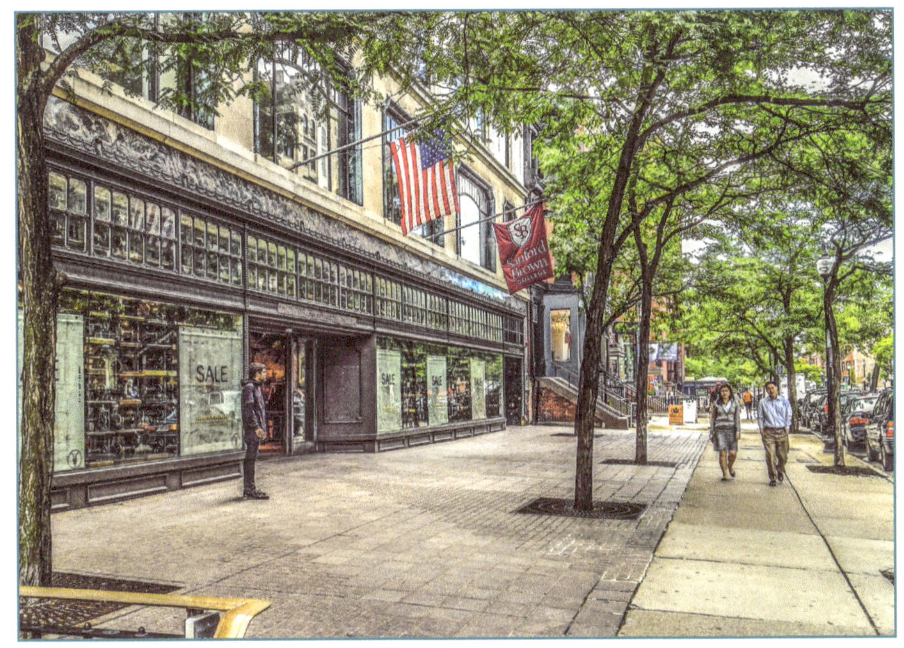

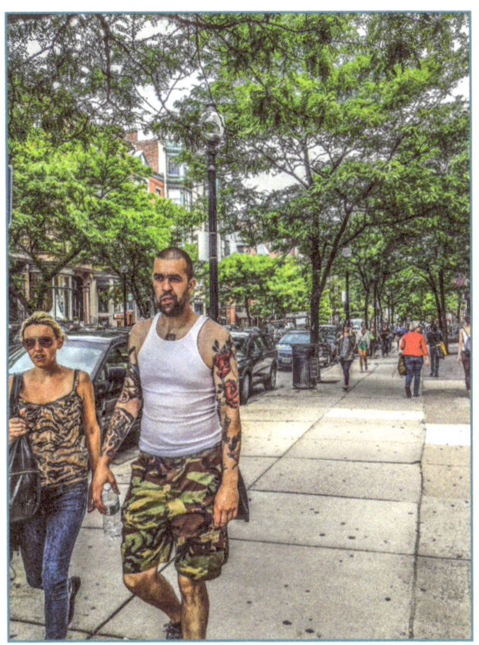

More than 45 million Americans are tattooed. Before October, 2000, tattoo parlors in Boston were outlawed for 38 years. Since then, ink shops have been popping up all over the area, particularly in neighborhoods like Cambridge and Alston.

The pricey procedure is a popular trend for athletes and celebrities alike, yet it is just as common on Joe Shmoe. Starting at about 100 to 150 dollars an hour, the age old practice of tattoo art is on the rise.

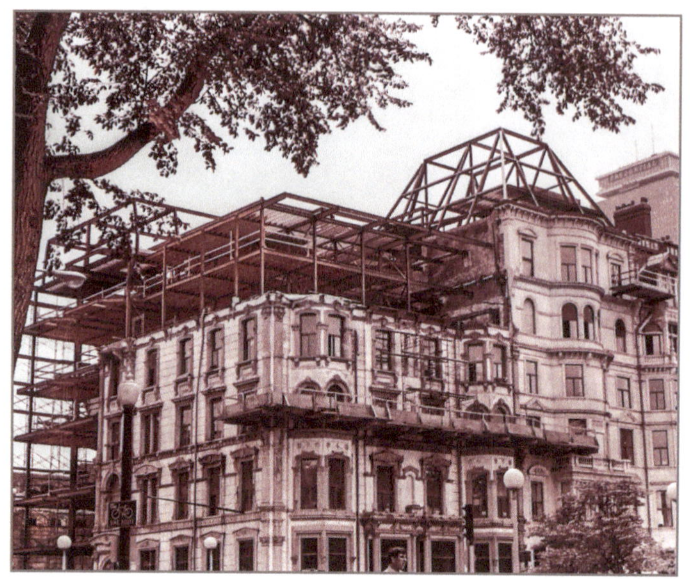

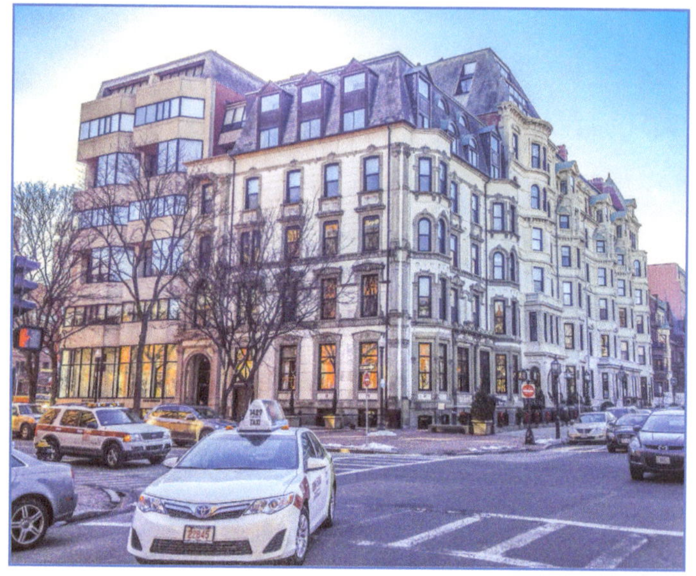

The Hotel Vendome had been the city's premier hotel. In 1882, it was the first commercial structure in Boston to be electrically lighted. It was lavish and elegant and hosted presidents, titans of industry, Mark Twains and Sarah Bernhardts.

The Vendome was a hundred years old and it was being converted into condos when tragedy struck on June 17, 1972, the day before Father's Day. A four alarm fire ripped through the unfinished building and caused serious structural damage.

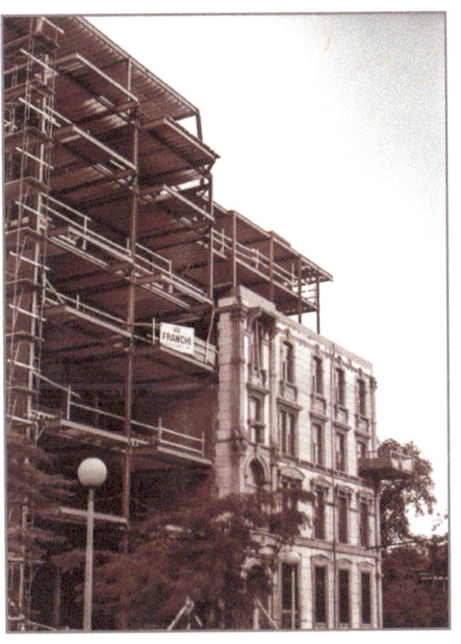

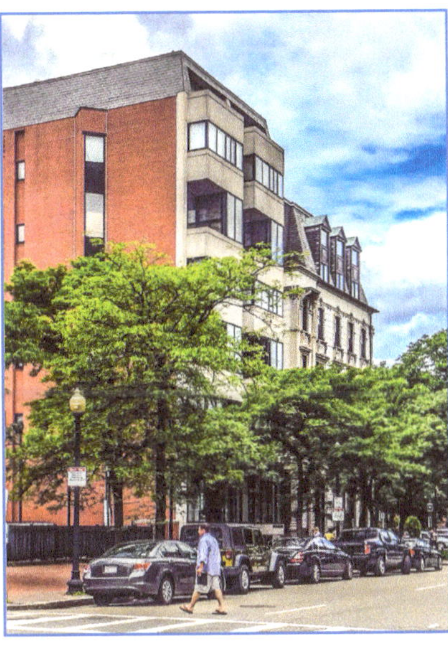

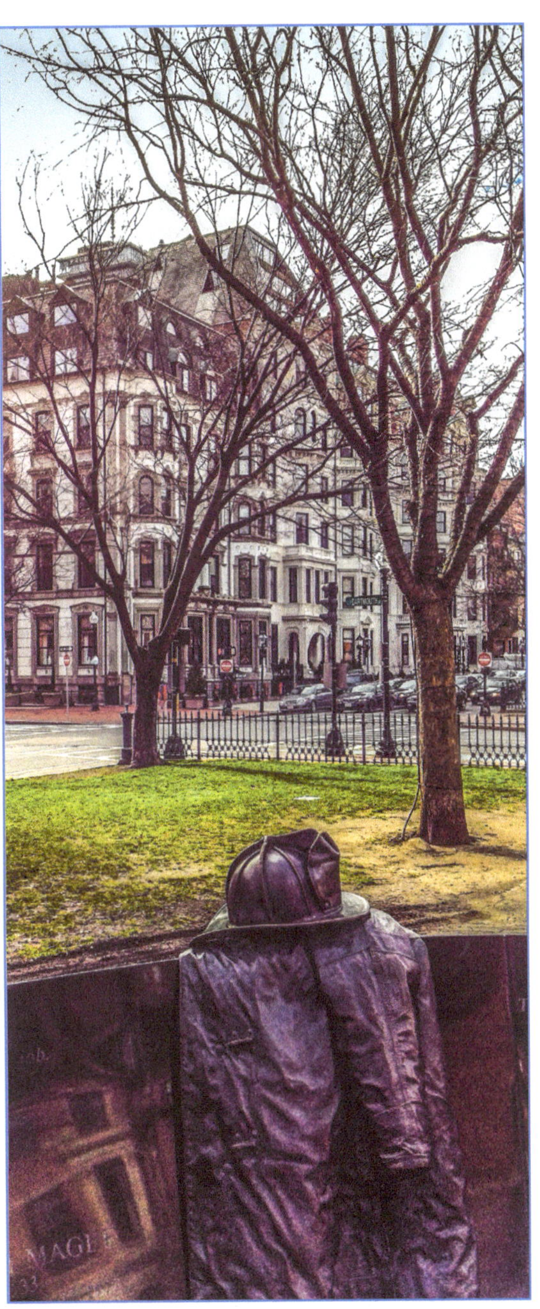

The fire was brought under control after two hours and cleanup had begun when five floors at the southeast corner of the building abruptly collapsed and buried 17 firefighters and a ladder truck. Nine firemen perished at the scene. It remains the worst fire fighting tragedy in Boston's history.

A memorial inscribed with the names of the fallen firefighters was installed on the mall along Commonwealth Avenue across from the hotel and dedicated on the 25th anniversary of the fire in 1997.

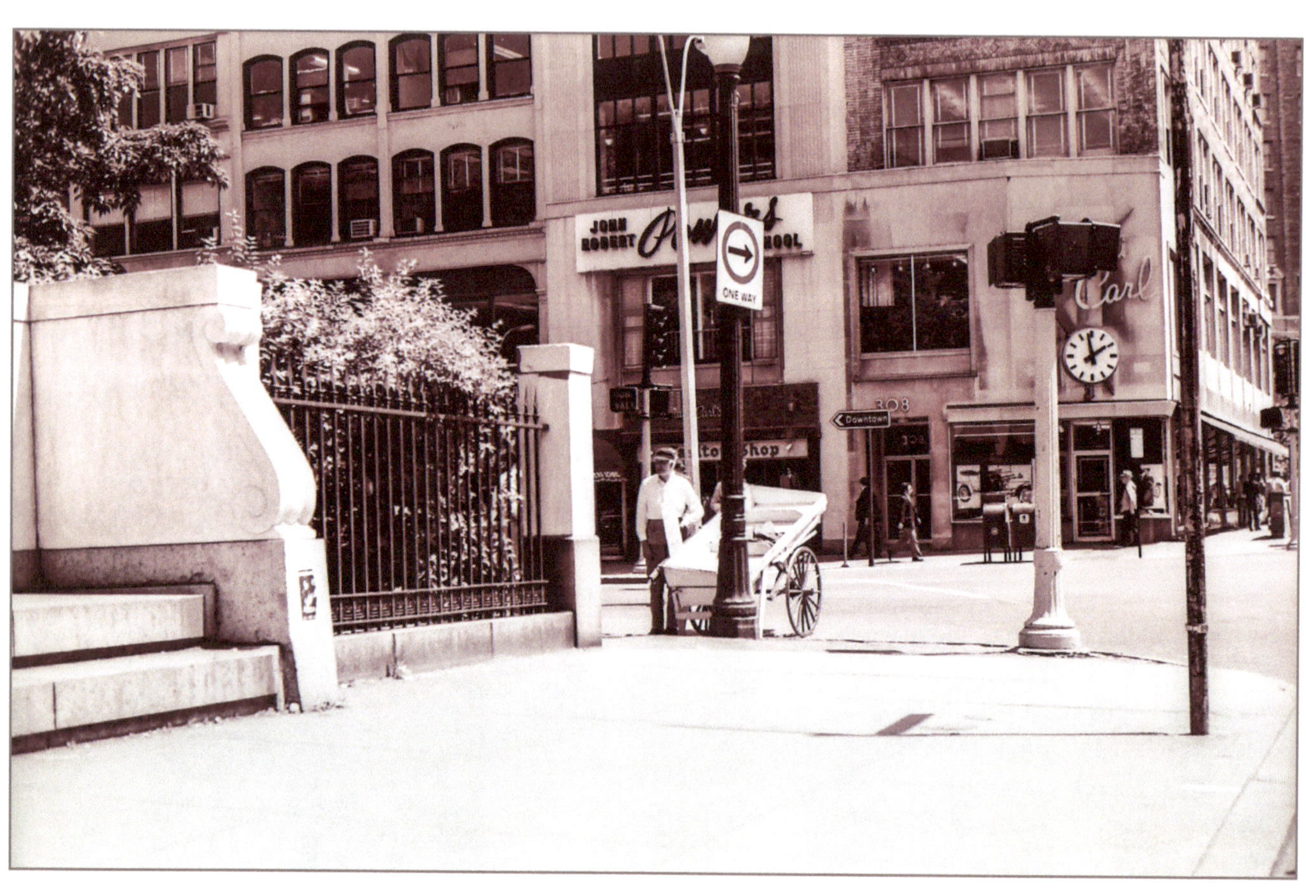
JOHN ROBERT
ONE WAY
Downtown
308

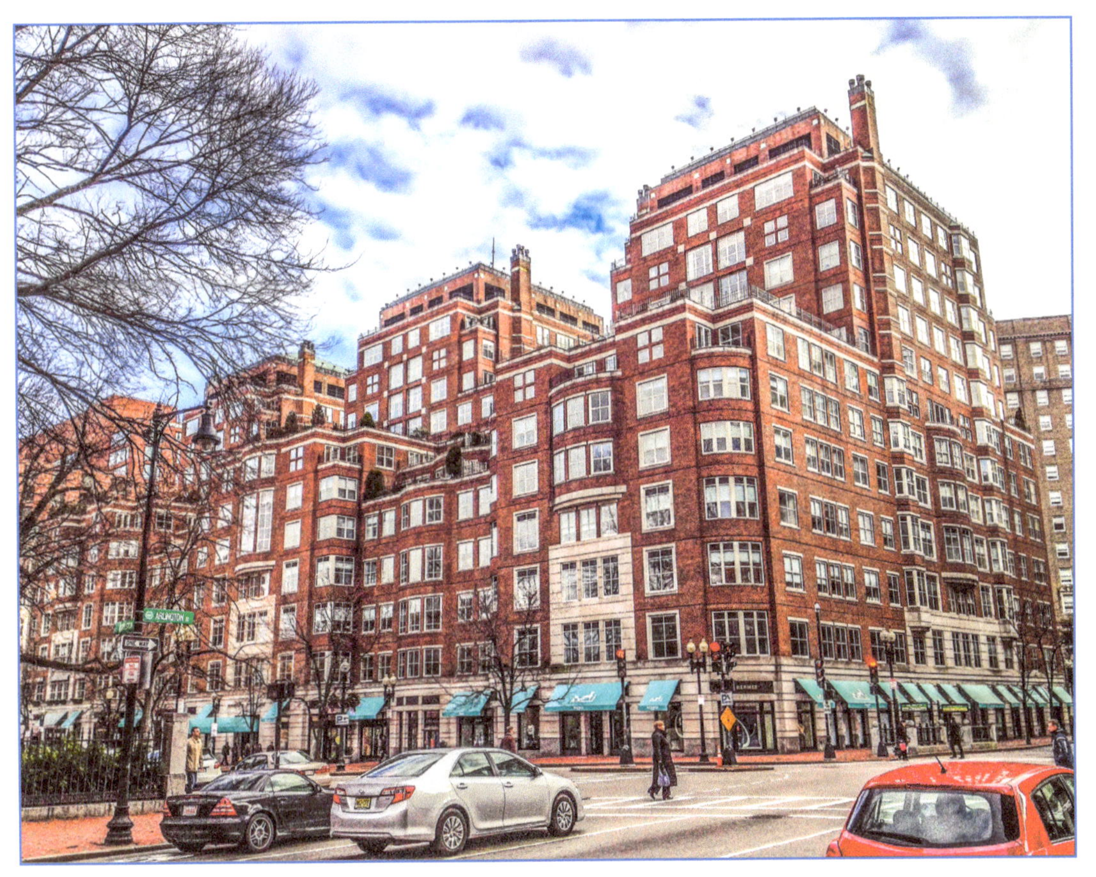

Boylston Street at the corner of Arlington Street is now anchored by luxury condos and expensive shops.

Boston was the 14th city to host a Playboy Club. A prudish reputation probably caused the city to have to wait until five years after the first Club opened in Chicago. The Boston edition arrived, not without controversy, in 1965 and settled in a renovated, multi-story building in a seedy Park Square, the progenitor to the Combat Zone.

The Four Seasons Hotel now sits splendidly where the Playboy Club was once considered an upgrade in a rundown neighborhood.

Gloria Steinem, a former Playboy Bunny, co-founded Ms. magazine in 1971.

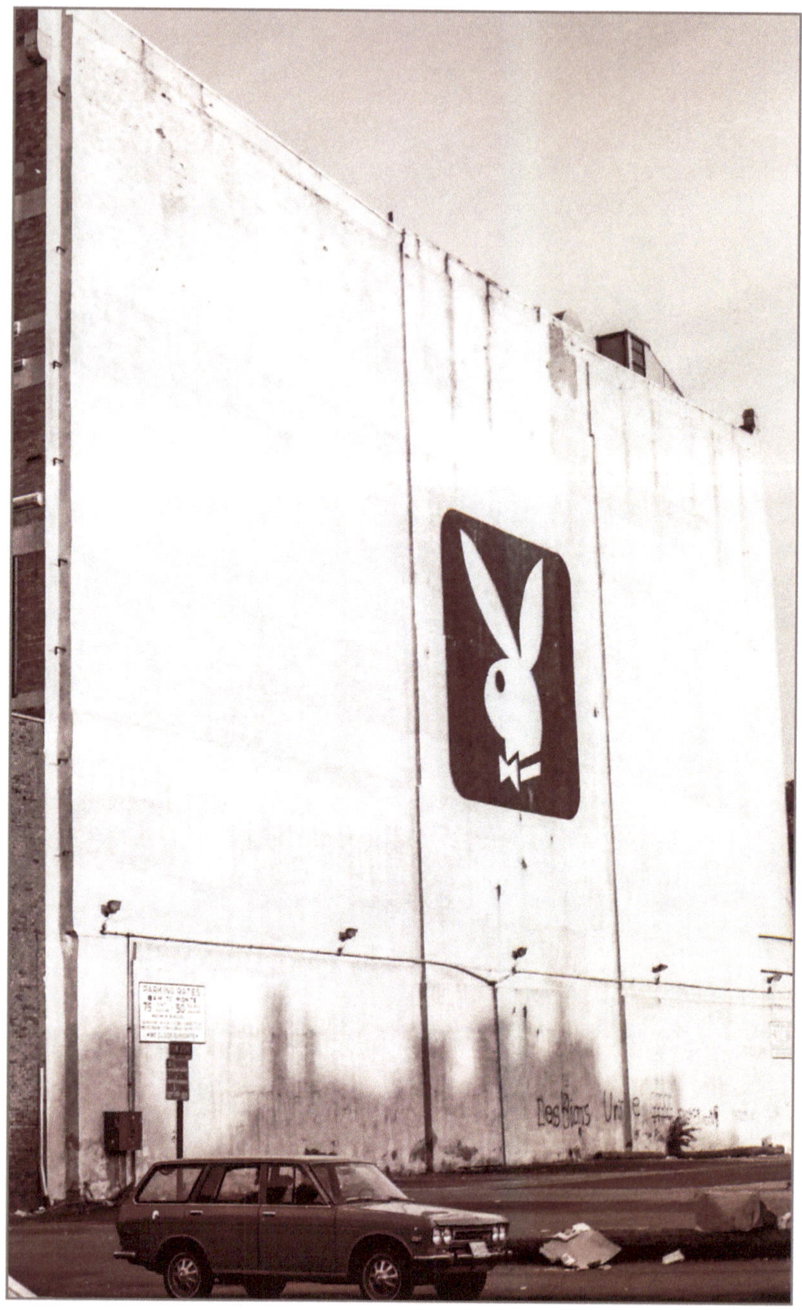

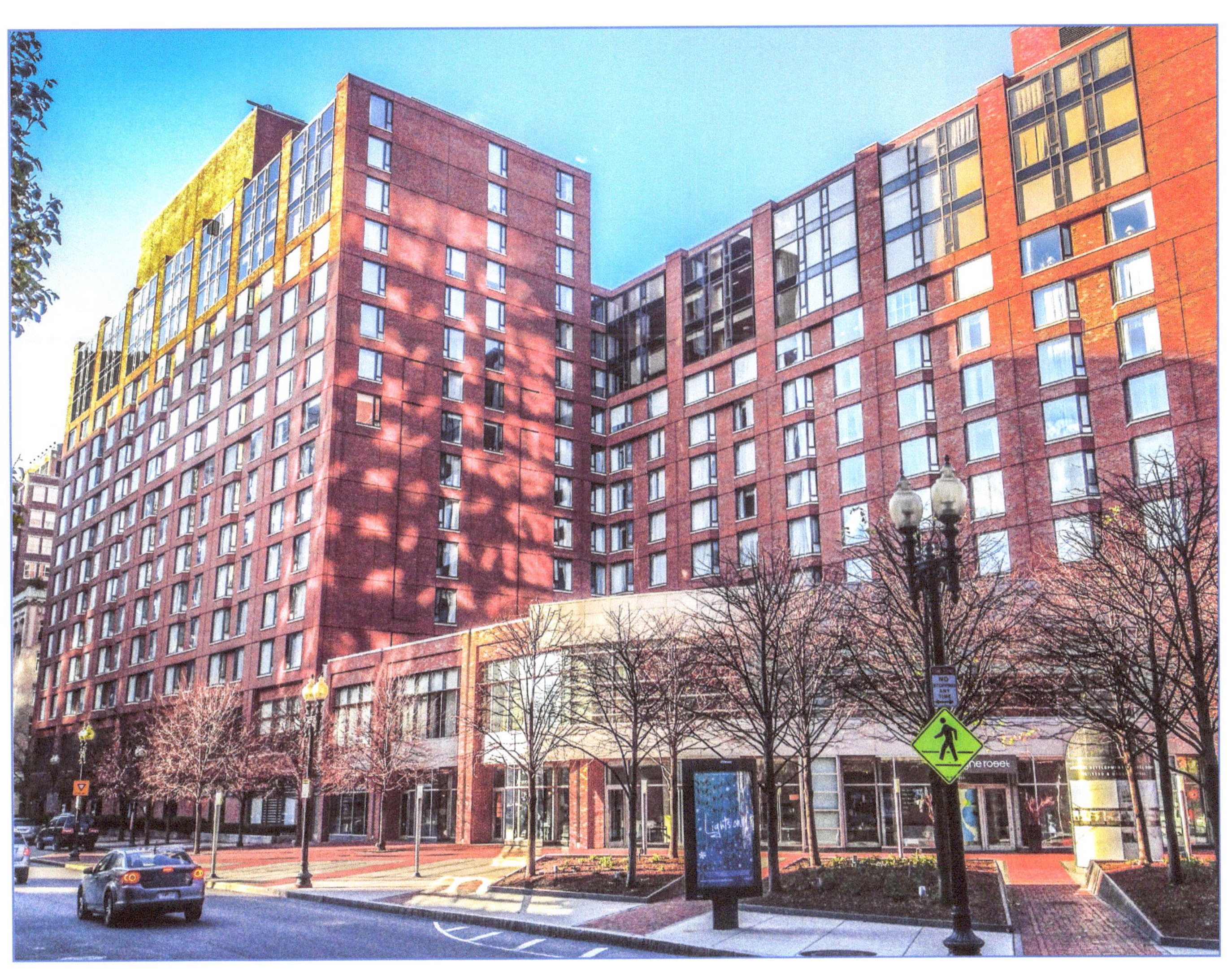

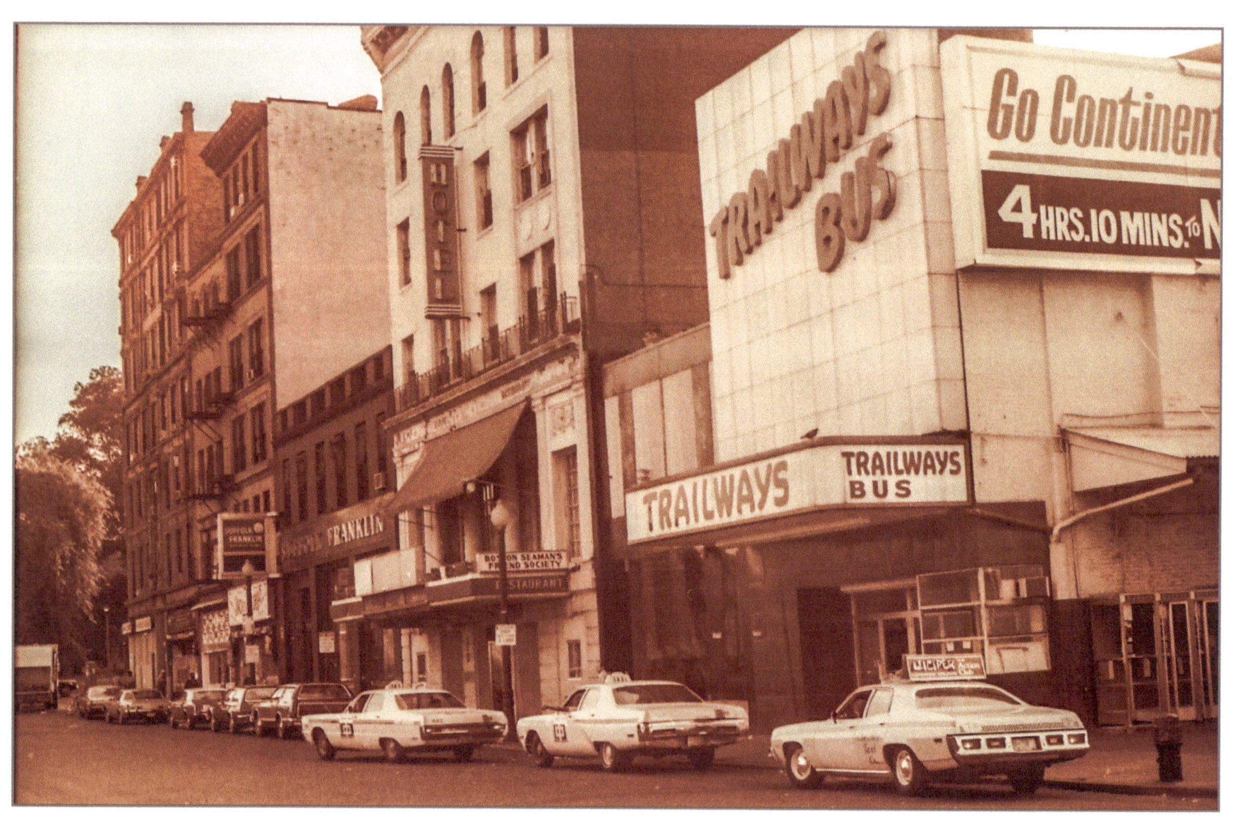

The Trailways Bus terminal in Park Square was replaced by the State Transportation Building.

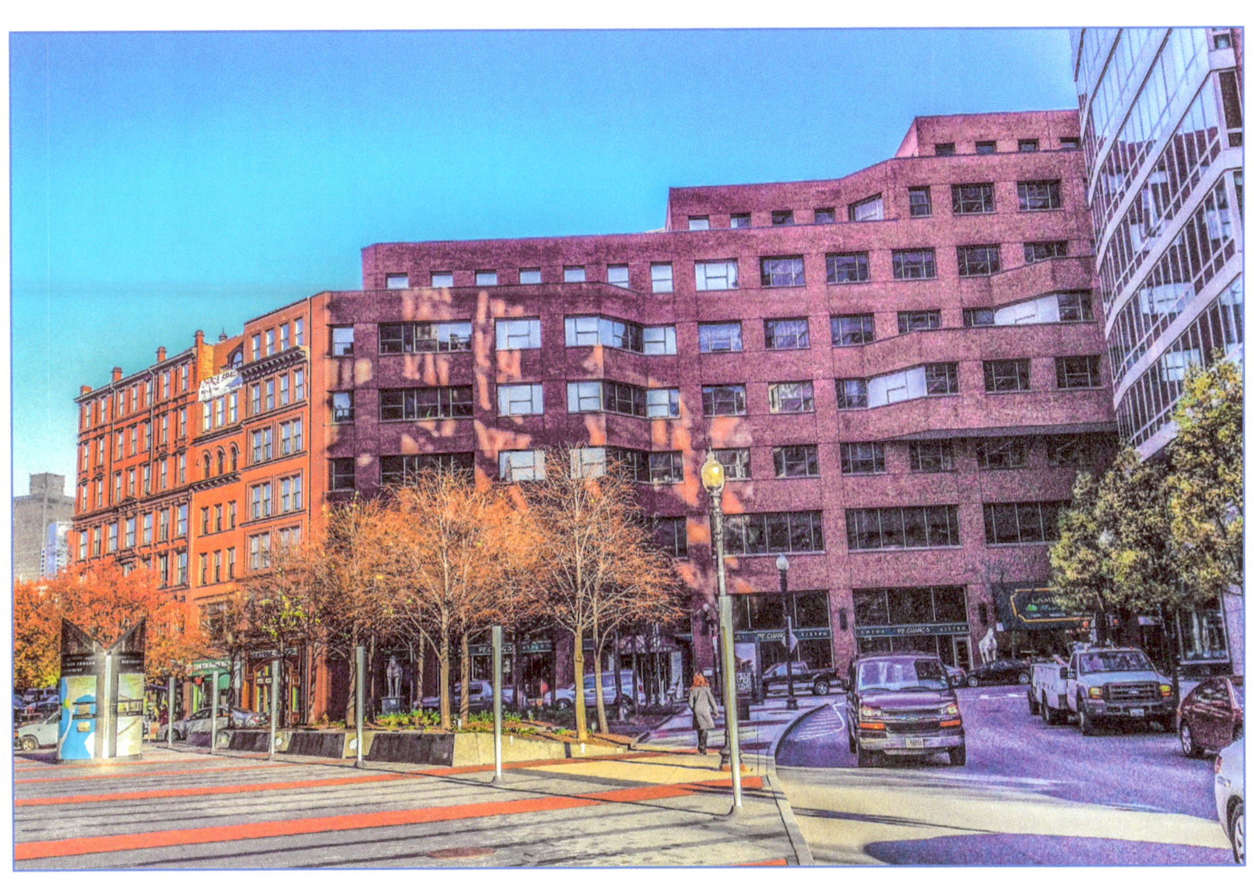

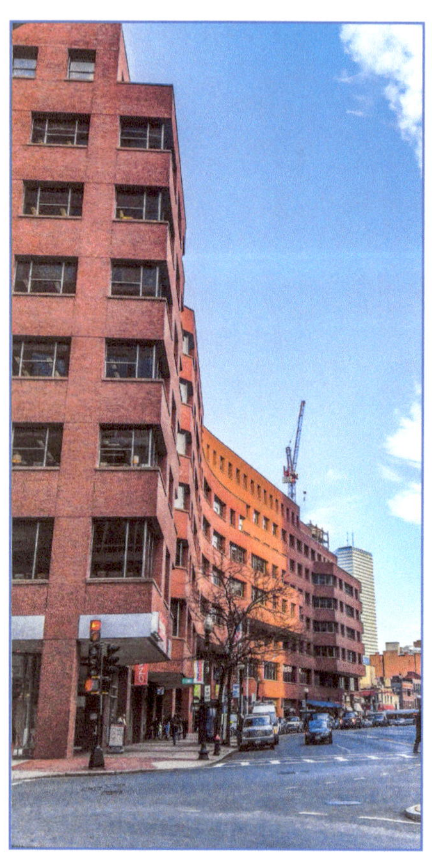

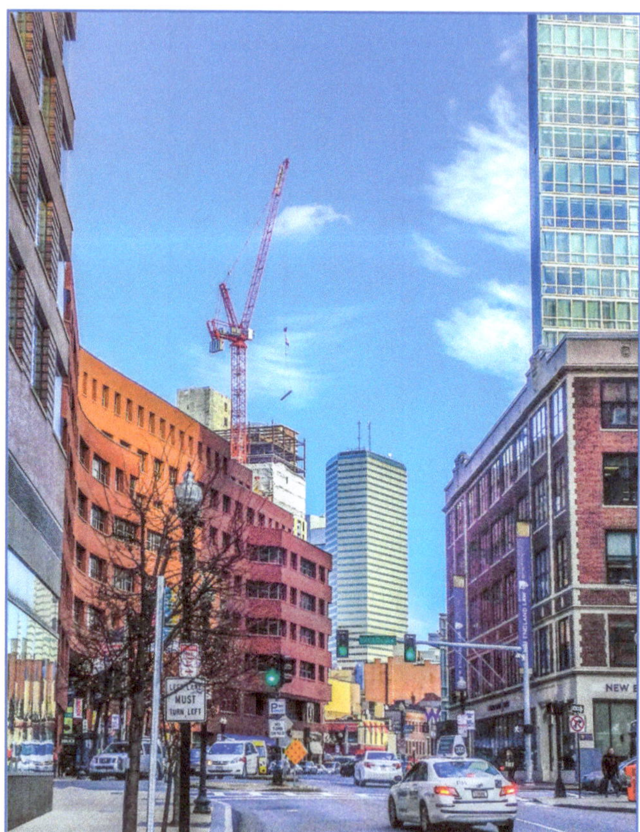

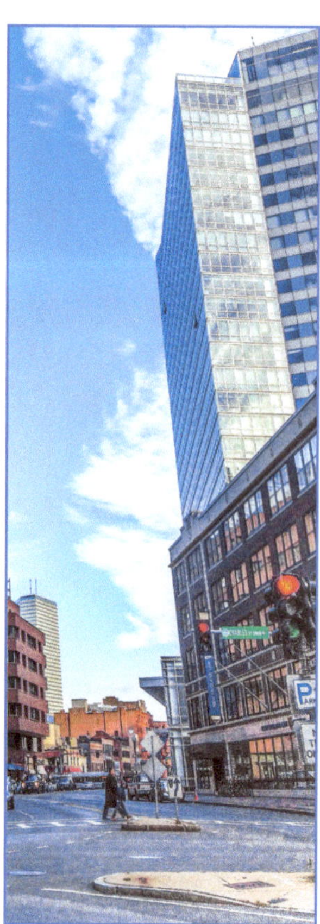

The State Transportation Building extends along Stuart Street to Tremomt Street replacing a block of period structures.

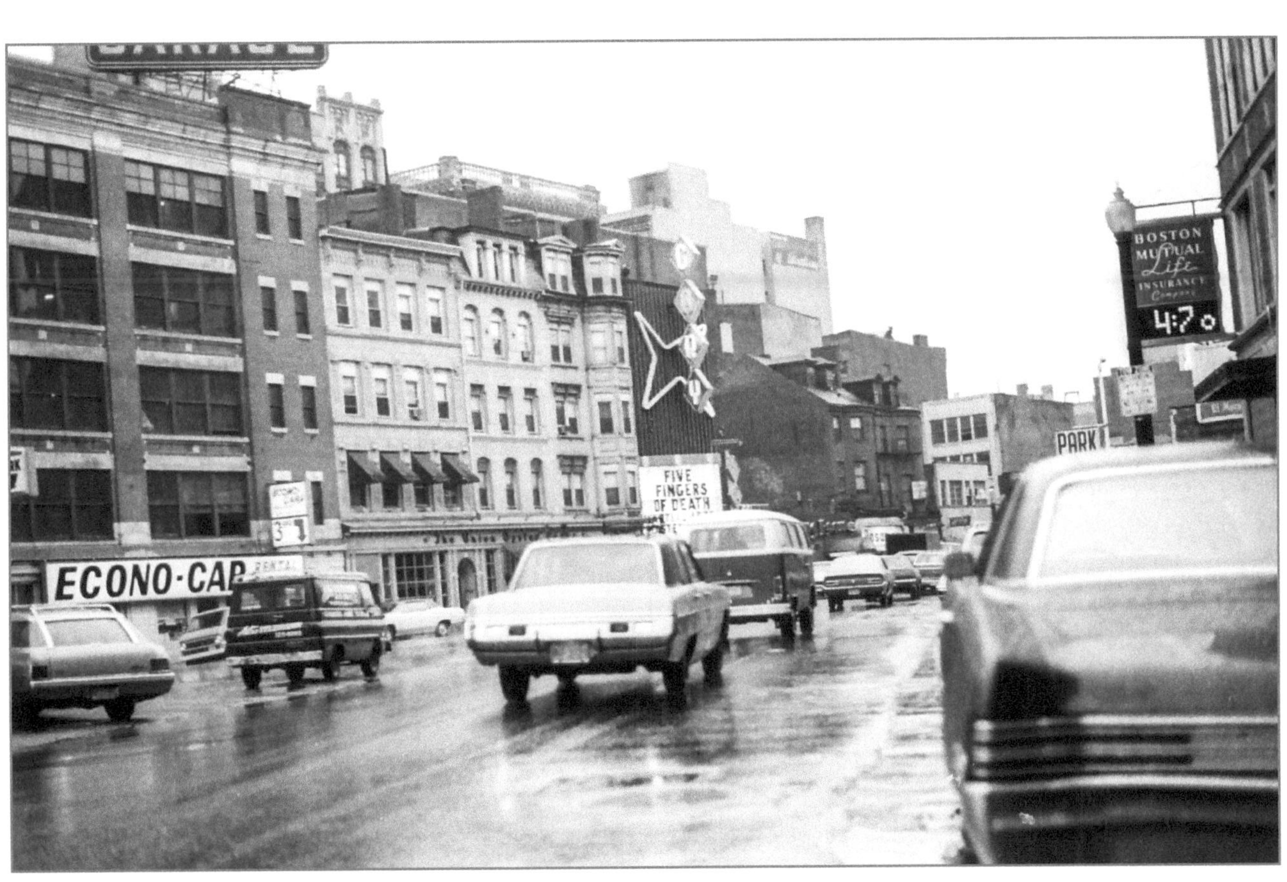
ECONO-CAR RENTAL
FIVE
FINGERS
OF DEATH
BOSTON
MUTUAL
Life
INSURANCE
4:70
PARK

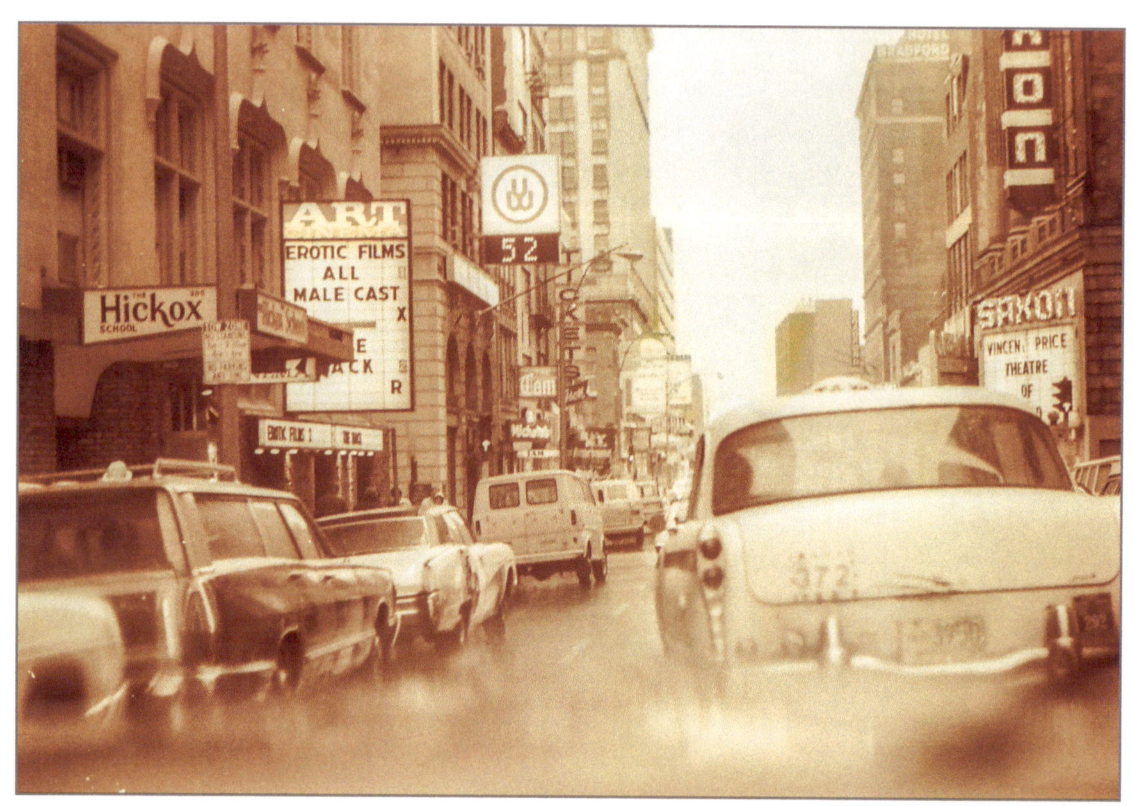

Tremont Street

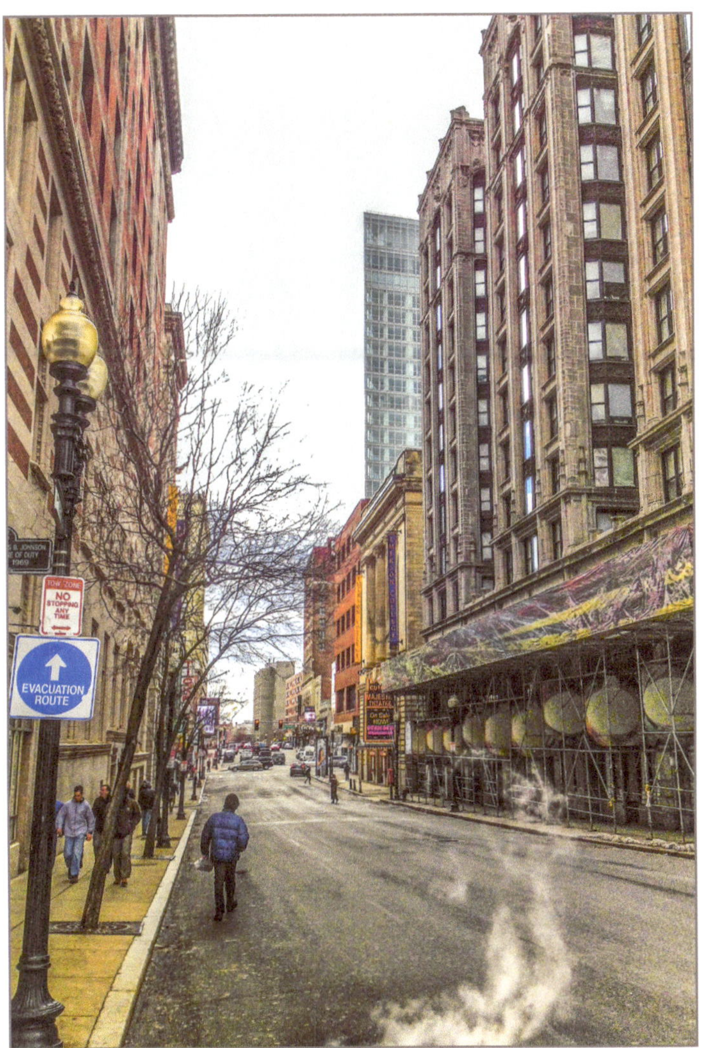

New York City added six all-electric Nissan Leafs to their official fleet of taxis in April, 2013. If they are profitable, the goal will be to replace one third of gas-powered cabs with an electric model by 2020.

The Electric Vehicle Company was the first company to commercially produce electric cars, more than 115 years ago. Their "Electrobat" taxicabs were used in New York City to replace horse and buggy cabs. But, oil was cheap and plentiful, and recharging was problematic, so electric vehicles became obsolete.

The Tesla Model S electric luxury sedan scored 99 out of 100 points in the May, 2013, Consumer Reports review. This is the highest rank CR has ever awarded a car. The only reported issue, recharging.

People might want electric cars but high prices and low battery range keep sales low and industry bankruptcies high.

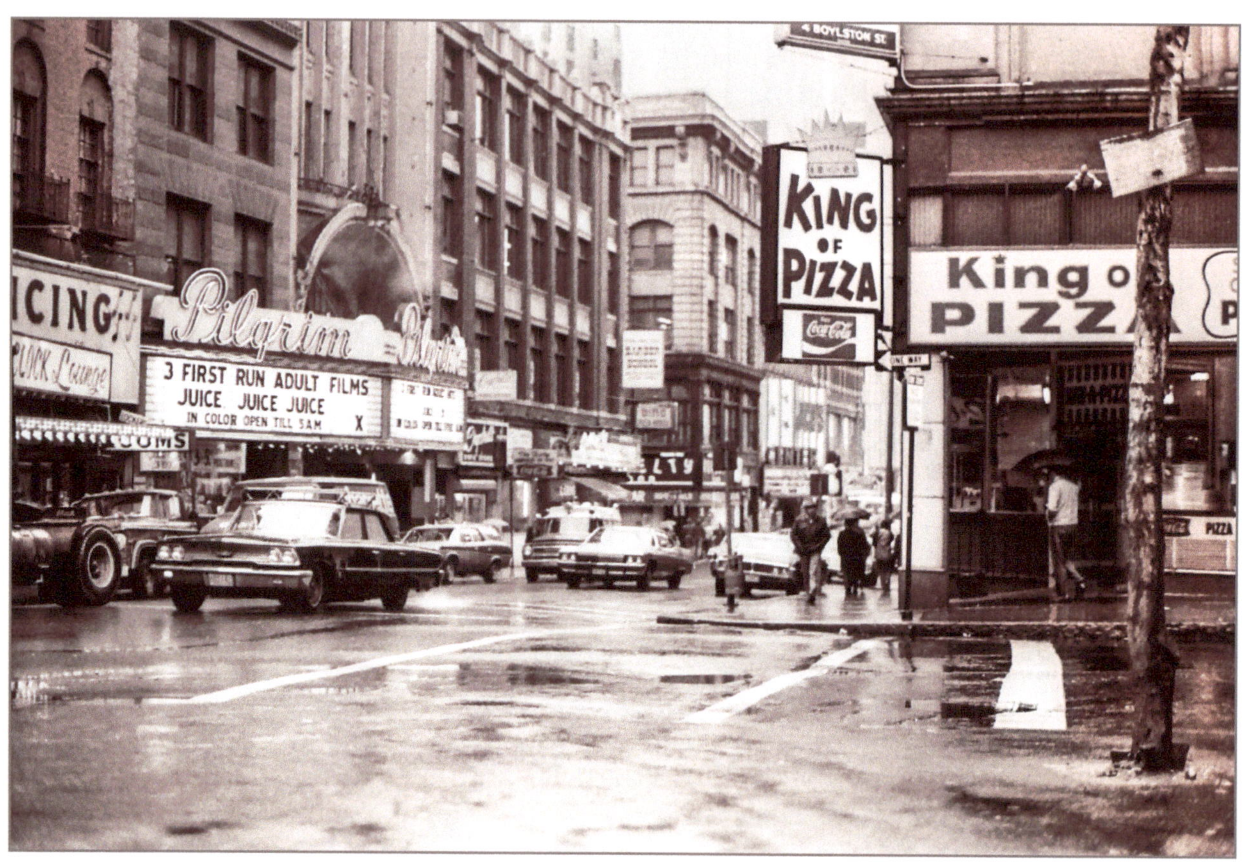

Washington Street from the corner of Boylston Street.

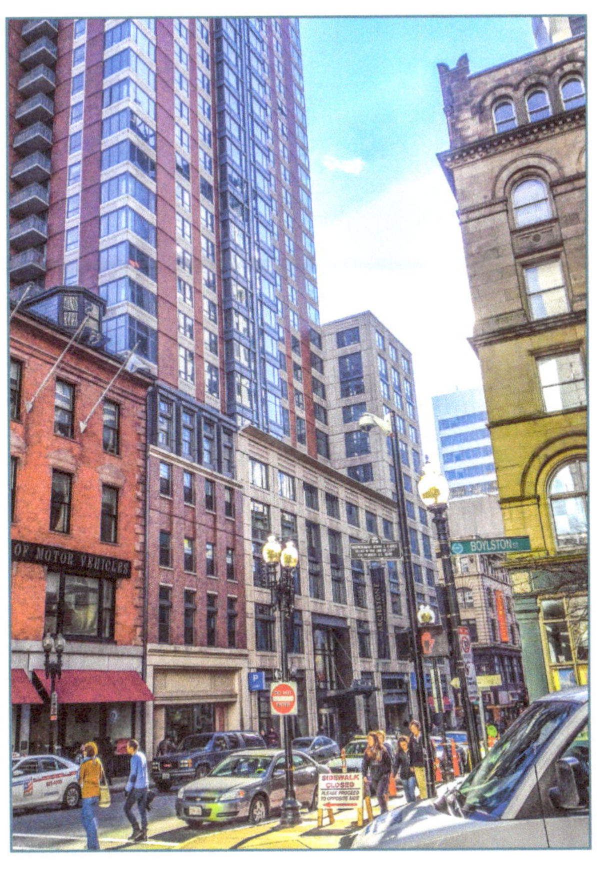
OF MOTOR VEHICLES
BOYLSTON

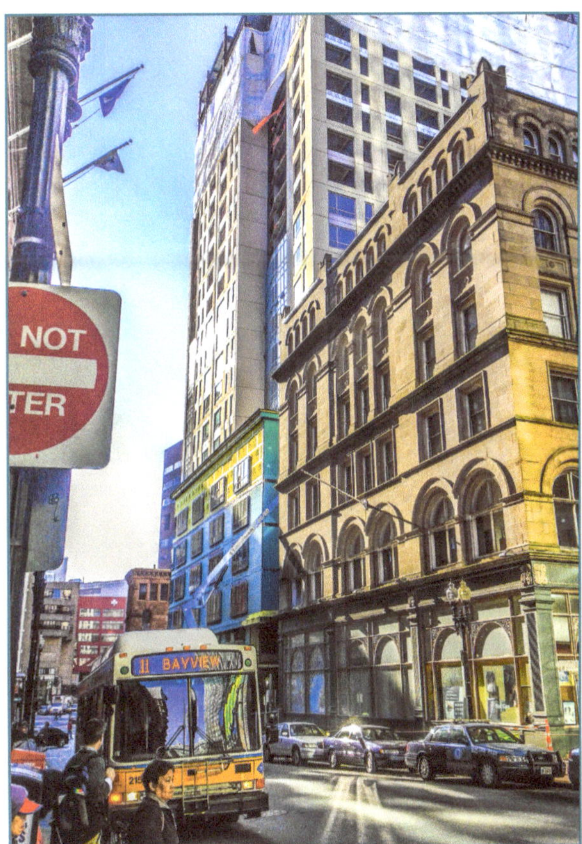
NOT
TER
11 BAYVIEW

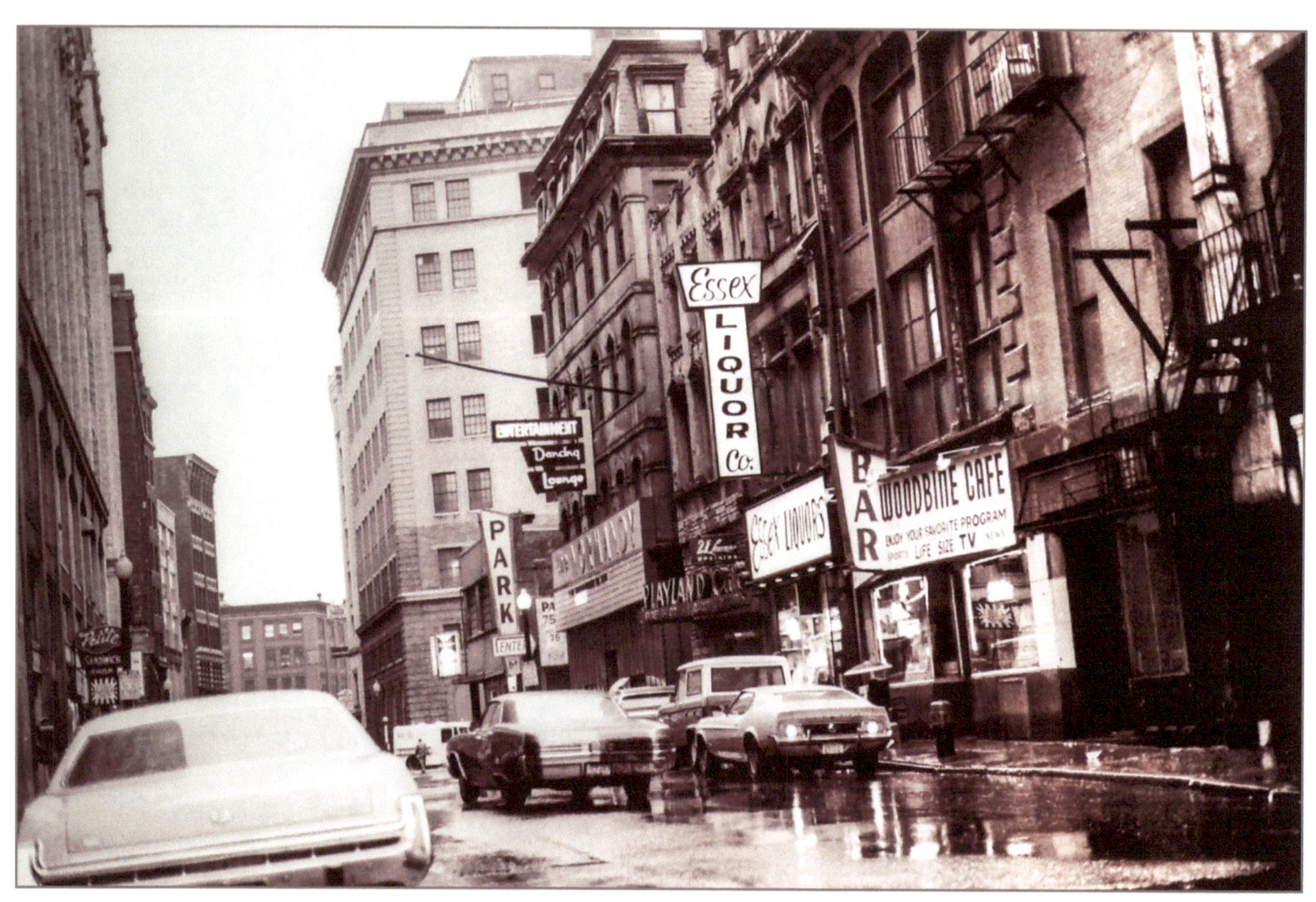

Essex Street in the Combat Zone.

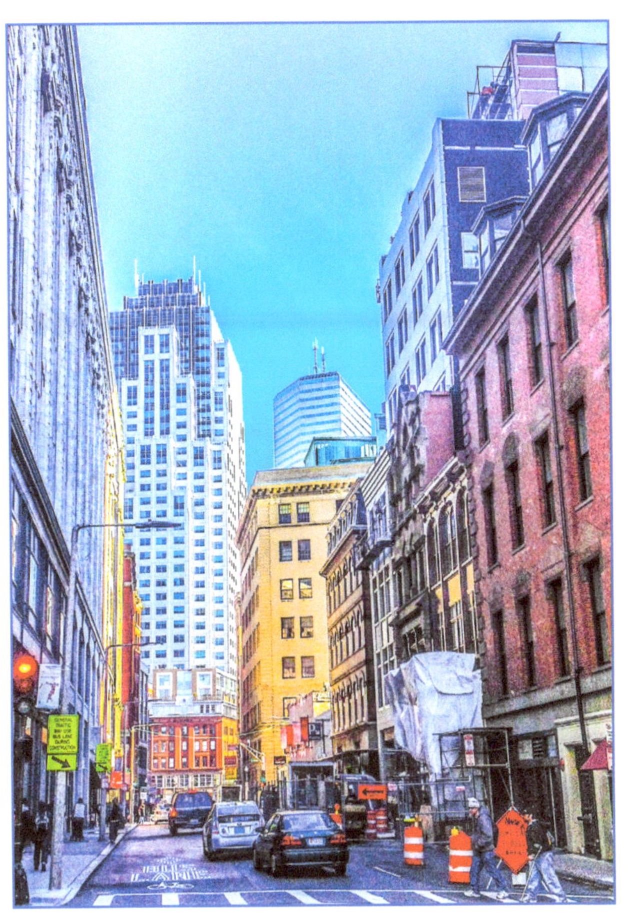

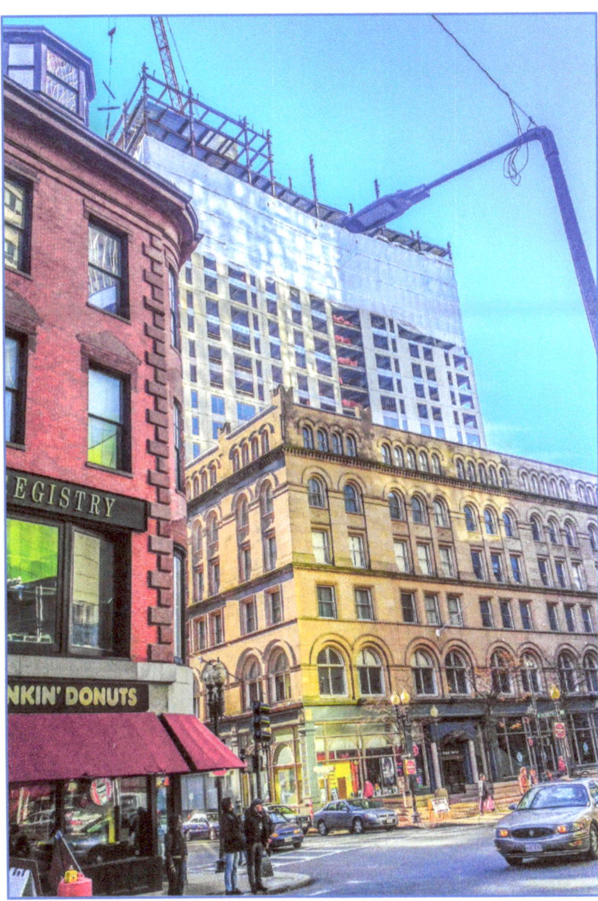
EGISTRY
NKIN' DONUTS

South Station was razed piecemeal and it was nearly demolished completely a couple of times before citizens' efforts in the early 1970's saved what was left of the building.

It is now on the National Register of Historic Sites.

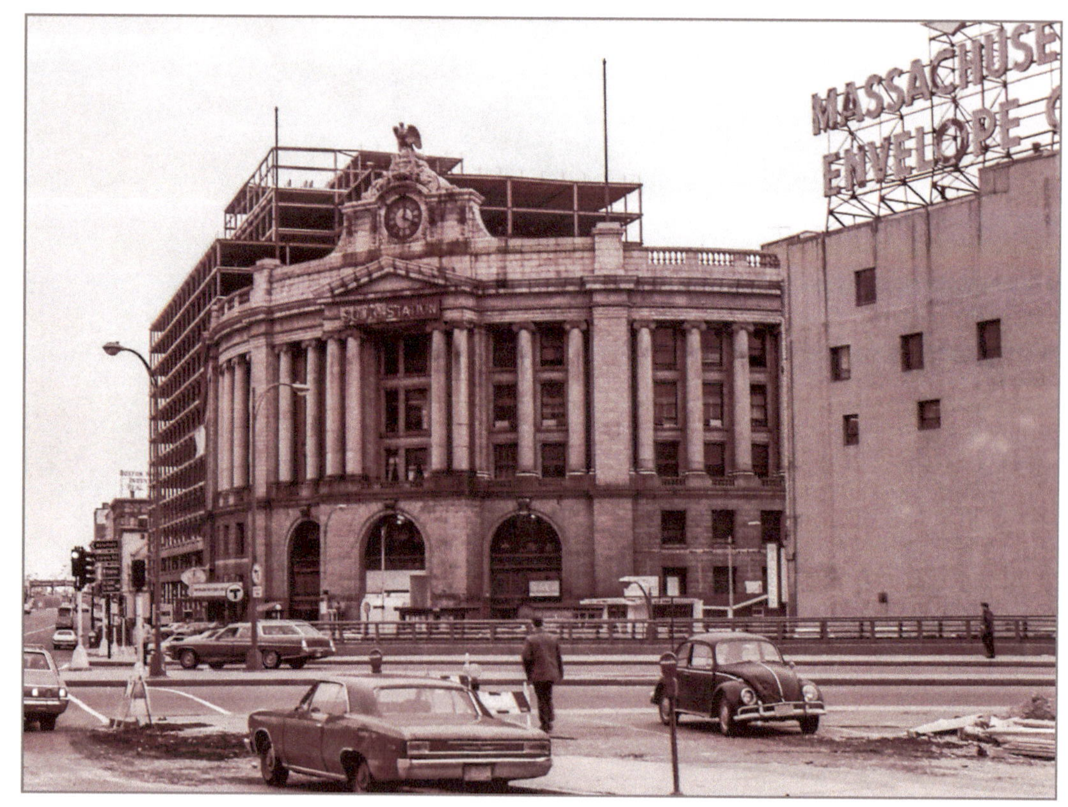

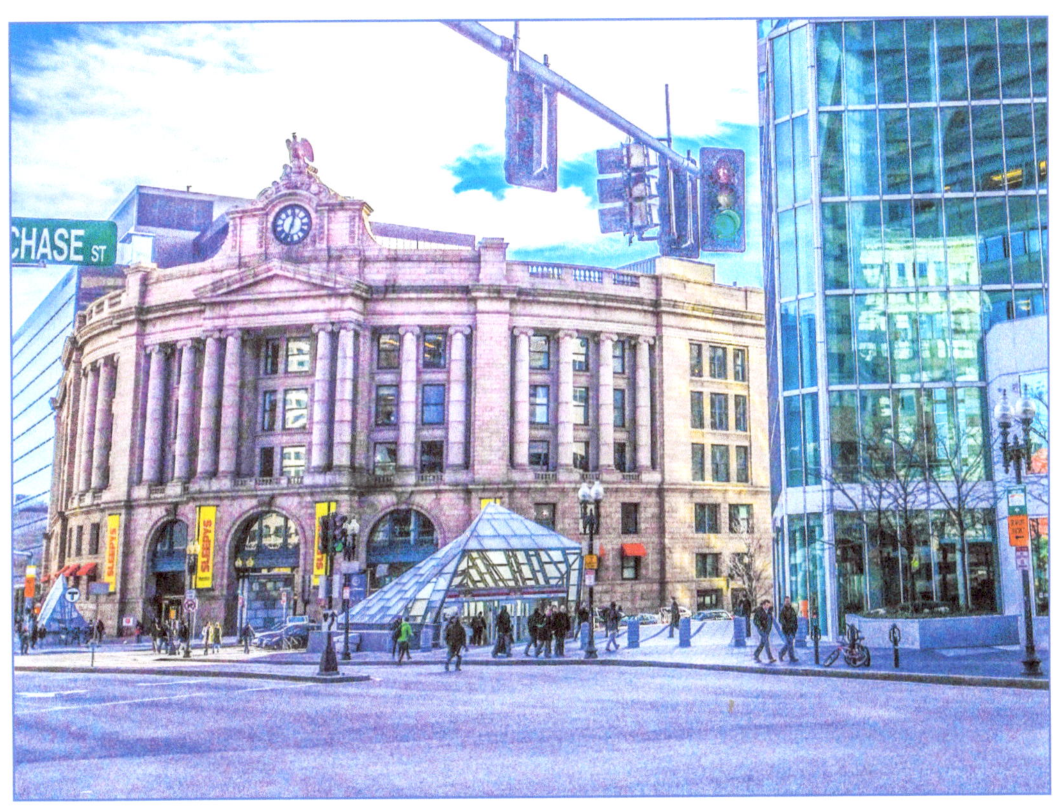
CHASE ST
SLEEPYS

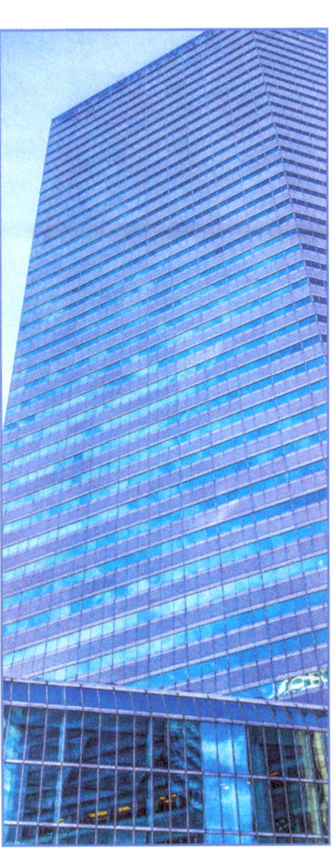

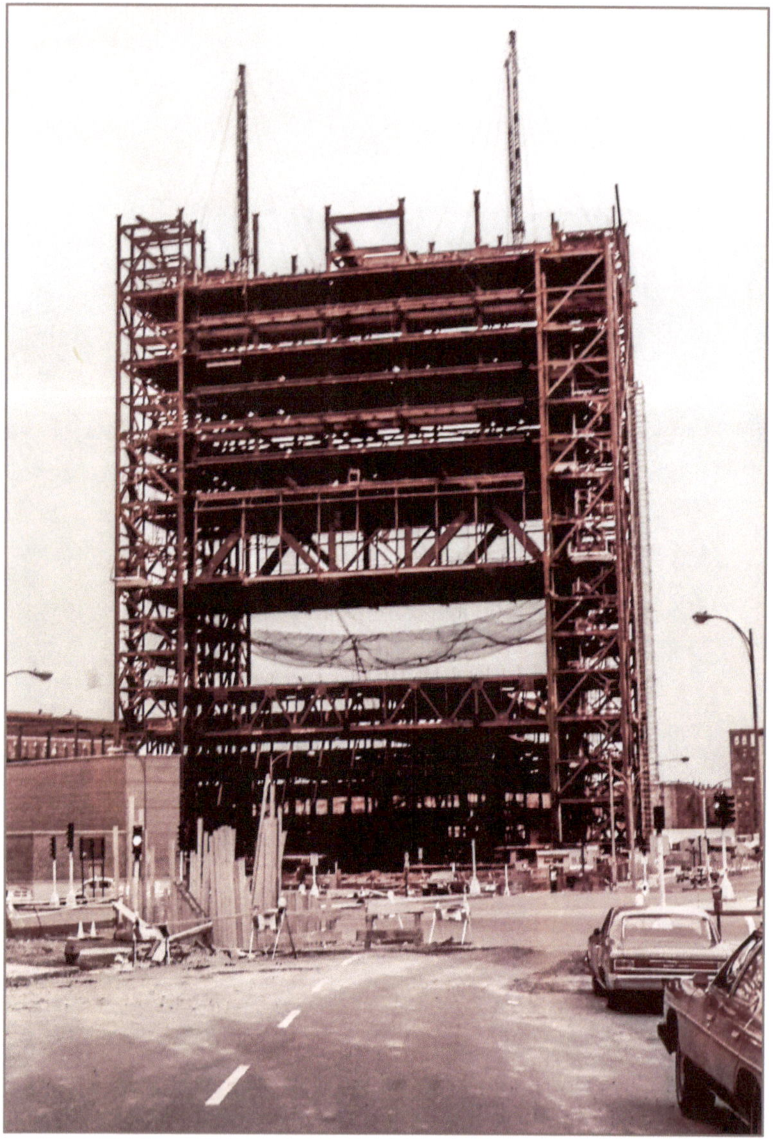

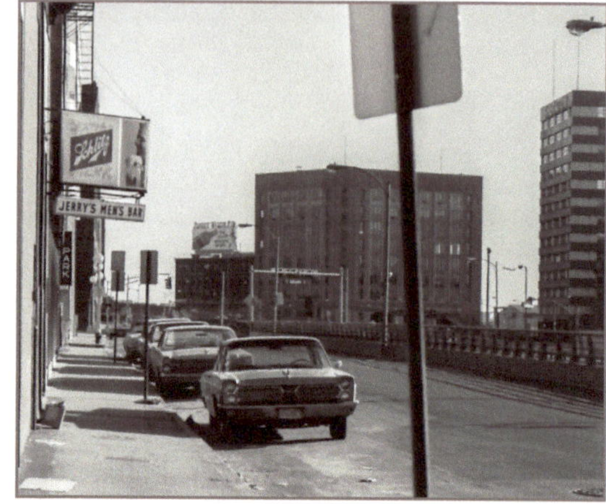

The skeleton of the Federal Reserve Bank rises in Dewey Square across from South Station in an area that was dotted with men's bars. The new bank was an important catalyst for change in the city.

Men's bars were dark inside and smelled stale from smoke and booze. They were ripe targets for feminist protests, although, higher end venues were more likely victims.

Locke-Obher's on Winter Place had wood paneling and polished, sparkling, sterling silver serving ware, but, women were not served.

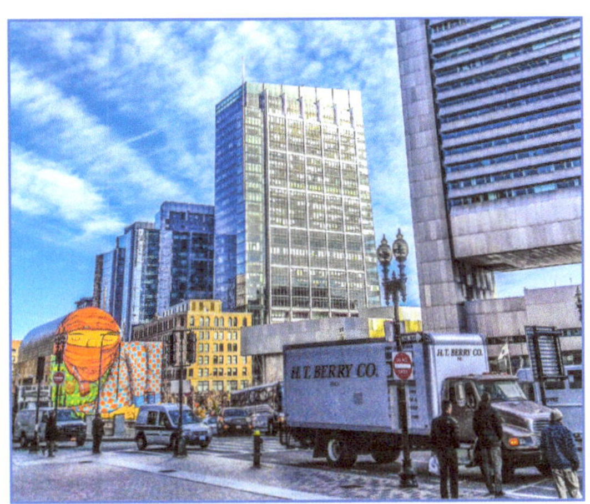

In the summer of 1970, an unruly hoard of angry feminists barged into the bar at Locke-Obher's, demanded drinks and then toasted each other.

The frenzy was unstoppable and less than grudgingly accepted by the previously all male bastion.

Across town at the Ritz-Carlton women wearing pants were not served in the dining room and unescorted women were not served at The Ritz Bar. Time dragged The Ritz into the future when, in 1975, they began accepting credit cards.

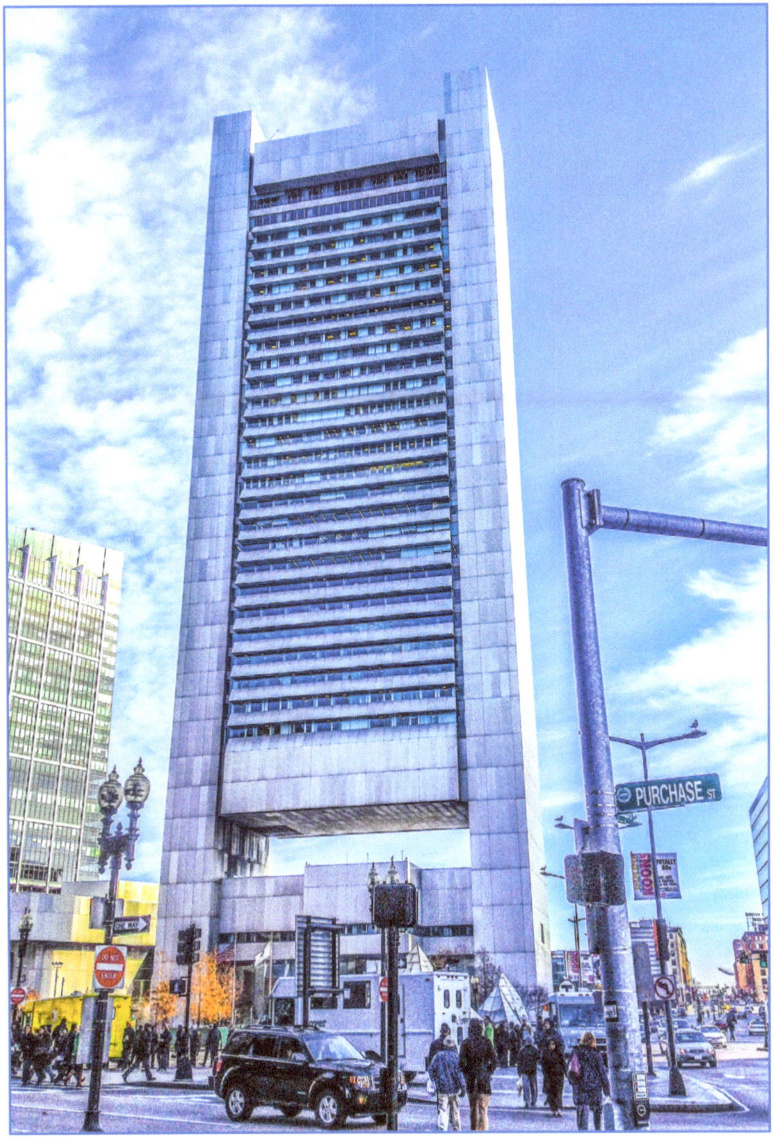

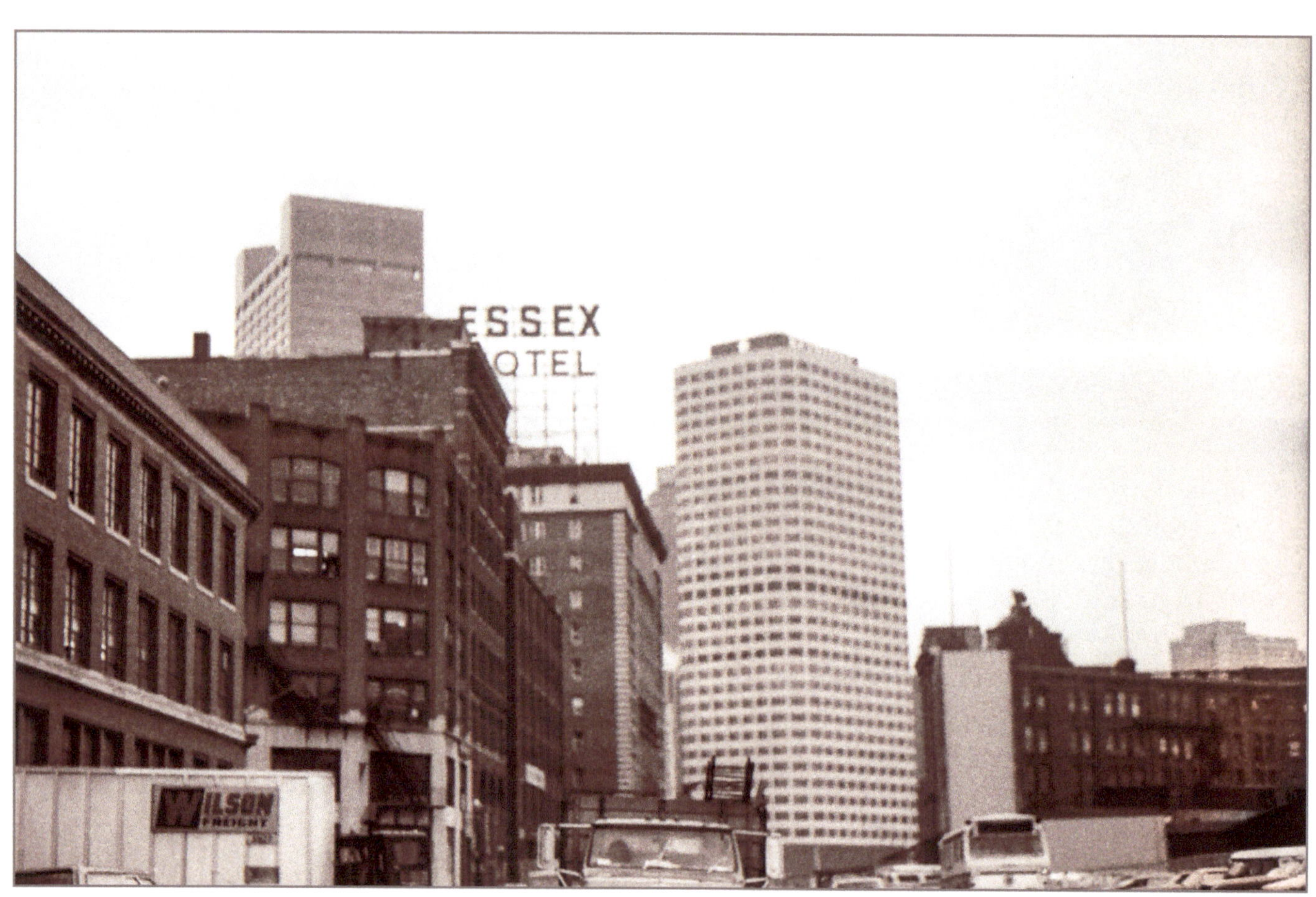

Atlantic Avenue with the Keystone Building in the center.

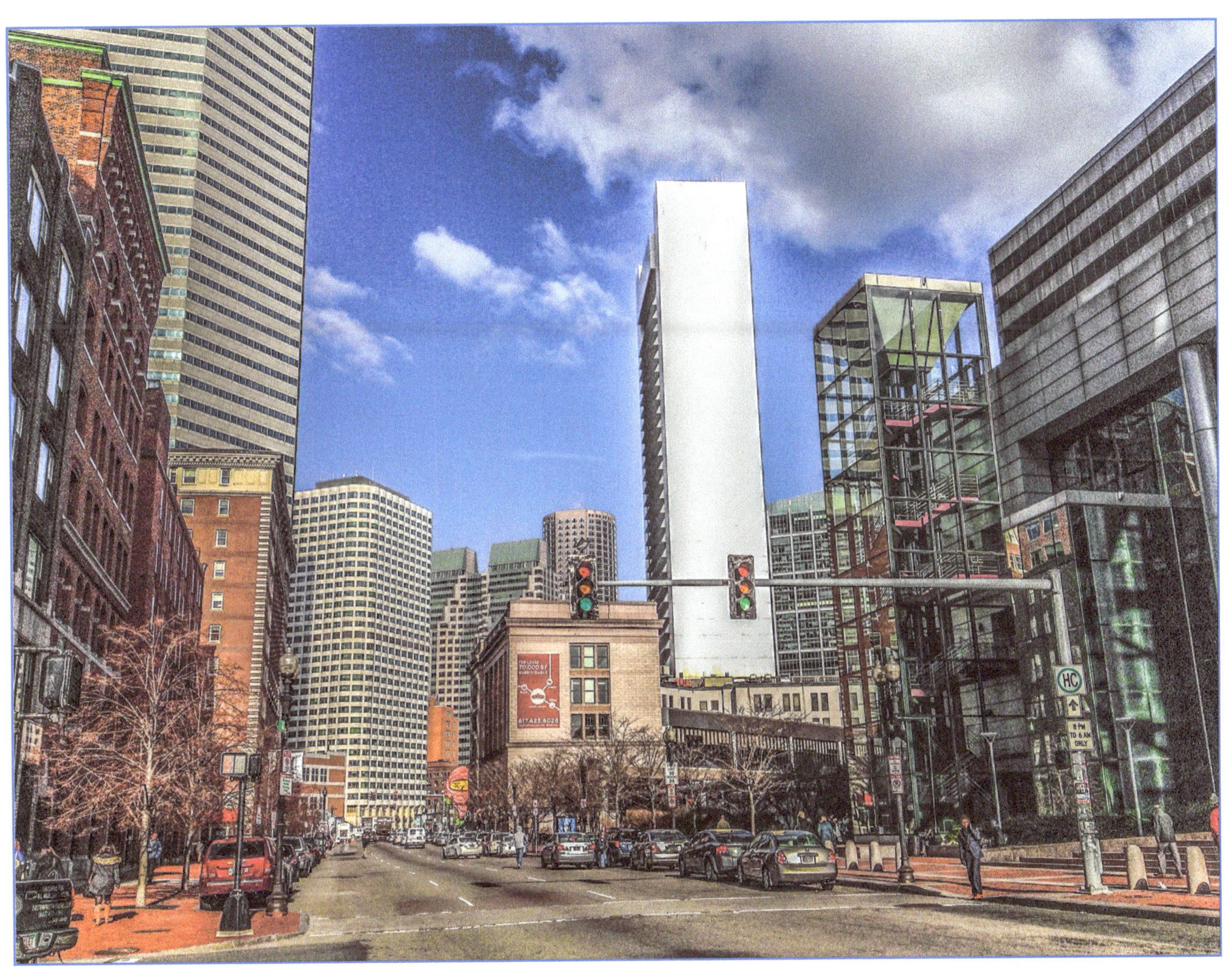
FOR LEASE
70,000 SF
617.423.6028
HC
8 PM TO 6 AM ONLY

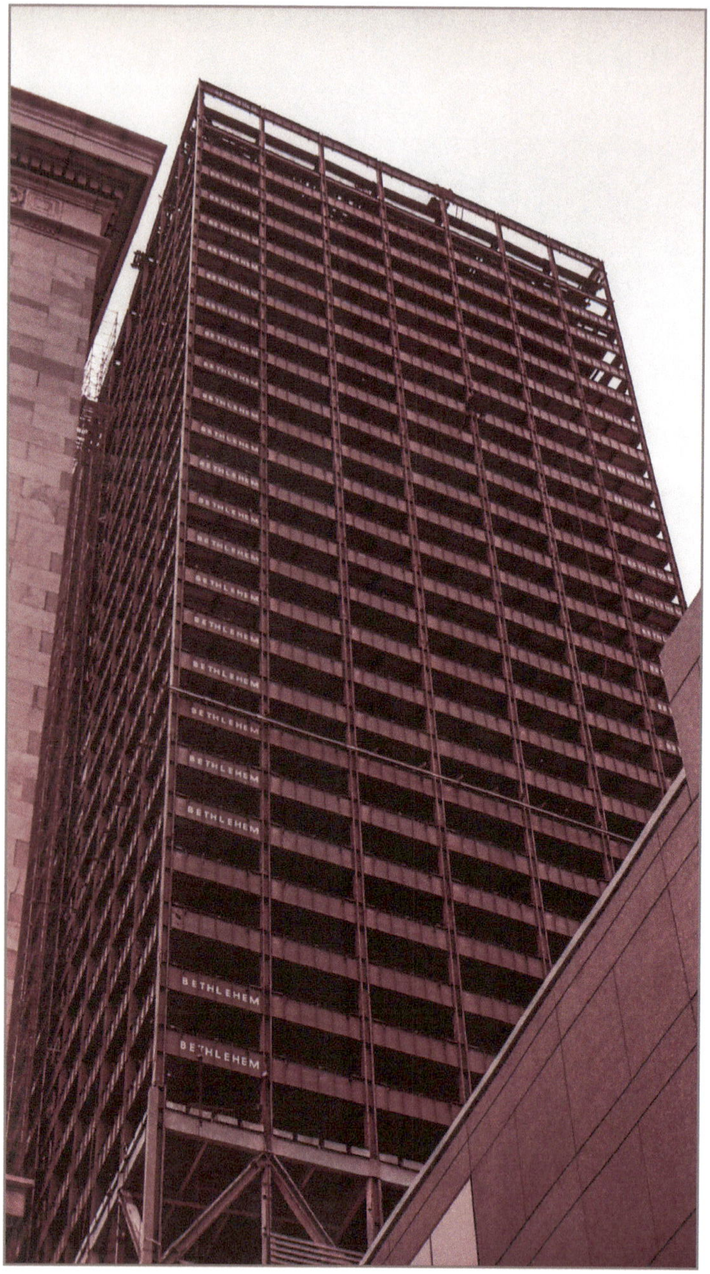

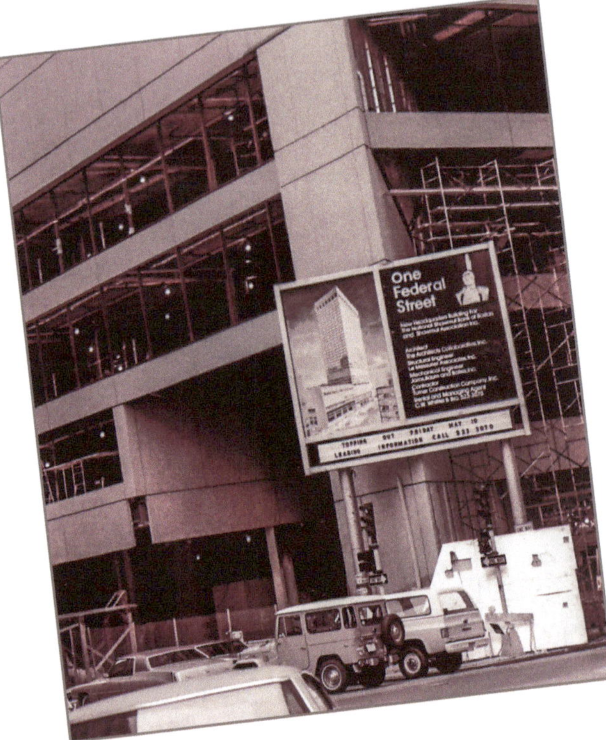
One
Federal
Street
TOPPING OUT FRIDAY MAY 19
LEASING INFORMATION CALL

Paul McCartney issued a press release on April 10, 1970, which announced that the Beatles had broken up. The hopes, dreams and rumors of a reunion flickered and dimmed until John Lennon was shot in 1980.

•

The life expectancy for US males in 1970 was 67.1 years.

•

DuPont received a patent for the 2 litre plastic bottle in 1973.

•

Hamilton Watch Company introduced the first electronic digital watch, the Pulsar, in April, 1972.

•

The United States Air Force developed the Global Positioning System (GPS), in 1973, using 24 satellites.

•

Baby Boomers are ageing. Since January 1, 2011, every month, 300,000 boomers will become eligible for Social Security and Medicare, until 2030.

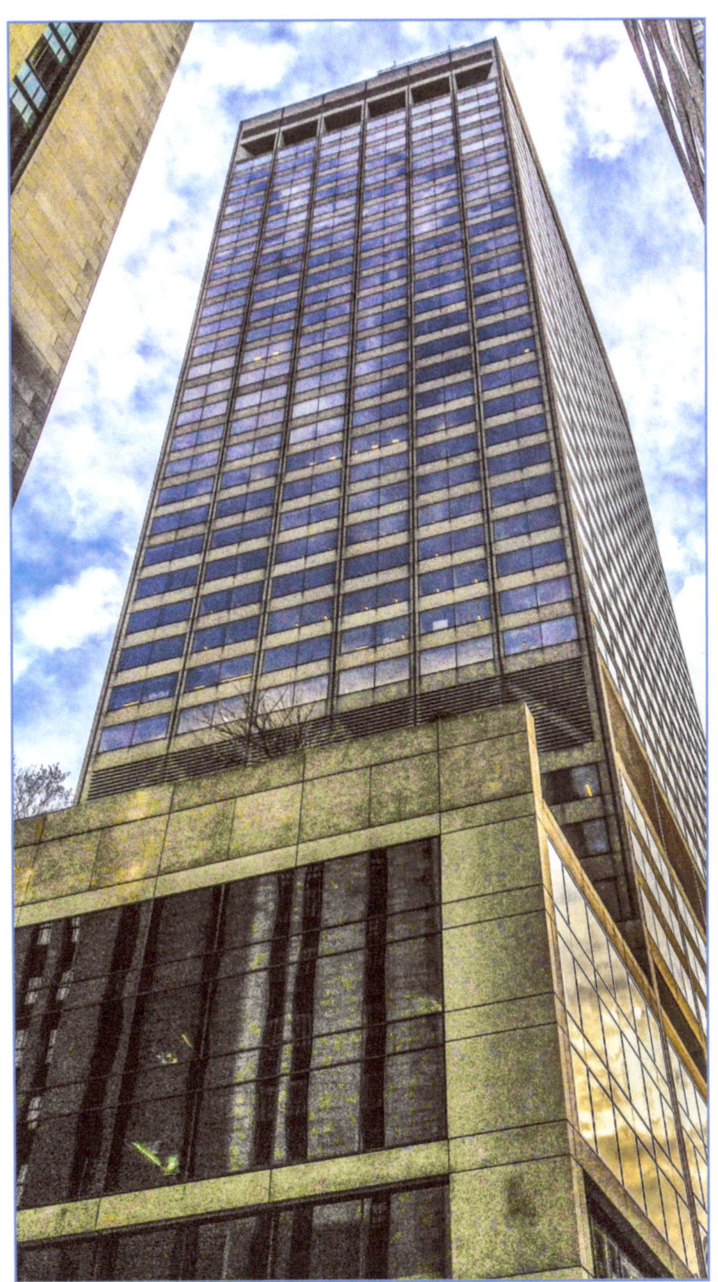

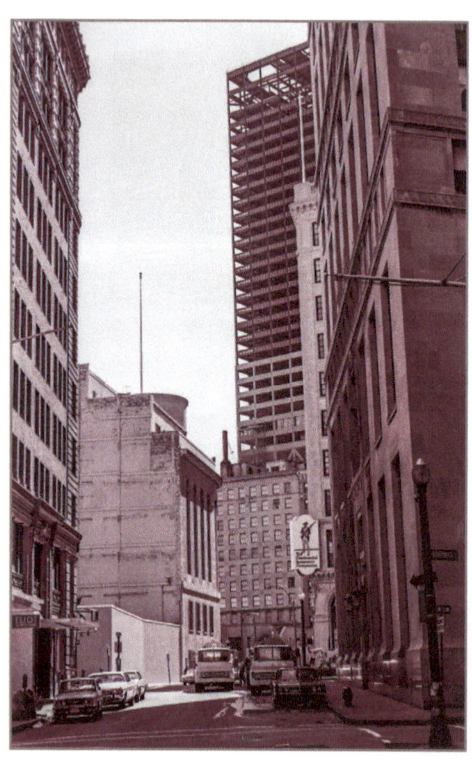

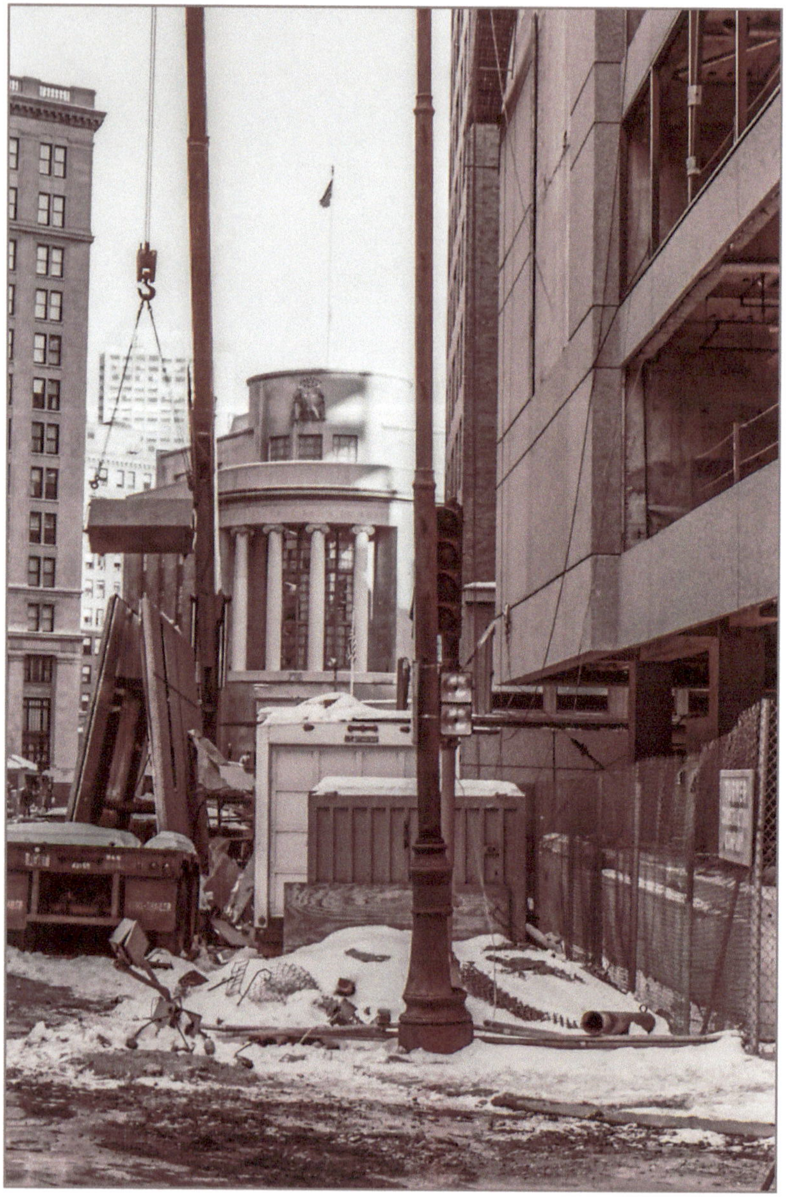

The Shawmut Bank is under construction on Milk Street and the old Federal Reserve Bank annex stands solidly on the other side of Post Office Square, although its fate has already been sealed.

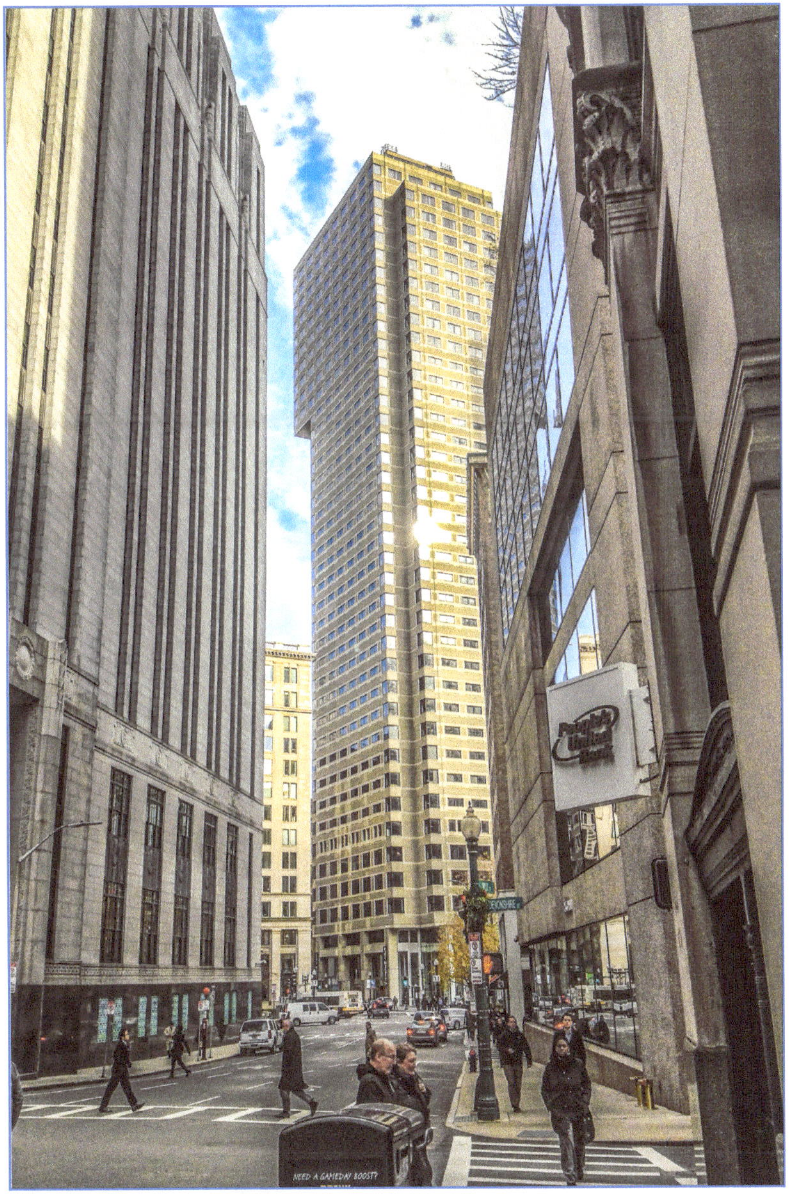

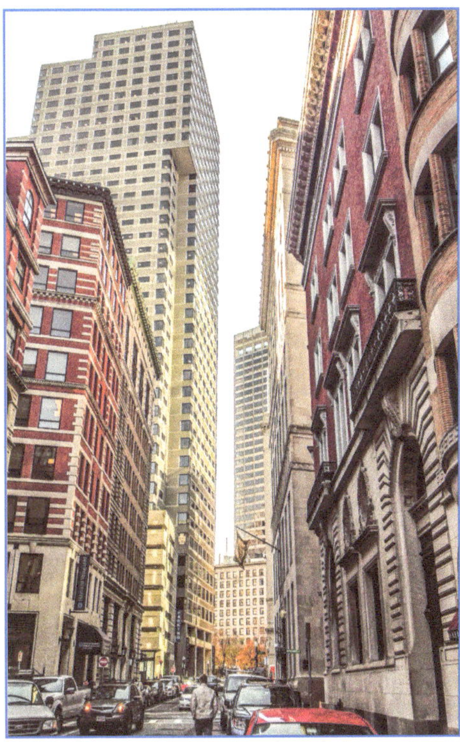

Above and far left, these pictures were taken two or three blocks further down Milk Street and looking back toward Post Office Square.

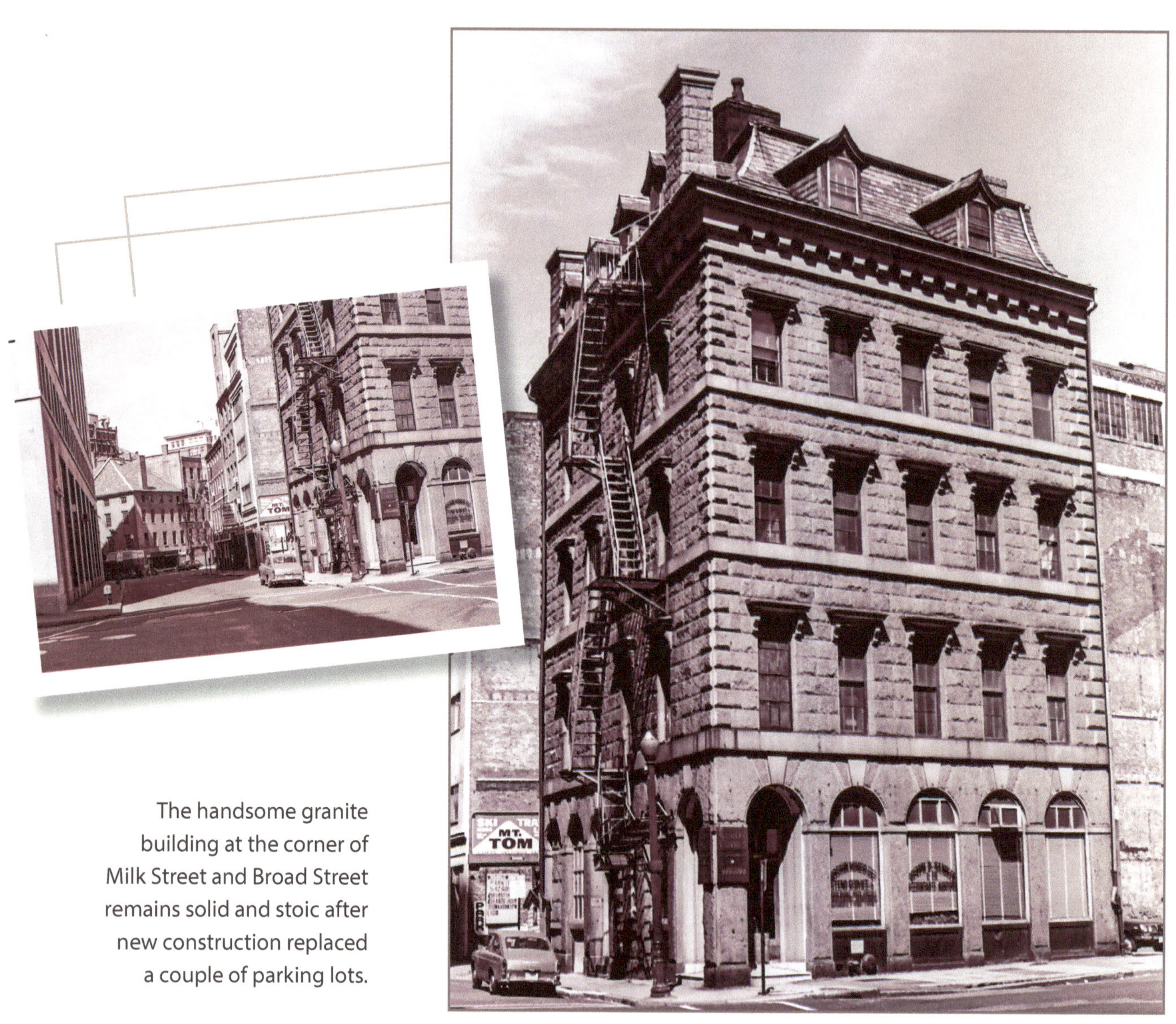

The handsome granite building at the corner of Milk Street and Broad Street remains solid and stoic after new construction replaced a couple of parking lots.

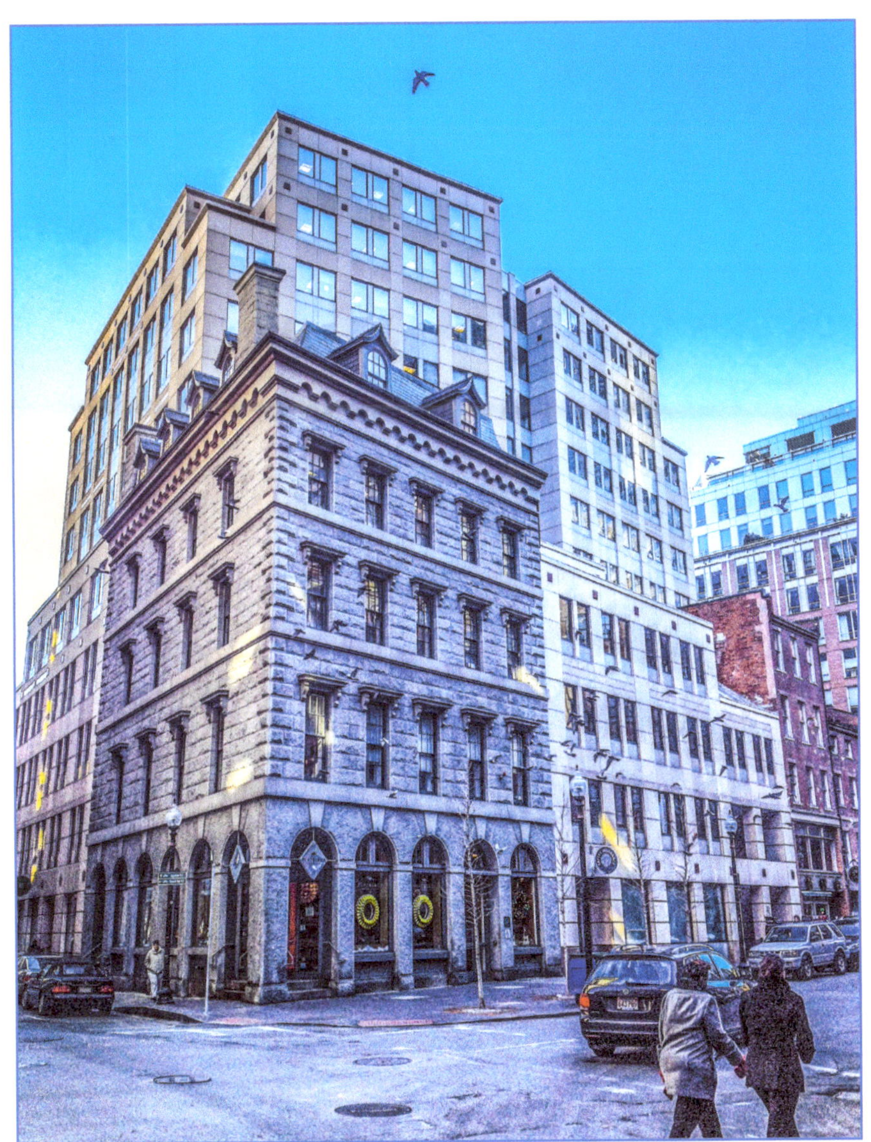

Social media has become an important form of communication. On Myspace, Facebook and Twitter, people are posting updates of their daily experiences.

Whether filtering a picture of your cat on Instagram or tweeting your feelings into 140 characters, people are instantly connecting to each other.

And accessing social media sites from mobile devices has become more convenient. You can stay connected to events in the community while on the go or Skype a street scene live from a cafe in Paris to Mom and Dad on Cape Cod. Social media is taking over the world.

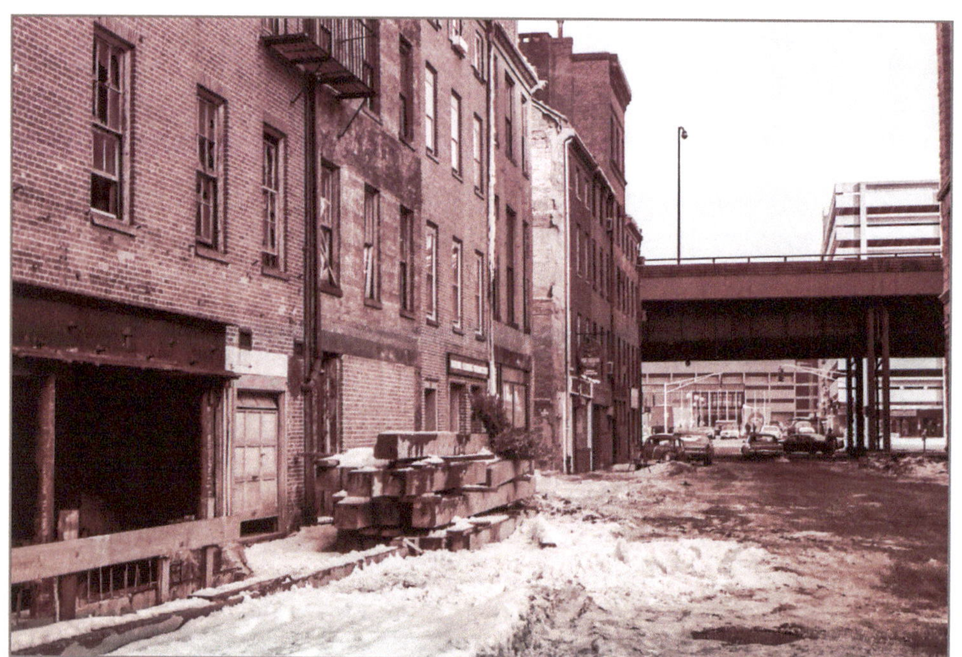

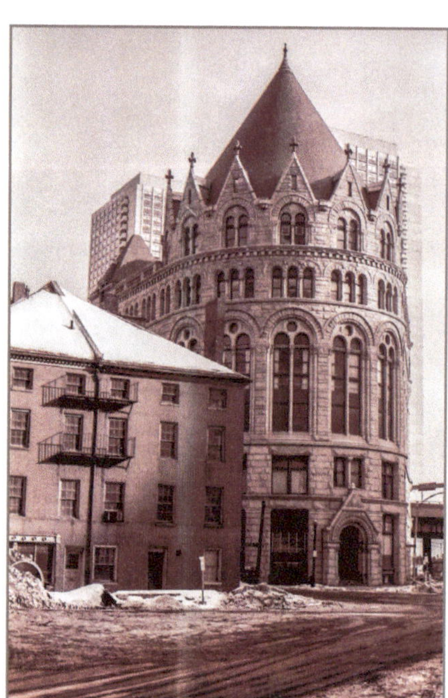

Milk Street continued under the Central Artery.

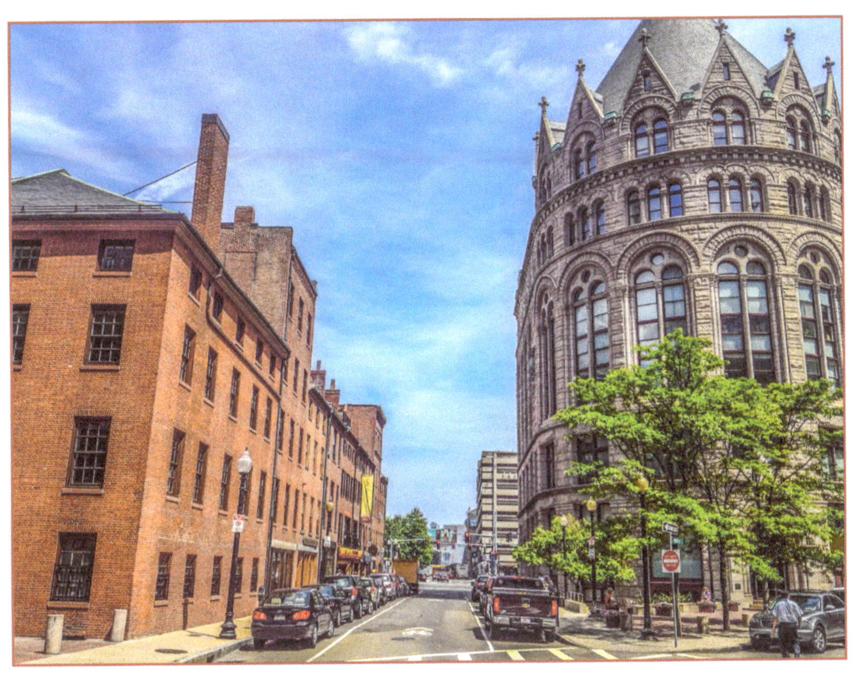

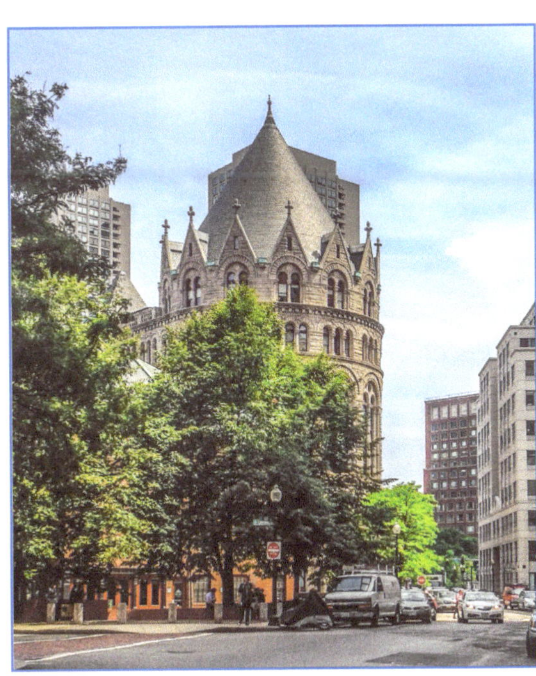

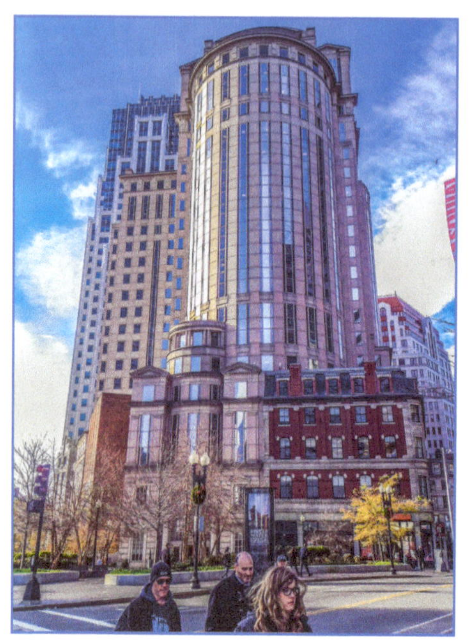

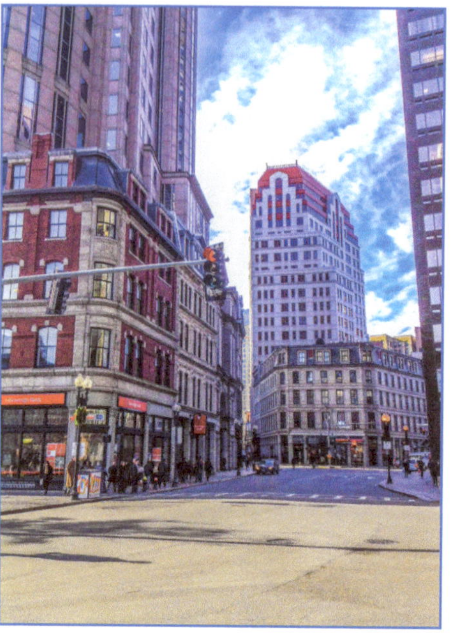

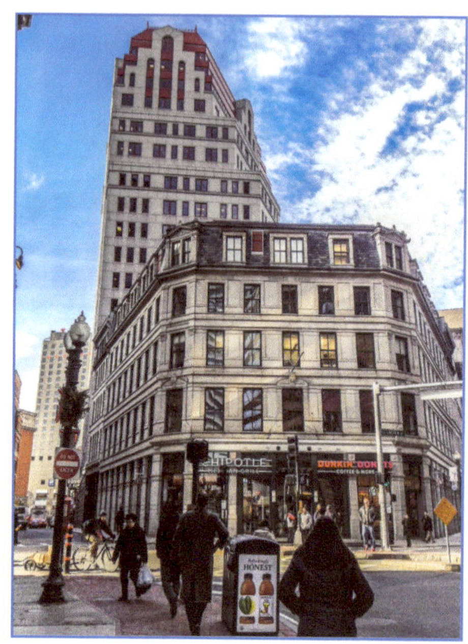

At far right, 100 Summer Street was nearing completion and, at 32 stories, dwarfed its neighbors, including the Church Green Buildings which were built after the Great Fire of 1872.

These buildings seem tiny today but they shine bright in a scene of goliathan contrasts. The district is listed in the National Register of Historic Places.

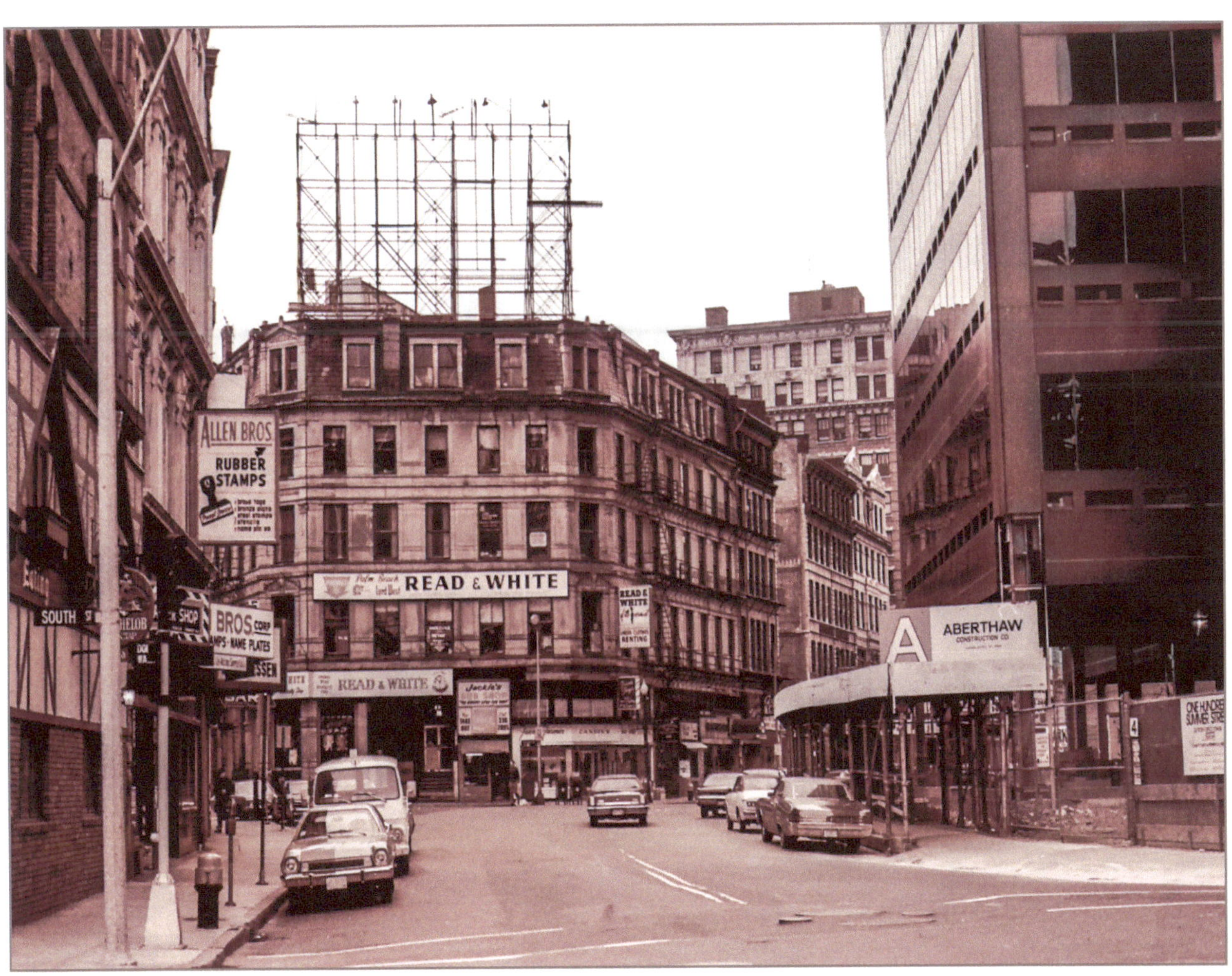
ALLEN BROS
RUBBER STAMPS
READ & WHITE
SOUTH
BROS. CORP
READ & WHITE
ABERTHAW
CONSTRUCTION CO.
A

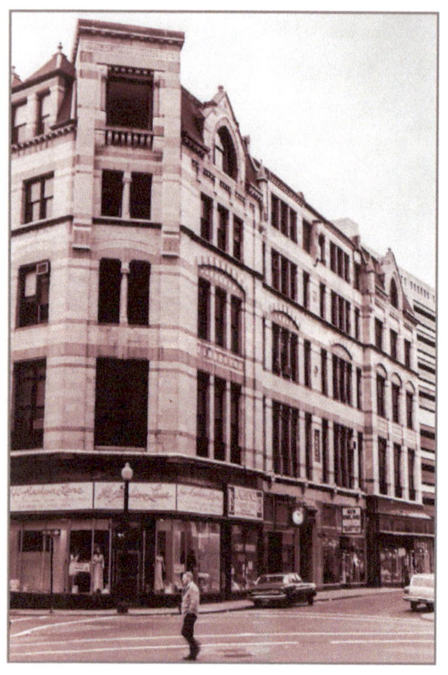

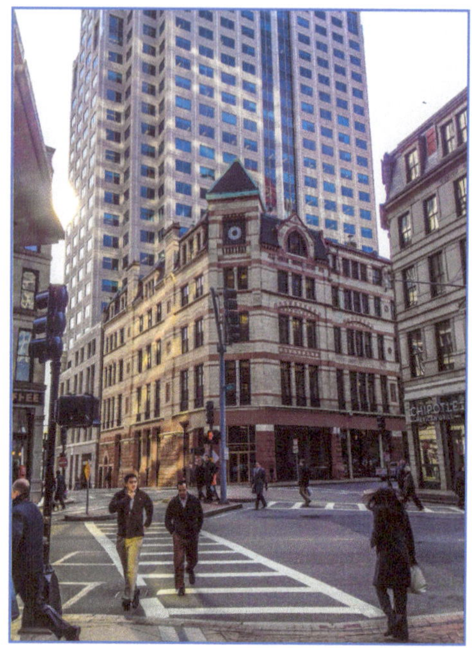

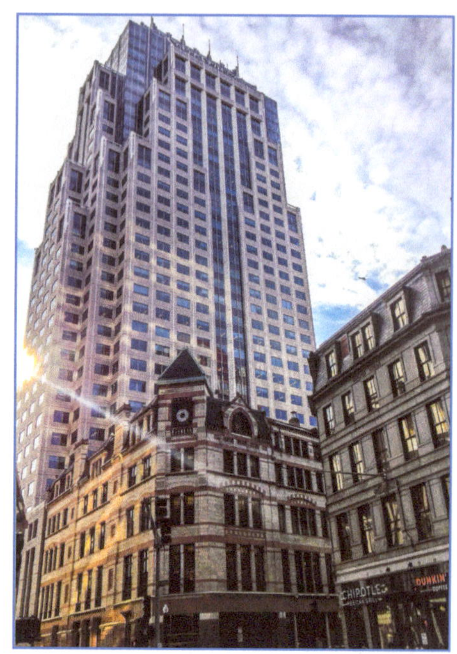

The Bedford Building at 99 Bedford Street was built after the Great Boston Fire of 1872. It was added to the National Historic Register in 1979.

At right, One Winthrop Square was also built after the fire which destroyed 65 acres of the commercial district. The area was rebuilt in short time with capital from Boston's wealthy merchants and businessmen.

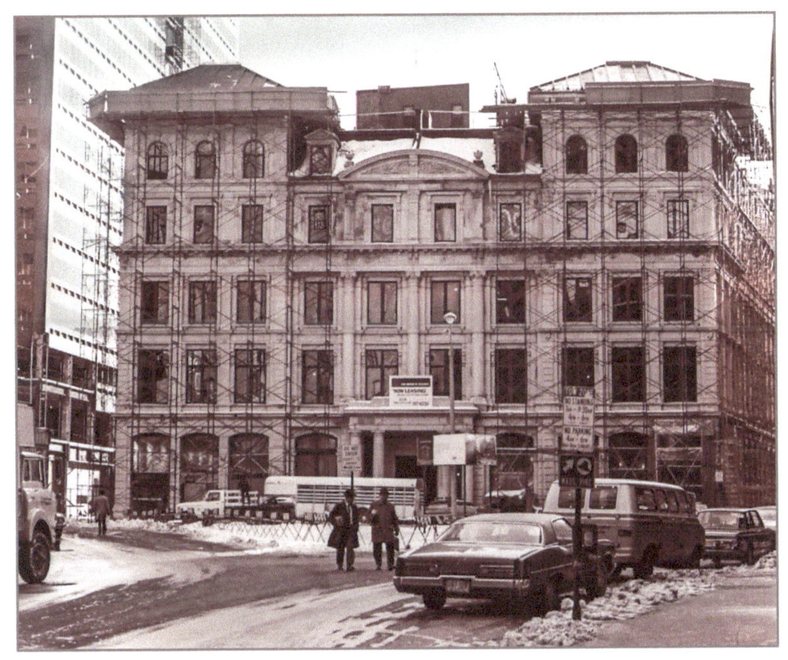

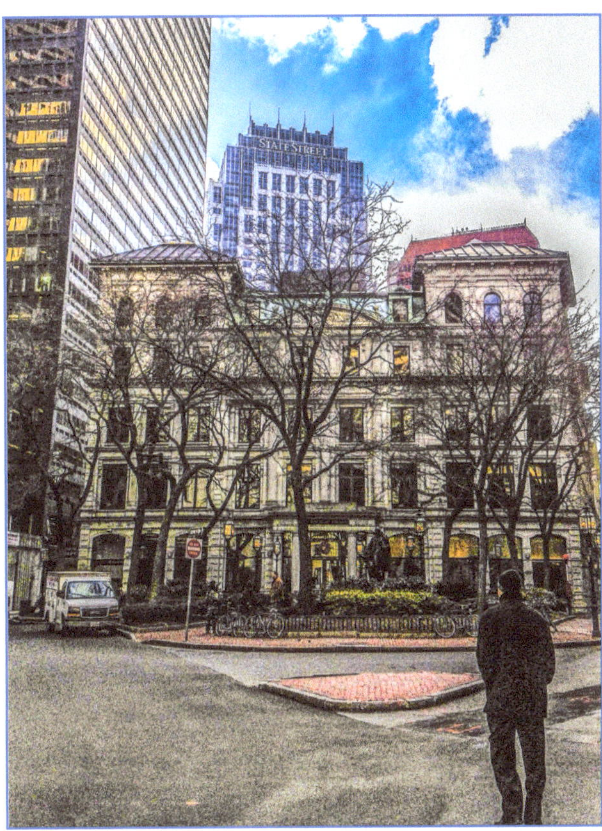
STATE STREET

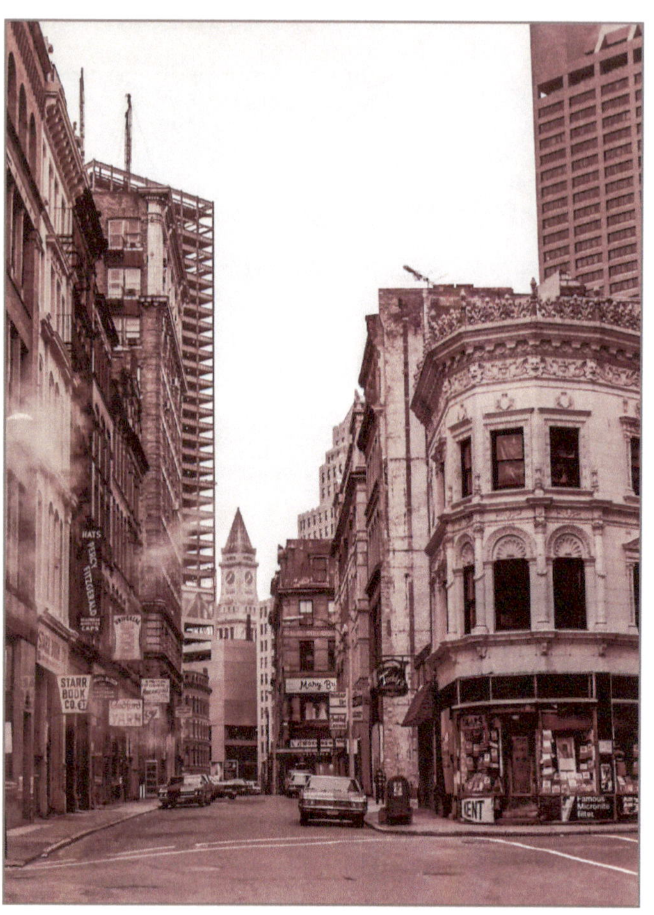

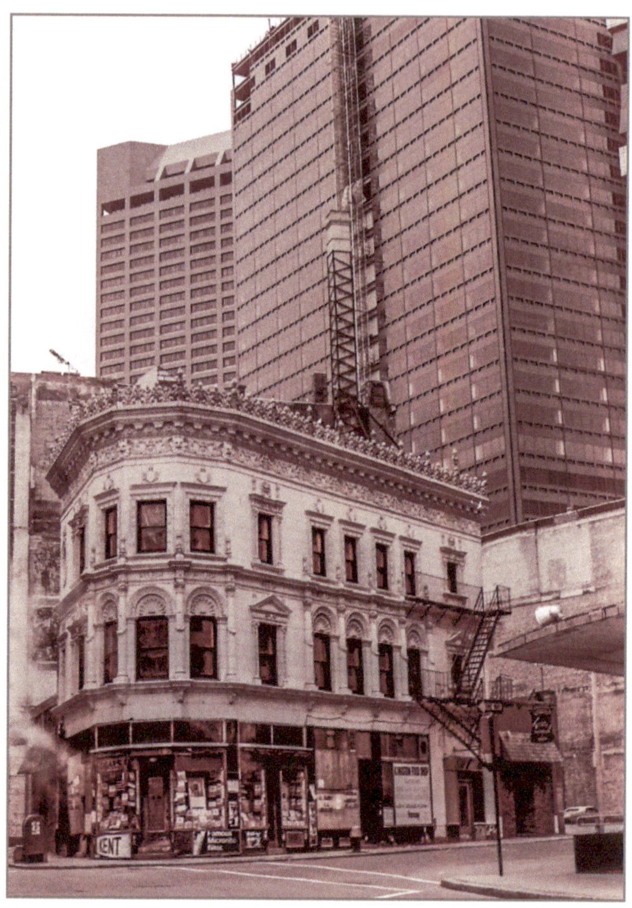

The Proctor Building was built in 1897 at Bedford Street and Kingston Street in what, at the time, was the leather district.

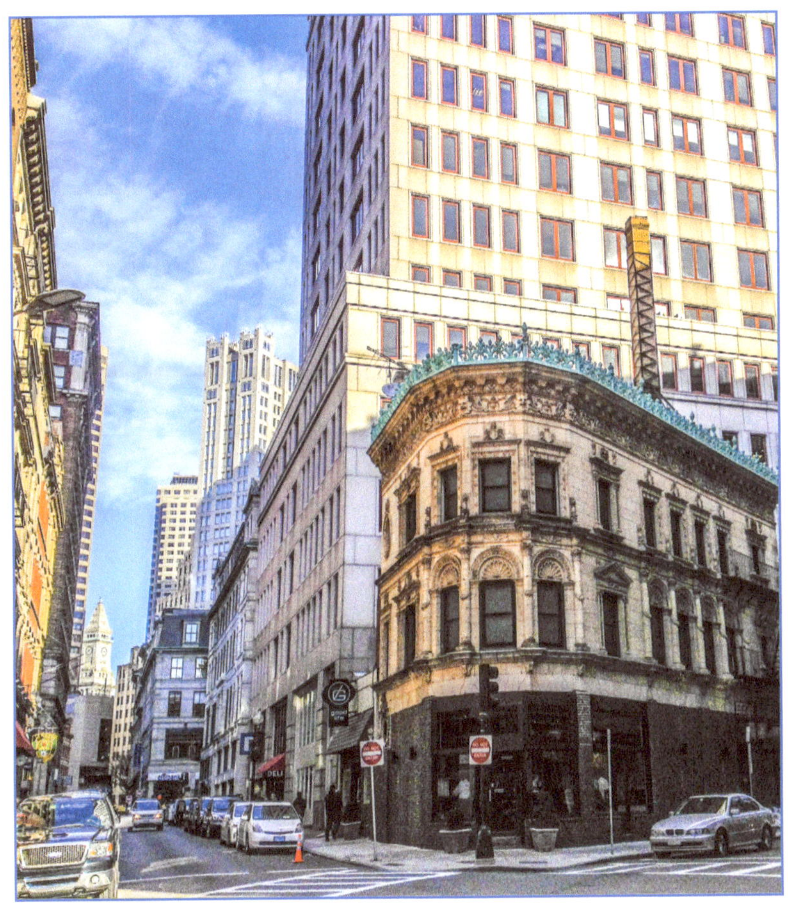
DELI

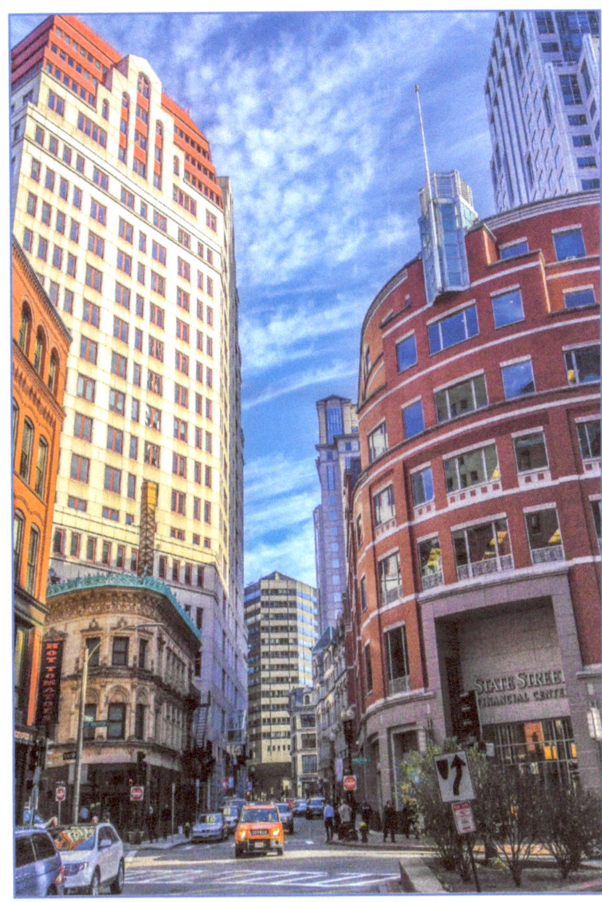
STATE STREE
FINANCIAL CENTE

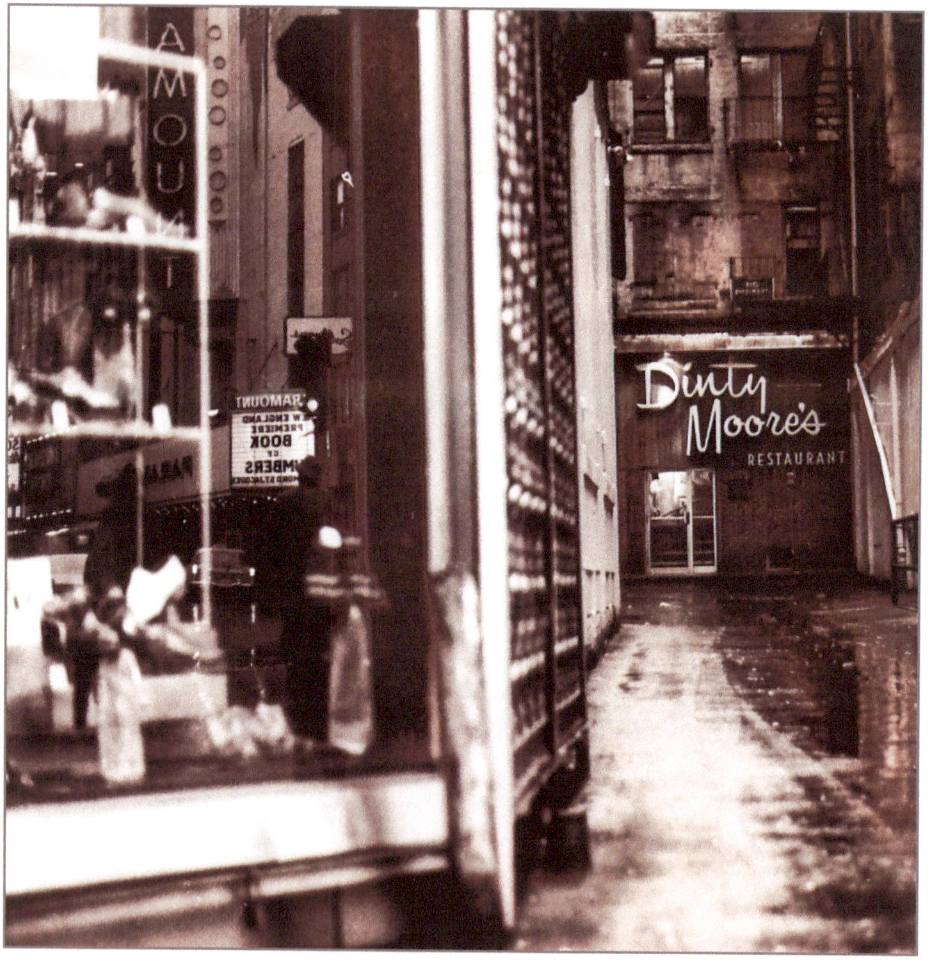

Dinty Moore's entrance was located in an alley just past the Paramount Theater on Washington Street. It was a popular steaks and chops restaurant out of New York that featured red carpets and red walls with white linen tablecloths where patrons drank martinis and manhattans with their meat.

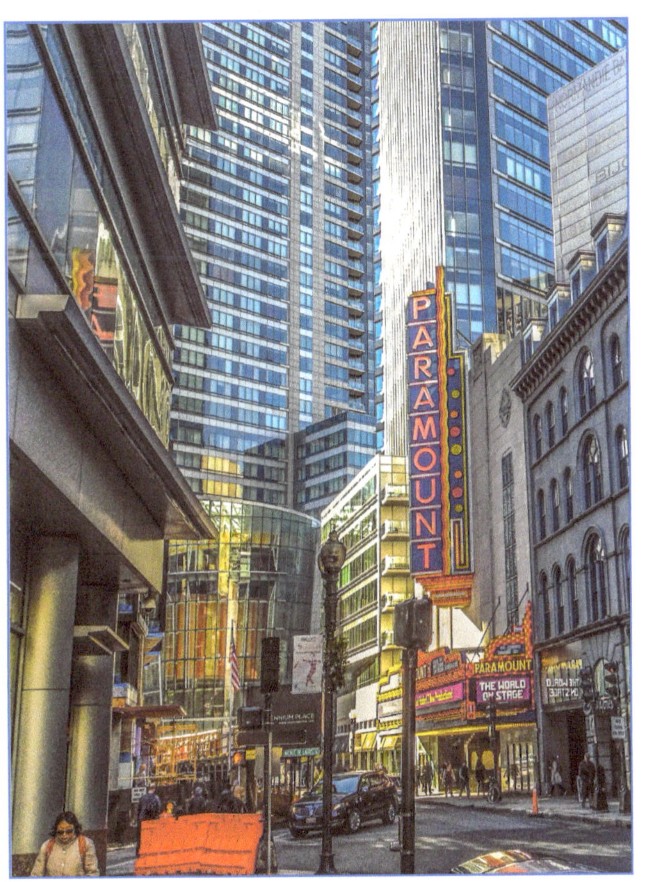
PARAMOUNT
PARAMOUNT
THE WORLD ON STAGE

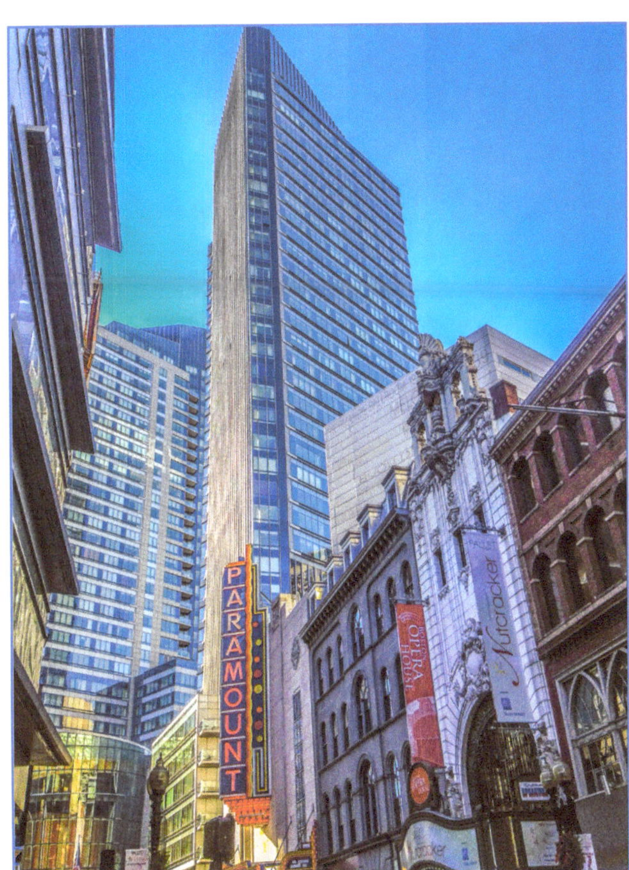
PARAMOUNT
BOSTON OPERA HOUSE
Nutcracker

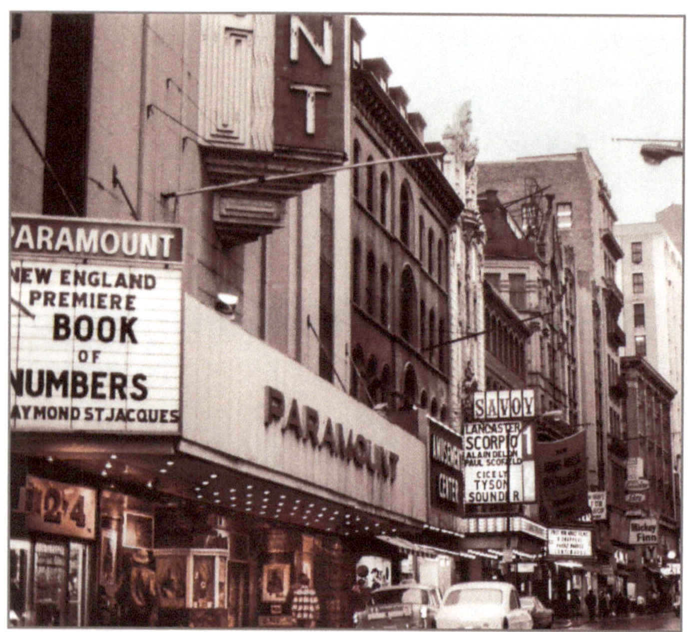

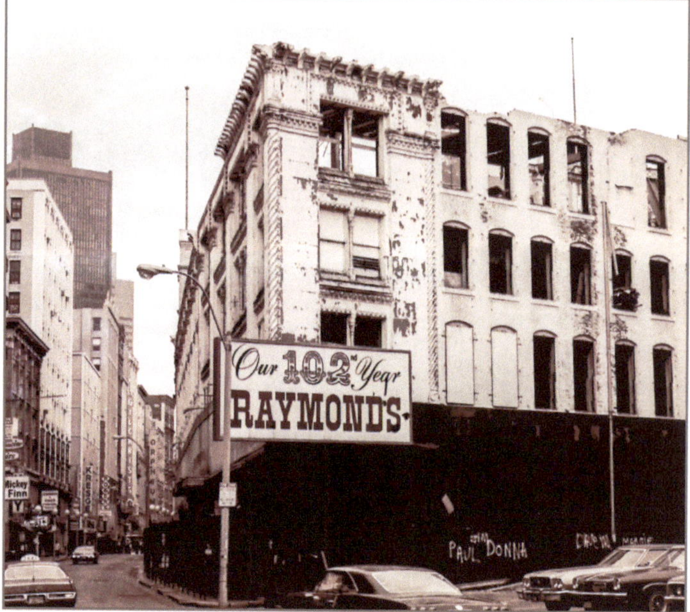

Raymond's had moved into the R.H. White building and it was part of a row of large department stores on Washington Street that was the major shopping destination before suburban malls made downtown redundant. Other stores included Jordan Marsh, Gilchrist's and Filene's.

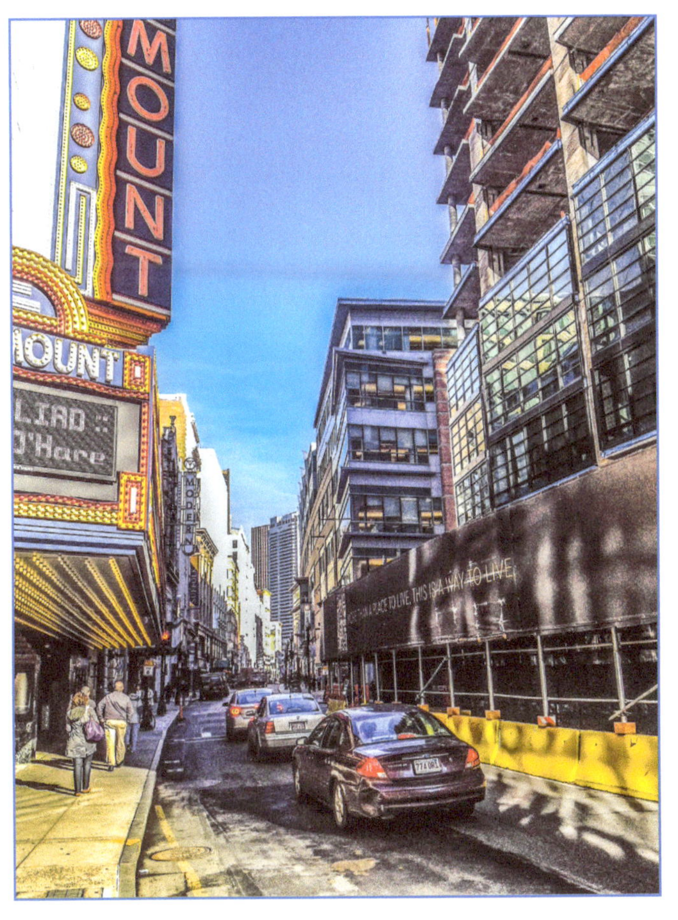
MOUNT

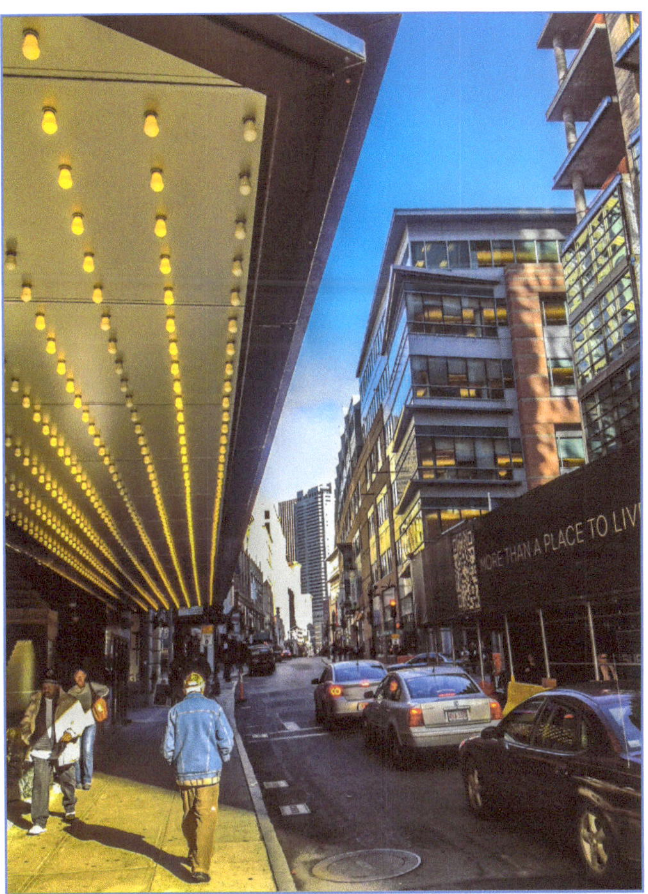

Higher education has become big business in downtown Boston. Emerson College and Suffolk University have expanded their physical footprints and changed the landscape.

Theaters have been reborn, buildings have been renovated for dormitories and classrooms and the new construction is architecturally significant. In blighted areas, vitality has replaced vulgarity.

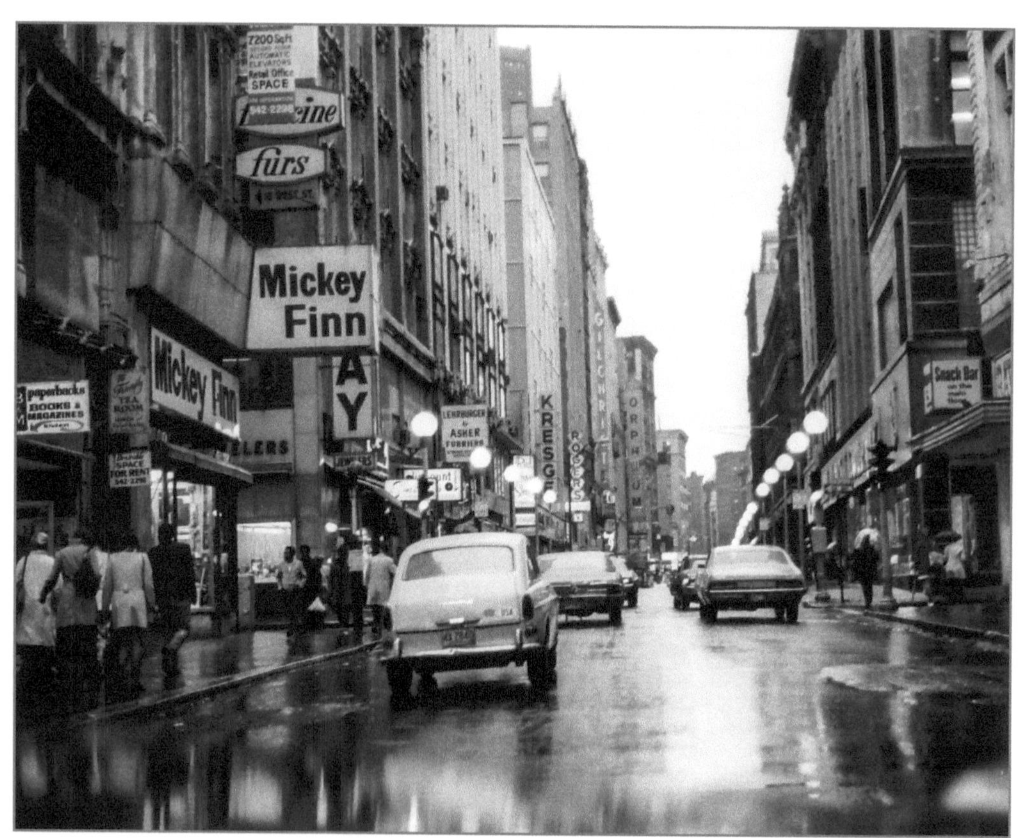

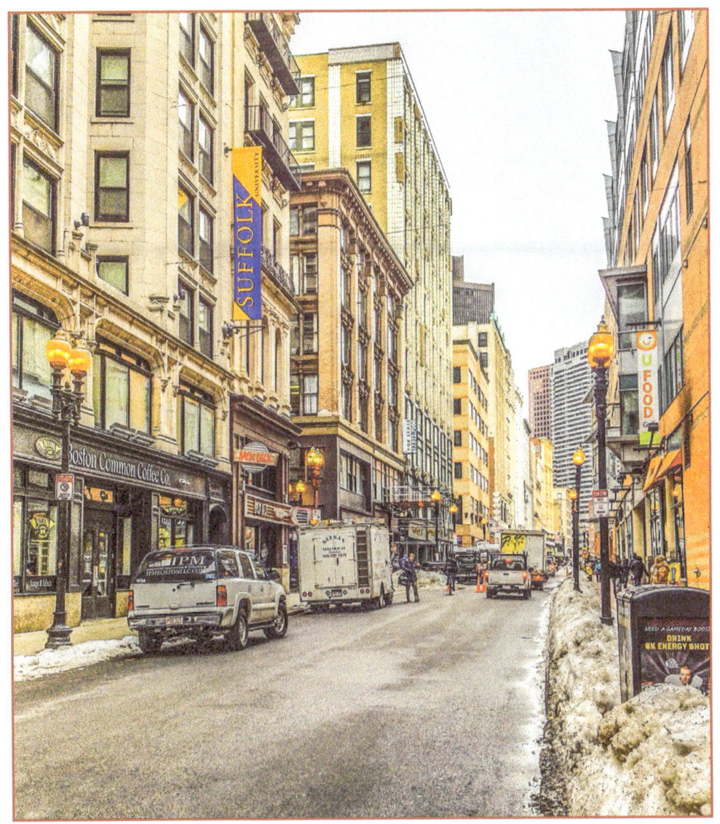

But the rising cost of higher education has been a real concern over the past decade. Although the number of young adults graduating from colleges and universities has been growing, the debt most of these students are left to pay has also been growing. However, we may be getting closer to outsmarting outrageous tuitions.

Harvard and MIT have formed a nonprofit partnership known as edX which offers curriculum courses free online. Students can receive a certificate and a grade, but not credit toward a degree.

Other universities have also developed programs offering free massively open online courses (MOOCs). This open system of learning and education gives opportunity to gain knowledge that was previously attainable only to those who could afford the cost.

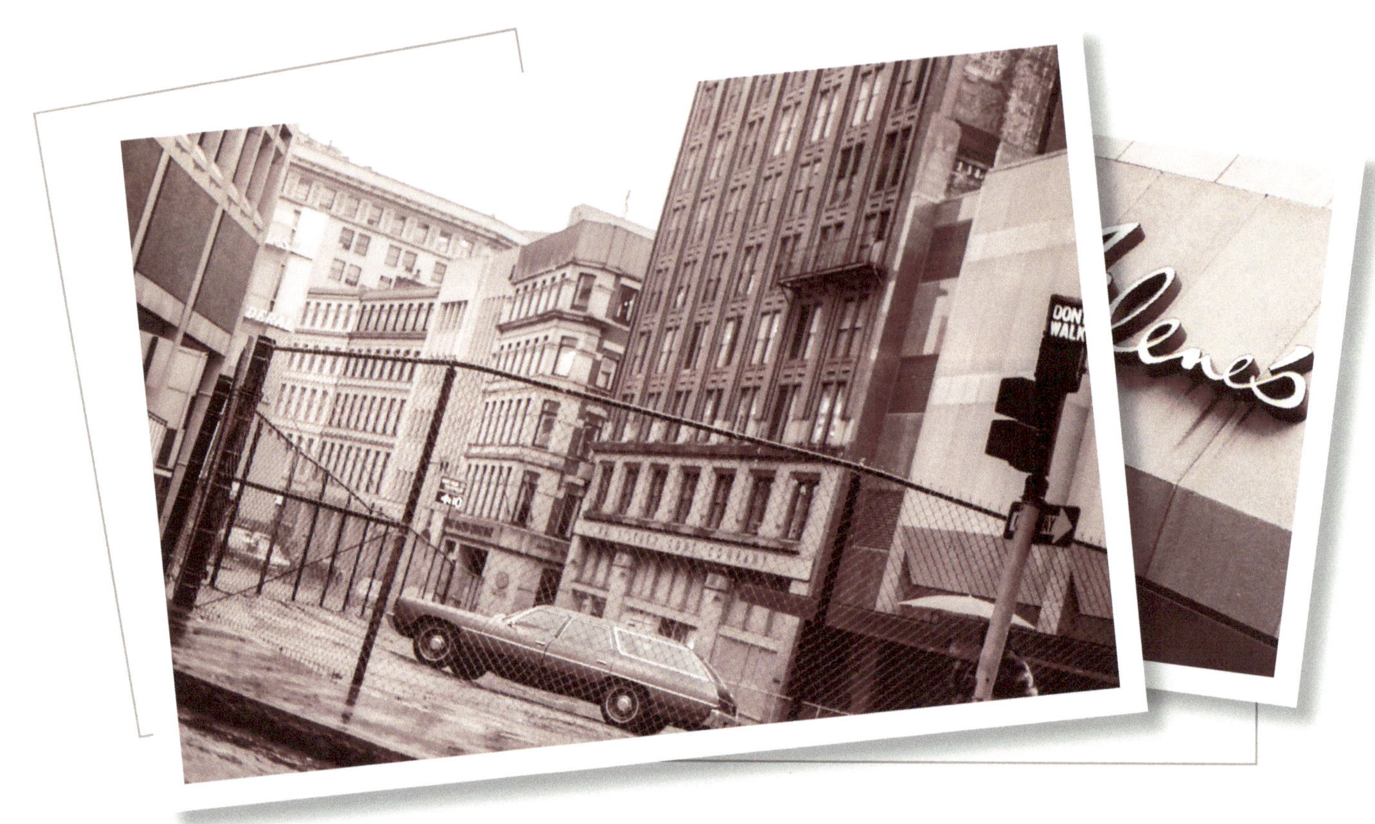

A 625 foot tower with nearly 450,000 square feet of leasable space will soon rise above the spot formerly occupied by Filene's at Washington and Franklin Streets.

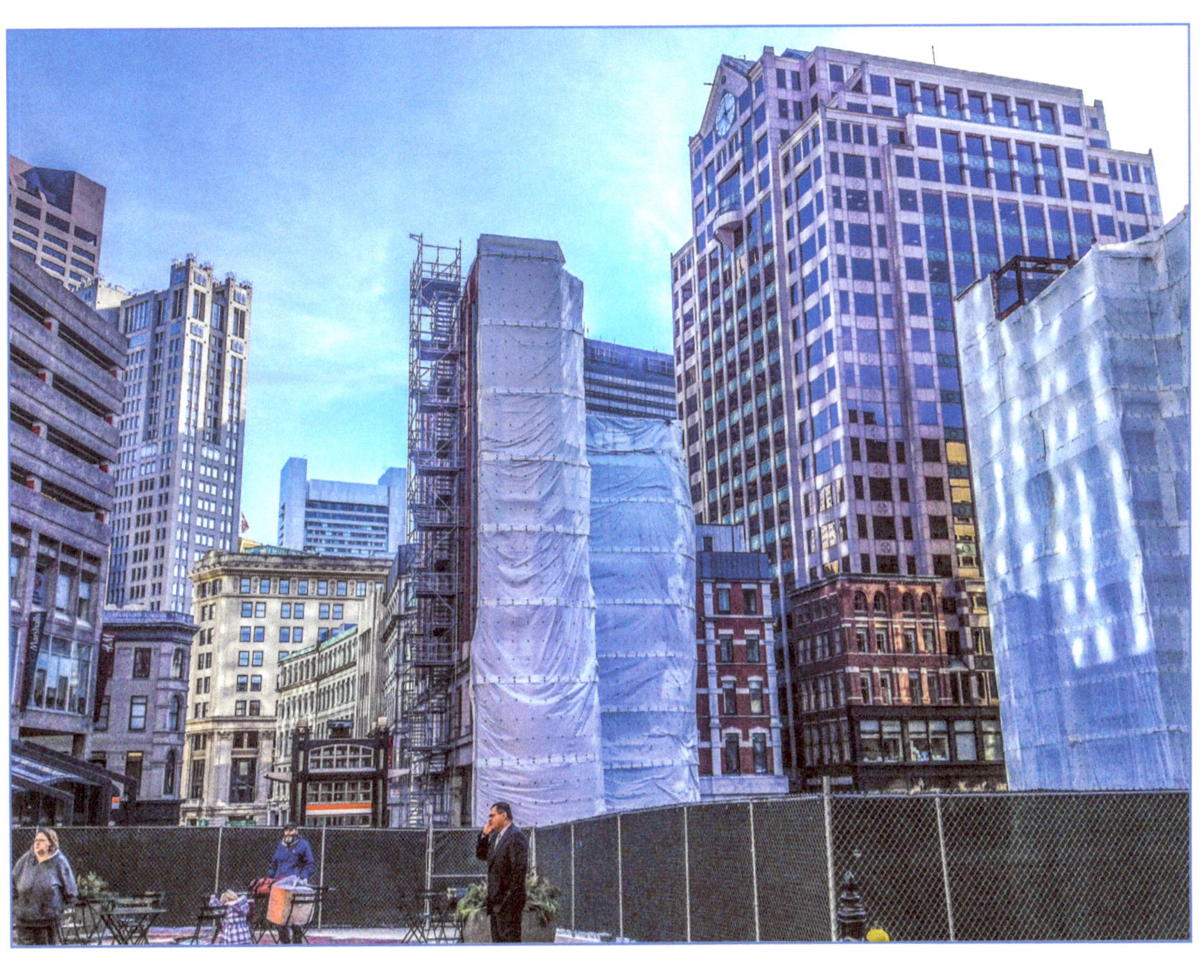

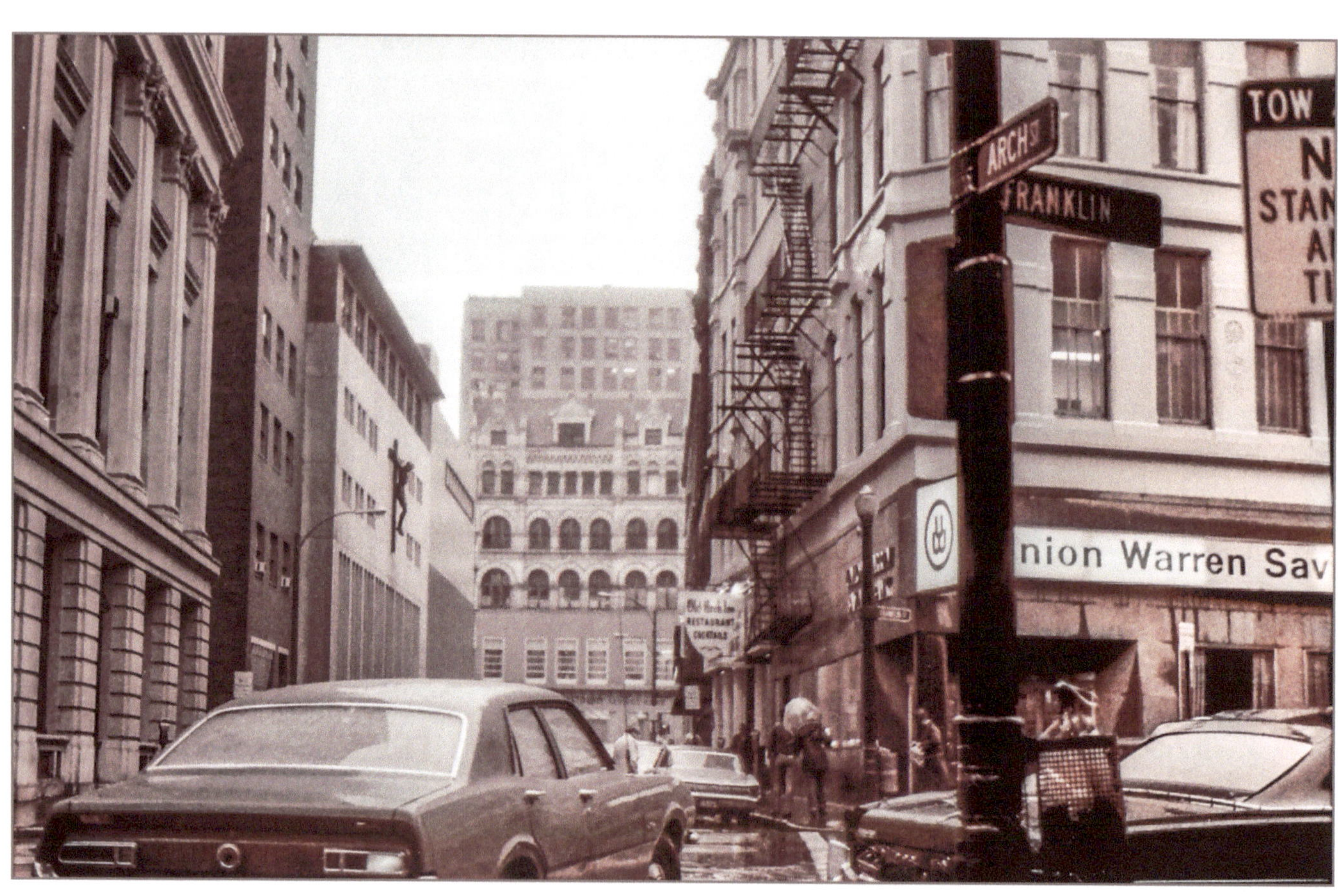
TOW
ARCH ST
FRANKLIN
nion Warren Sav

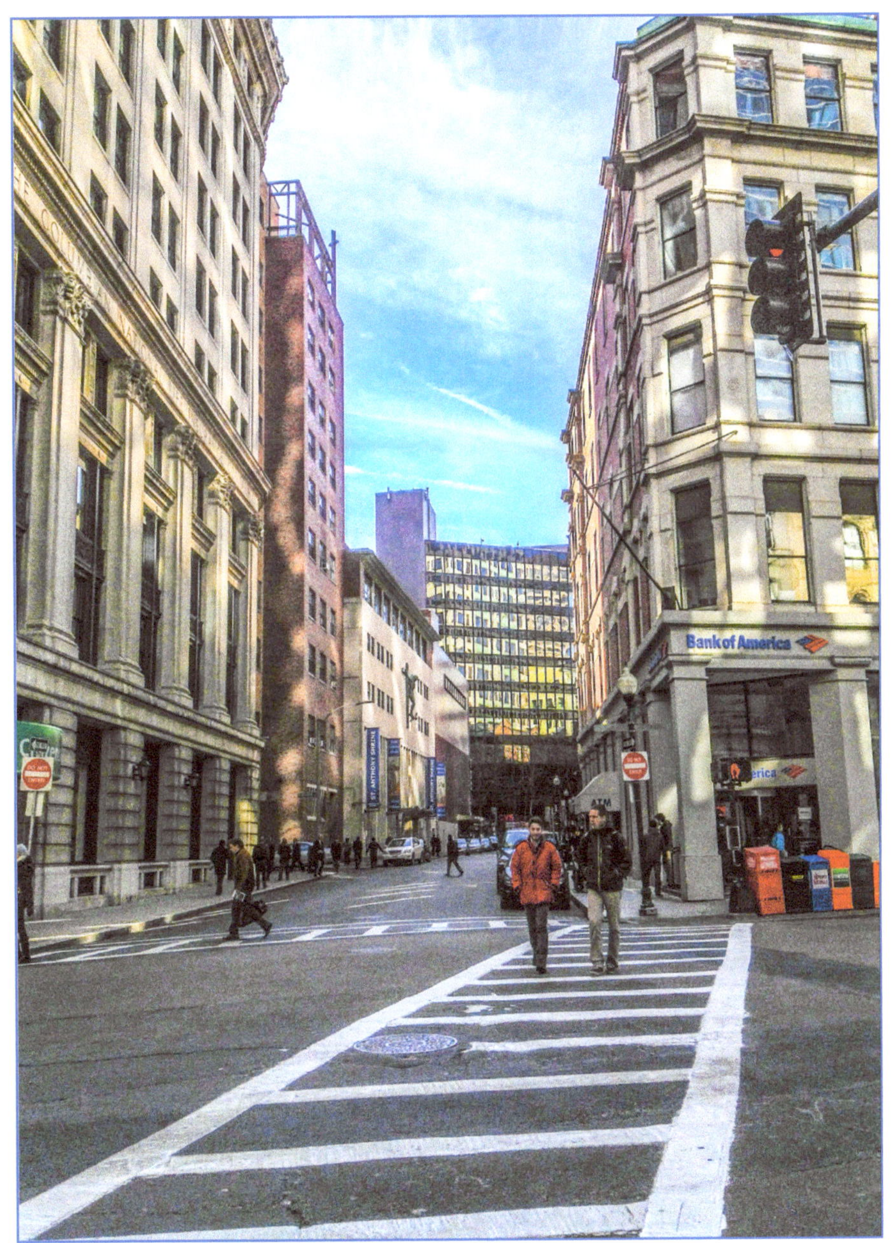

Bank of America existed only in California in 1972. It was before deregulation and all banks were restricted geographically by state lines.

In Massachusetts, banks were only allowed to do business within county lines. The Suffolk Franklin Savings Bank, The Norfolk County Bank & Trust Company and the Middlesex Bank were all named for the places where they were permitted to operate.

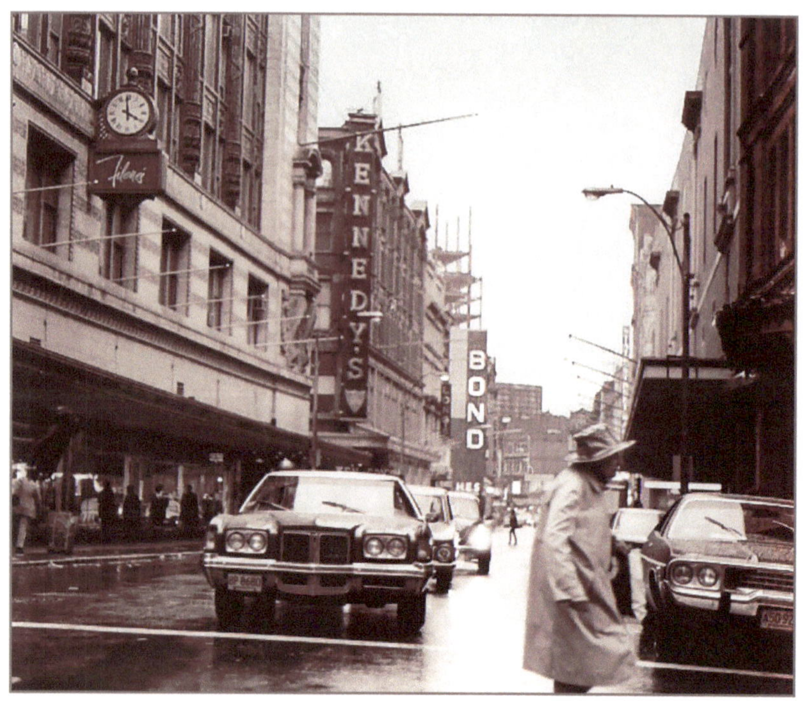
KENNEDY'S
BOND

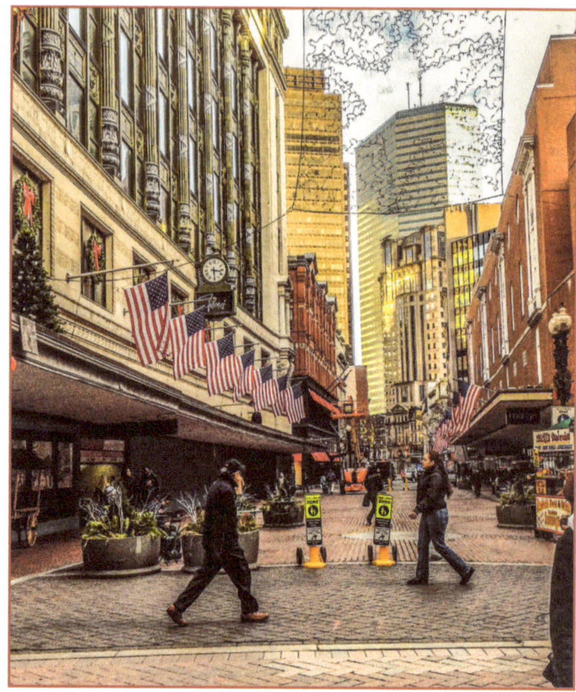

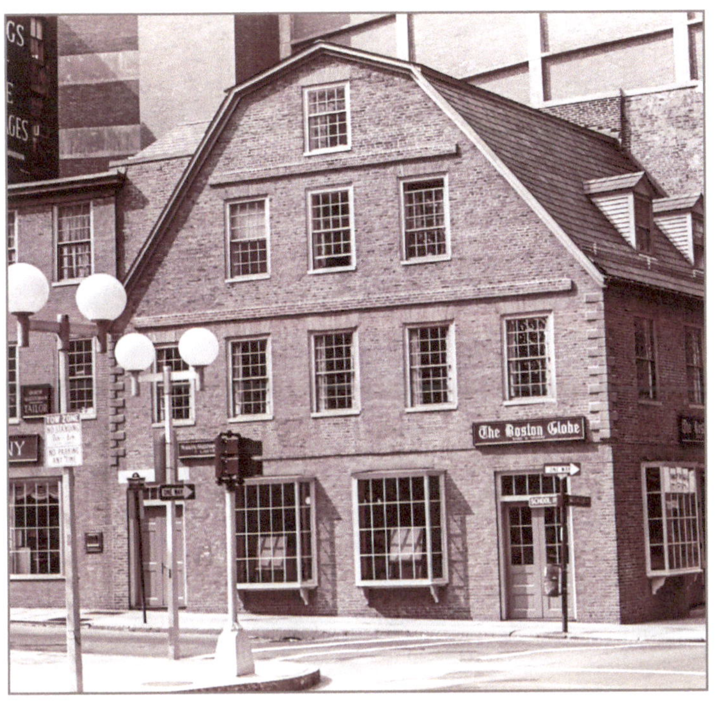

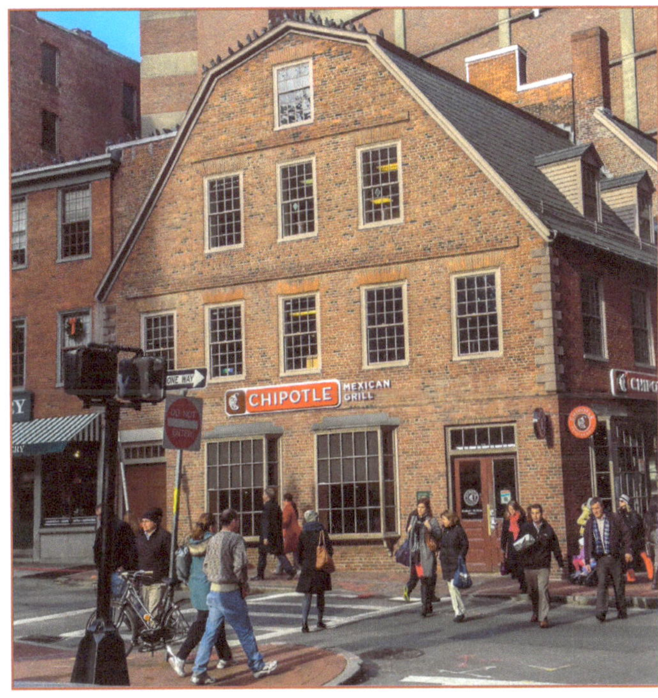

The Old Corner Bookstore at Washington and School Streets was built in 1712 and it is the oldest commercial structure in Boston.

At left, Summer Street looking toward South Station.

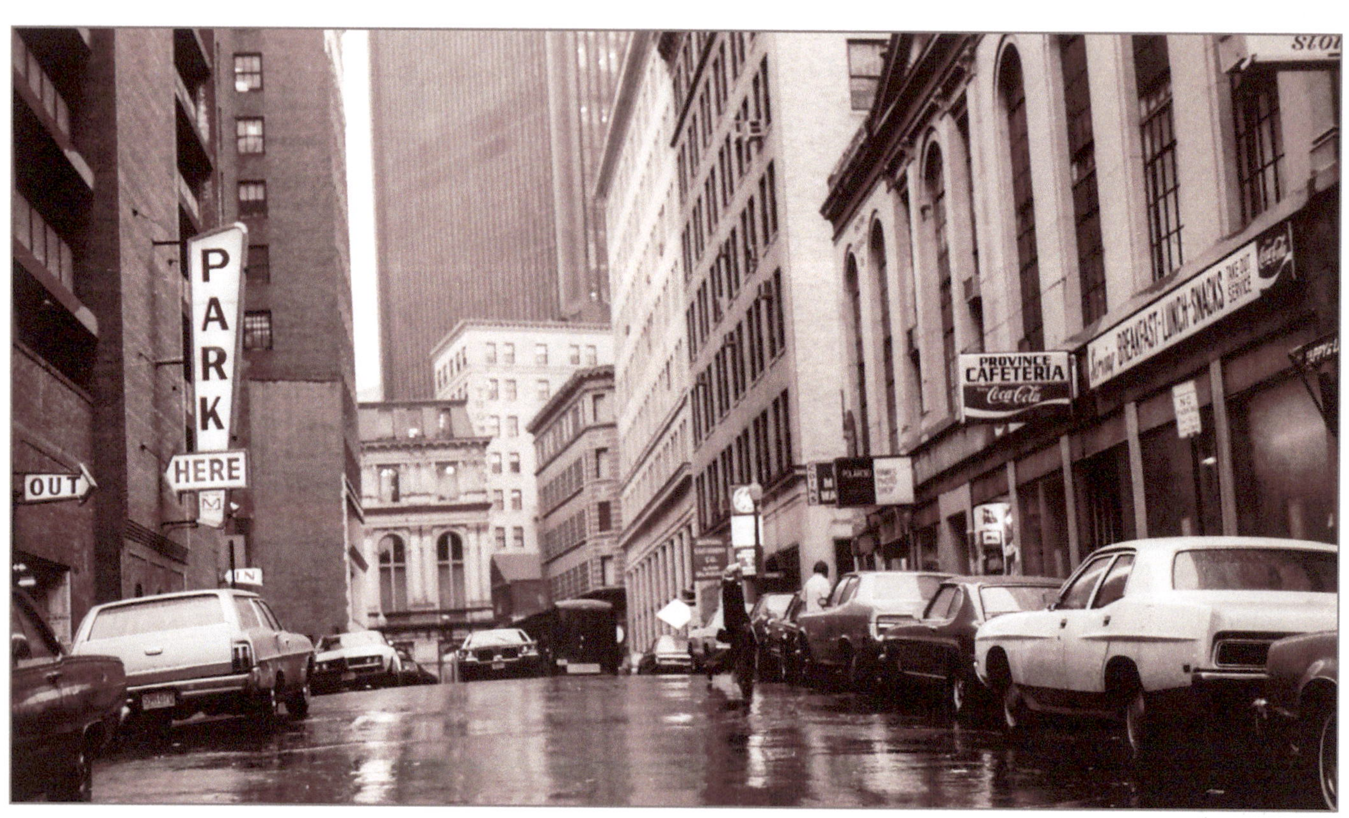

Province Street looking toward Old City Hall.

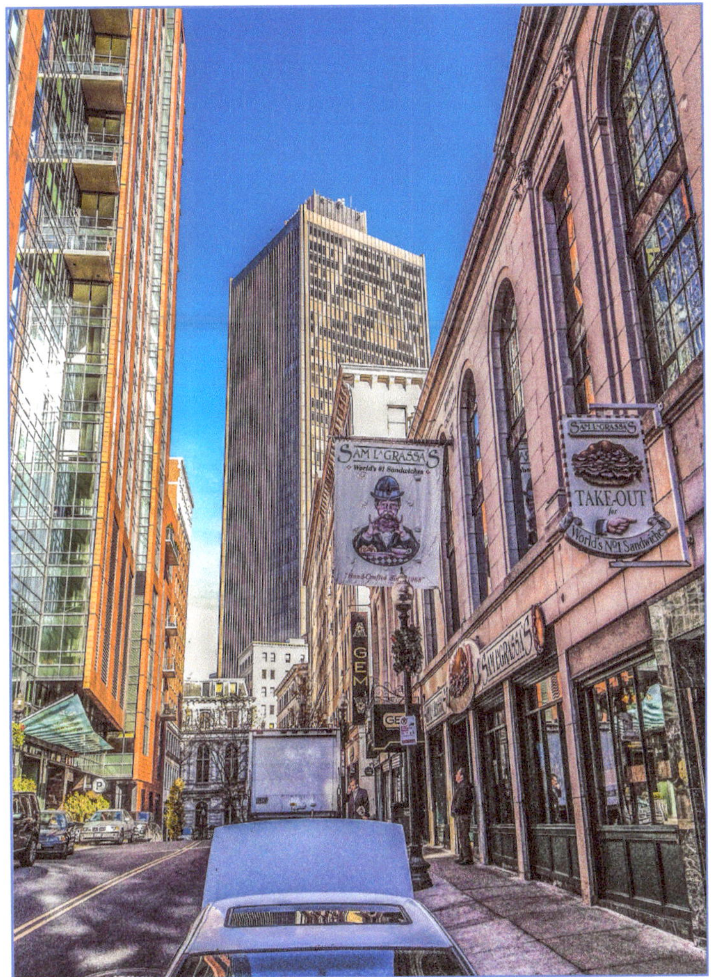

Forty years ago microwave ovens were still an up and coming idea for normal counter-top use. Now, something similar in size, but much larger in terms of scientific development, looms on the household horizon.

Families will use 3D printers to make snacks for their children to eat and toys for them to play with. And future versions of these 'maker-bots' will produce air and space crafts as well as medical and dental parts compatible for use within the human body.

Anything that is capable of being drawn on a computer is capable of being printed out into physical matter. Entire rooms can be printed with light fixtures already hung on the walls.

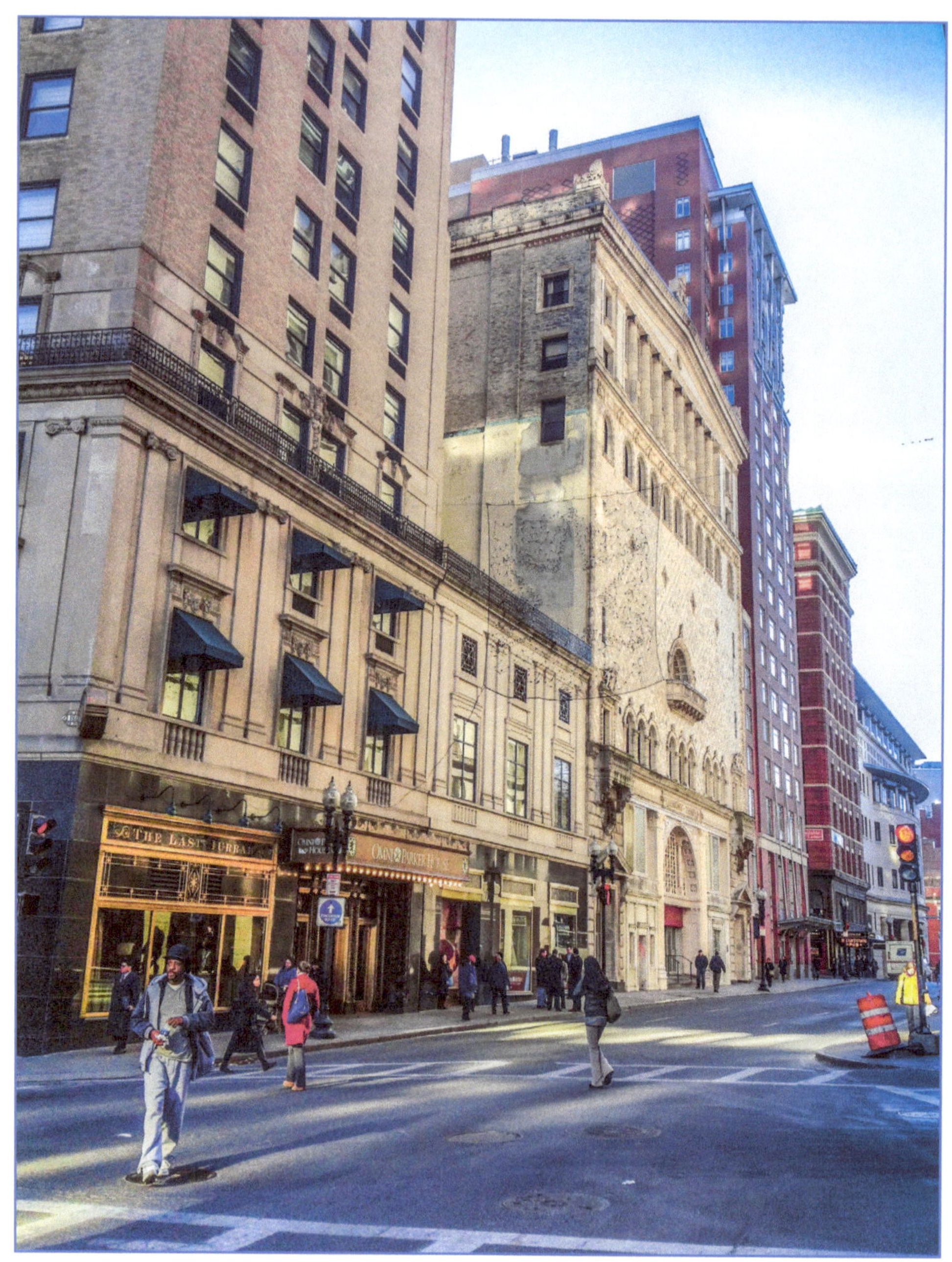
THE LAST
OMNI PARKER

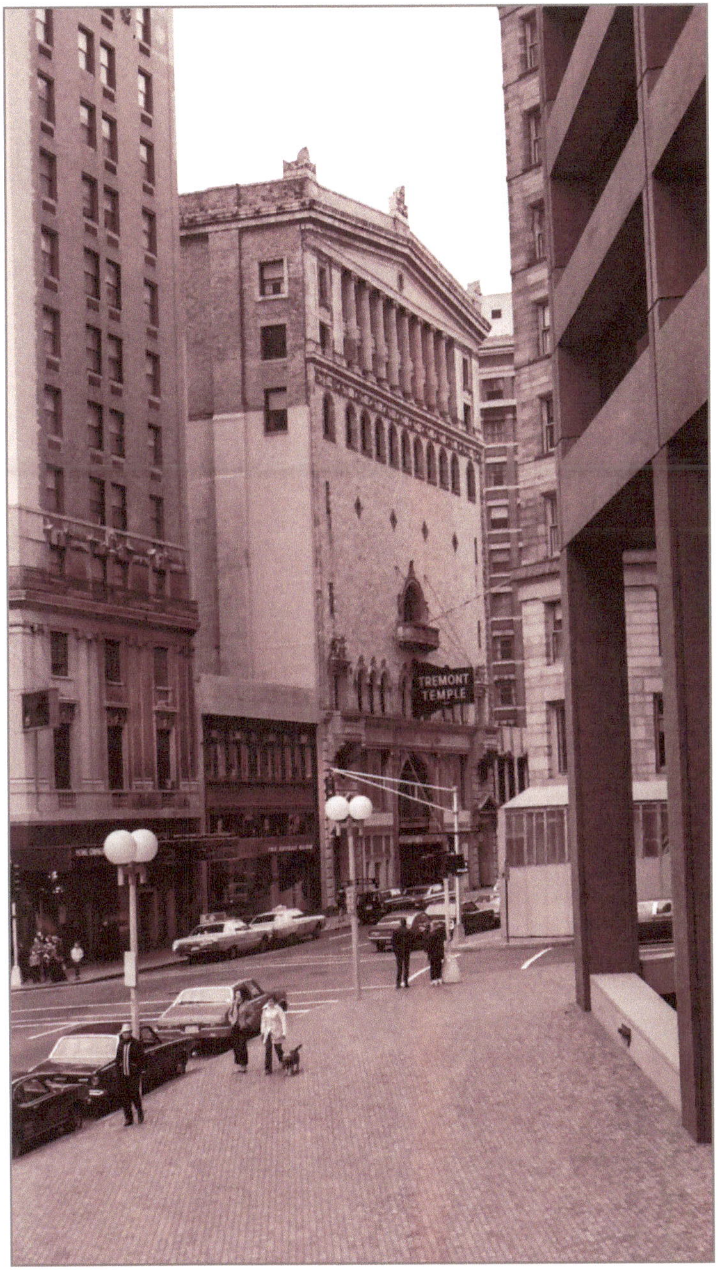

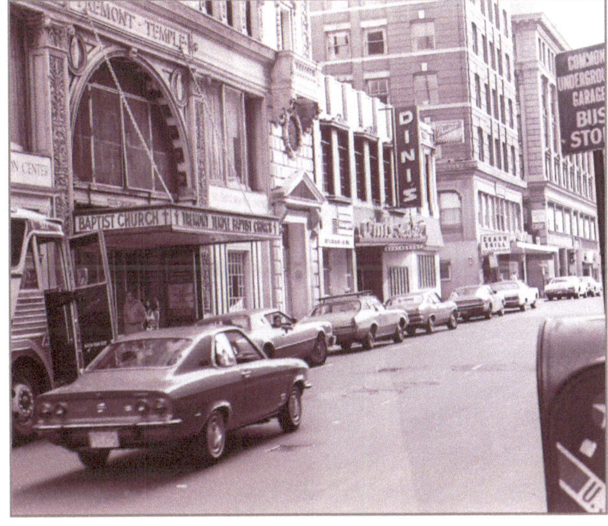

Dini's, above, had been the self-proclaimed "Home of Boston's Famous Scrod". Although, usage of the term "scrod" had actually originated at the Parker House on the other side of the Tremont Temple.

Far left, the arched doorway of the Tremont Temple Baptist Church gleams on a reconstituted Tremont Street.

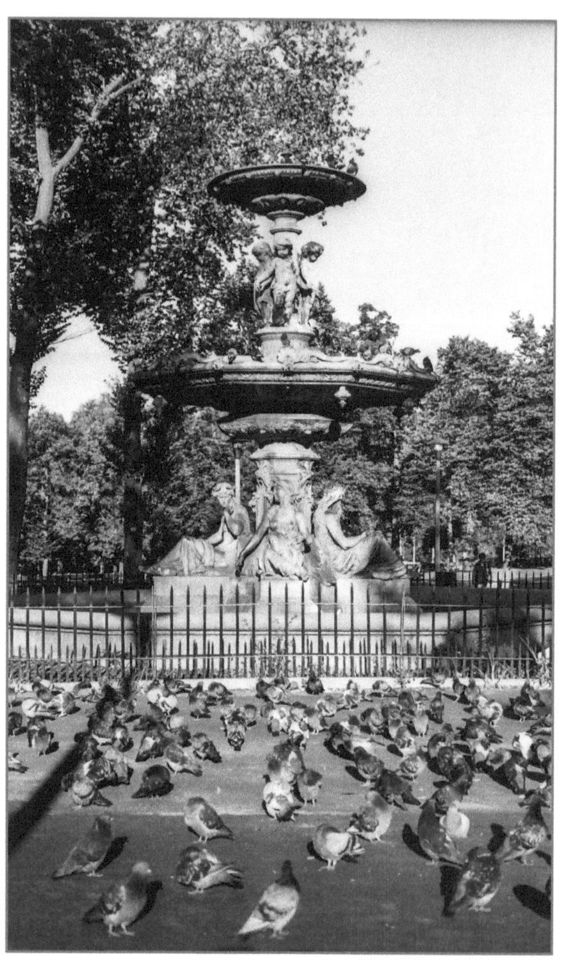

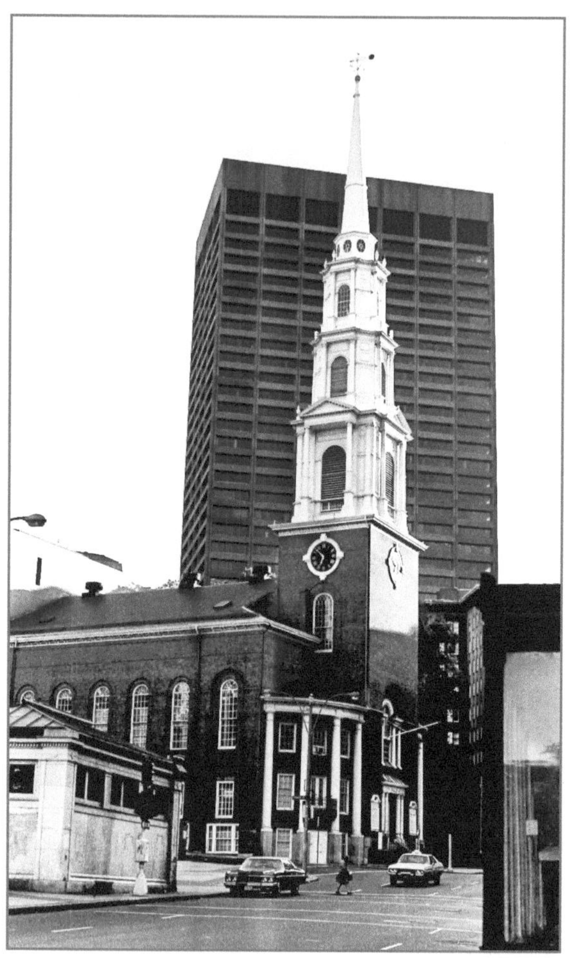

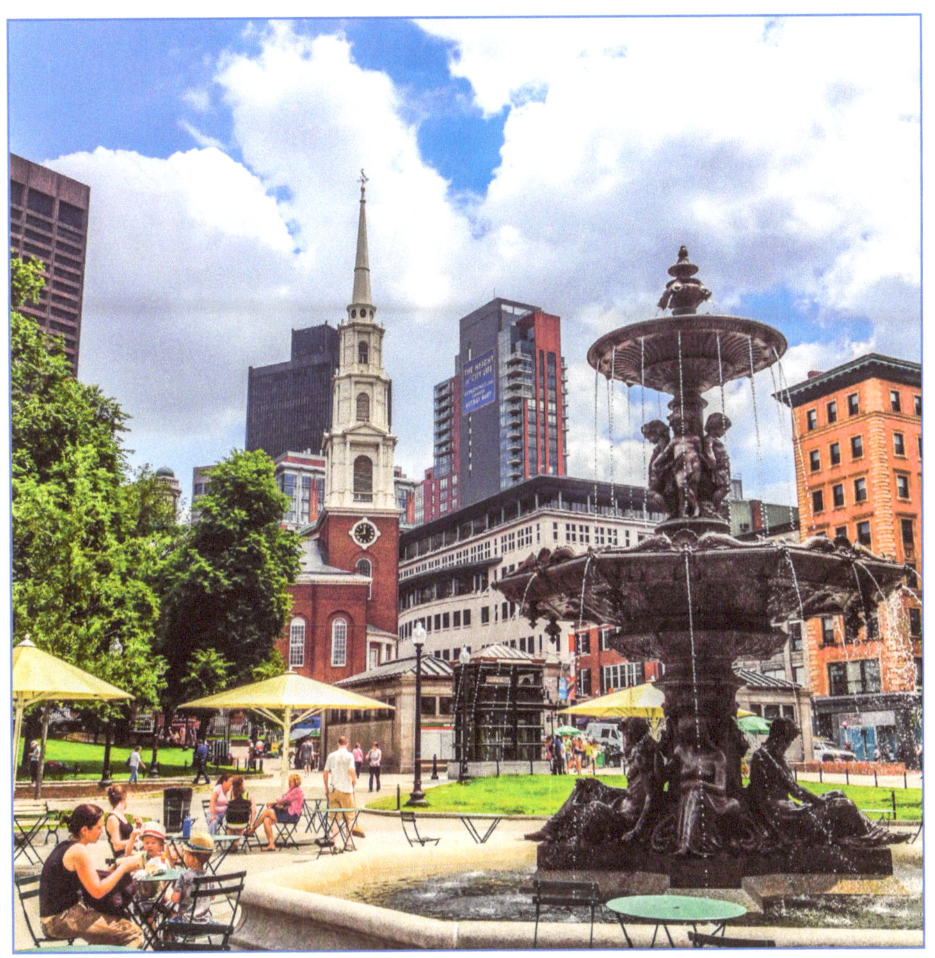

Vietnam was the major story of a generation that saw political assassinations, civil rights and LSD.

Wives had marched in protest of the war on the Boston Common, across from the Park Street Church, while their drafted husbands fought and died. Soldiers came home to hatred and derision when their fathers had returned from war as heroes.

Hawks and doves divided the country. Draft cards burned, protests swelled and hippies exhorted, with two fingers, "peace, brother" and "have a nice day".

President Richard Nixon visited China in February, 1972, in what he described as "the week that changed the world". At that time, US trade with China was statistically 0.0% of the total of US trade.

In 2012, China was our second largest trading partner overall and we import more goods from China than from any other country. Annual trade with China now totals more than $500 billion.

In June, 1972, five men were arrested breaking into the offices of the headquarters of the Democratic National Committee at the Watergate complex in Washington, D.C. and the unraveling of Richard Nixon, and his presidency, began.

Nixon won re-election that November in a landslide. He ran against Democrat George McGovern and he carried every state except Massachusetts.

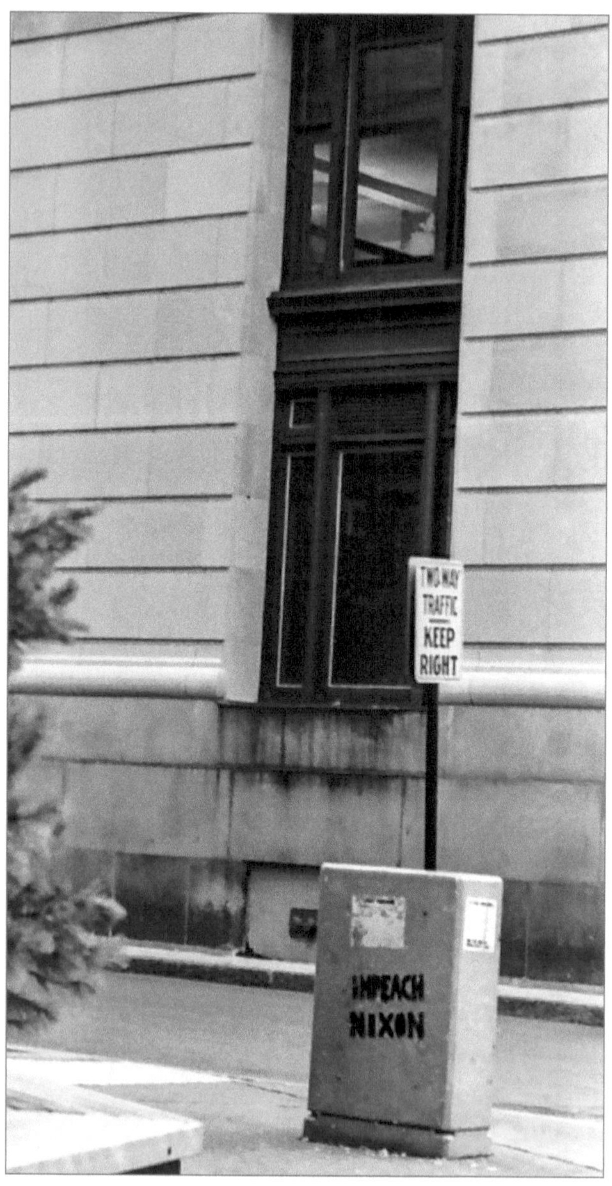

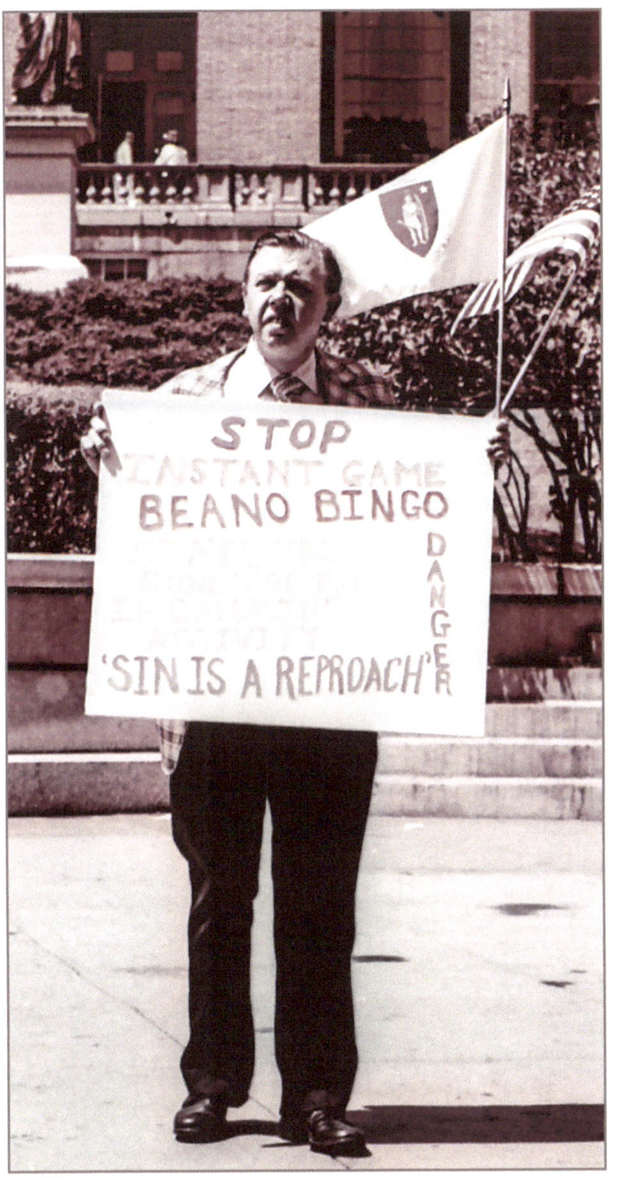

In January, 1973, the United States signed a cease-fire agreement with North Vietnam and Nixon's five year old promise to end the war had materialized.

However, Nixon's achievements would have to wait to be judged by history. He was about to be judged by Congress and his presidency could not withstand the barrage of an impending impeachment for obstructing justice. Nixon was forced to resign in August, 1974.

The Massachusetts Legislature passed a casino gambling bill in 2011, which the Governor signed. It calls for three casinos to be built in the state. The legislation gives preference in the licensing process to a federally recognized Native American tribe.

The Mashpee Wampanoag intend to build a $500,000,000 casino and family water park in Taunton, MA.

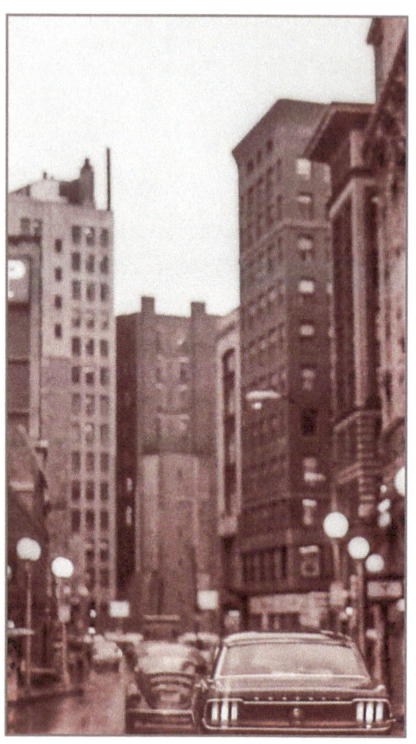

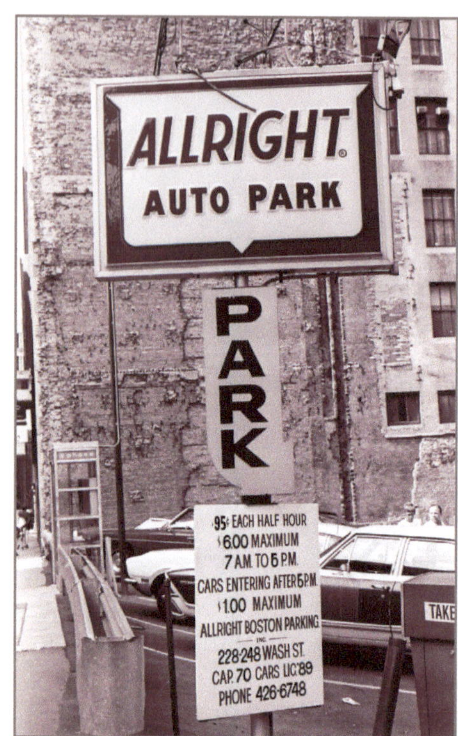

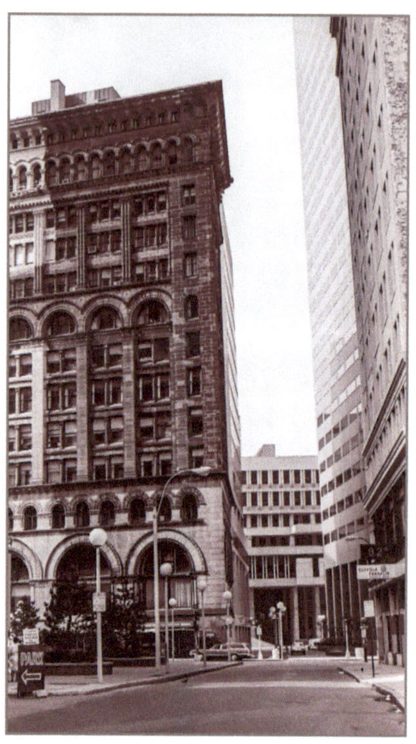

Did 1972 mark the beginning of the end for the ubiquitous phone booth? That was the year that Motorola demonstrated the first cellular phone to the FCC. People could call each other without wires, in about 25 years.

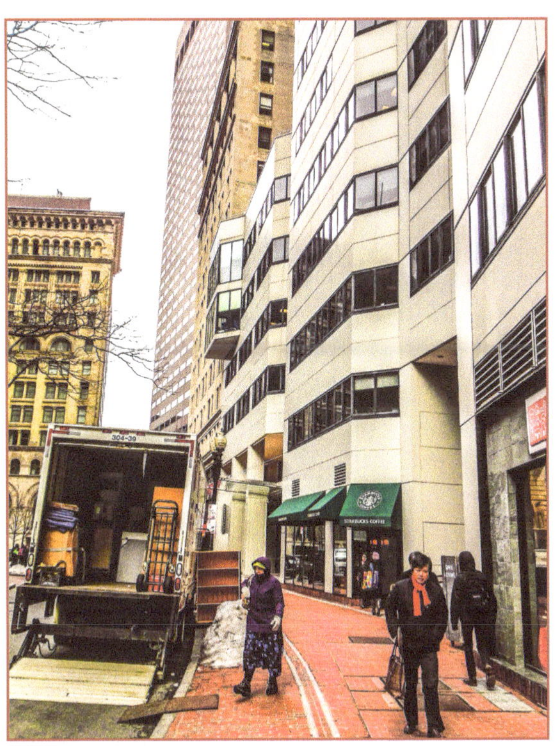

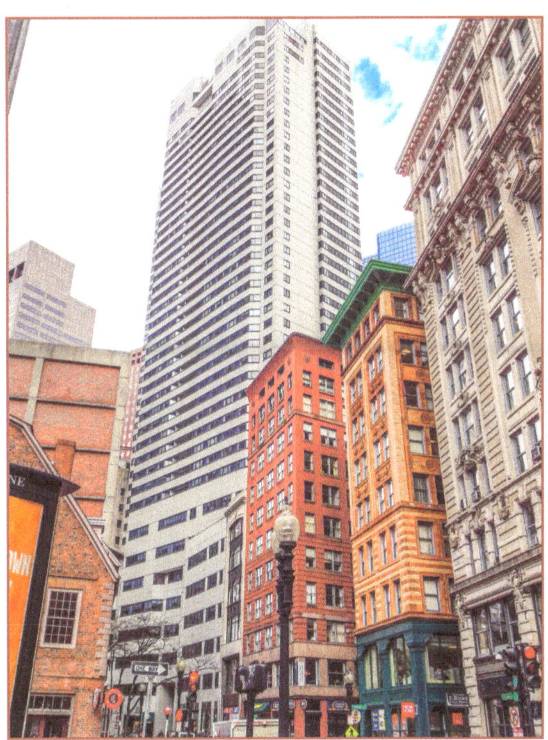

One Devonshire Place has replaced a parking lot on Washington Street which had previously been part of Boston's Newspaper Row and was the former site of The Boston Globe.

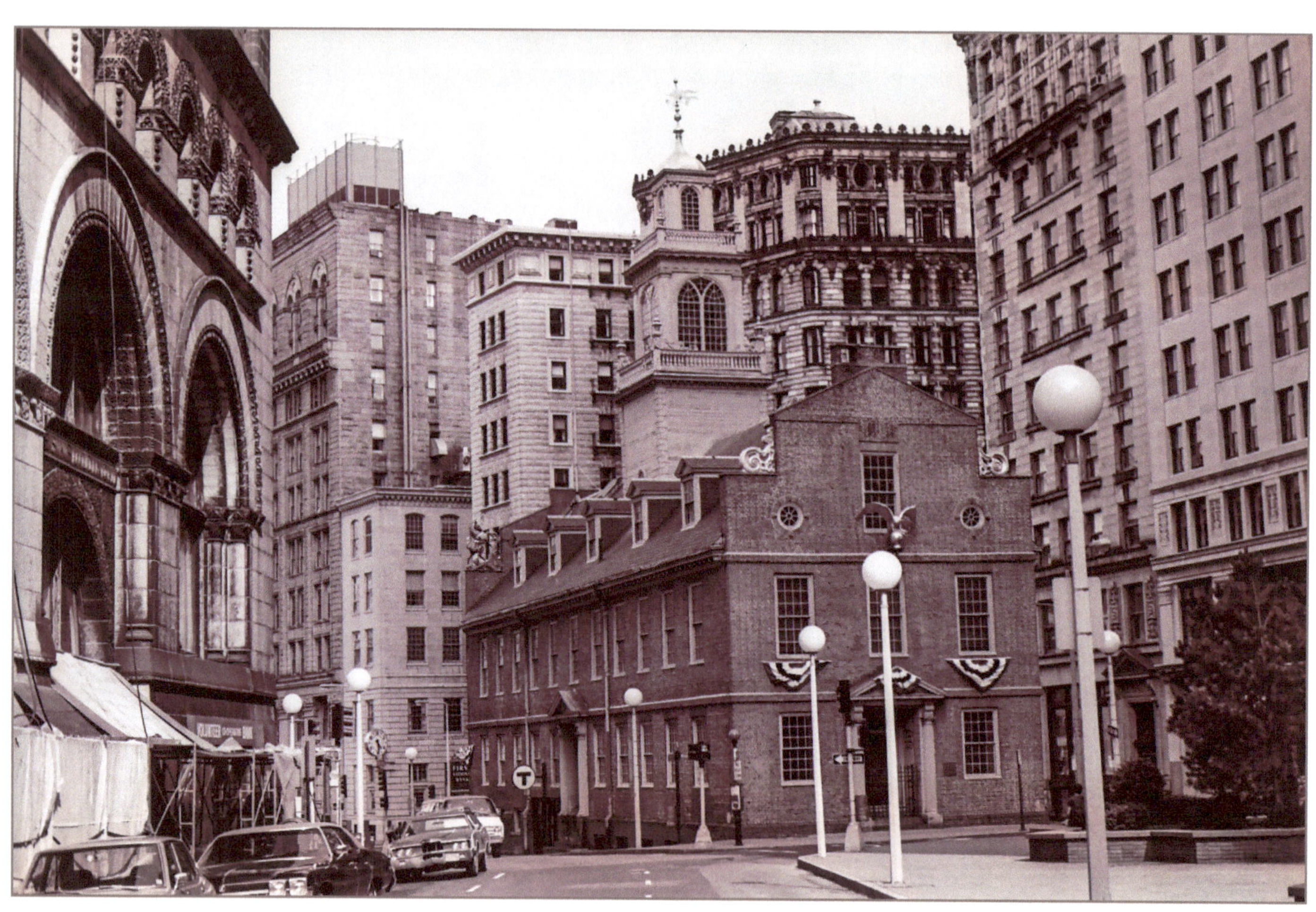

Old State House

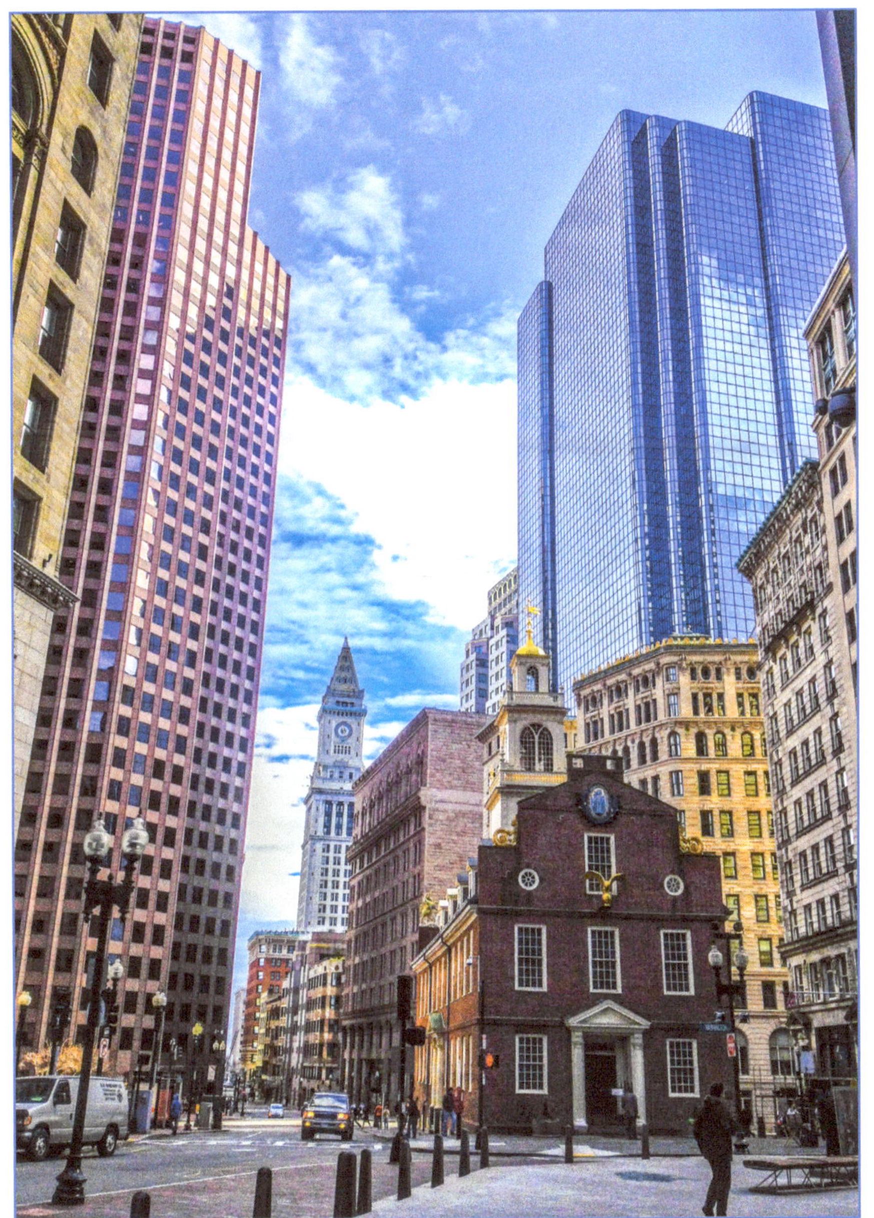

Nanotechnology is small stuff. A sheet of paper is about 100,000 nanometers thick. It was only 30 years ago that a microscope was developed that can see a nanometer. Previously, it was not even a notion in science fiction.

Nanoscience aims to alter materials on the atomic and molecular level. Nanoscopic machines will be invisible to the human eye and it will take trillions of them to create something tangible. Patients will ingest nanorobots to reconstruct diseased cells.

The potential of nanotechnology to recreate any known material, from food and water to body parts and cells, may be a far off concept, but it is a concept that would fundamentally change our world.

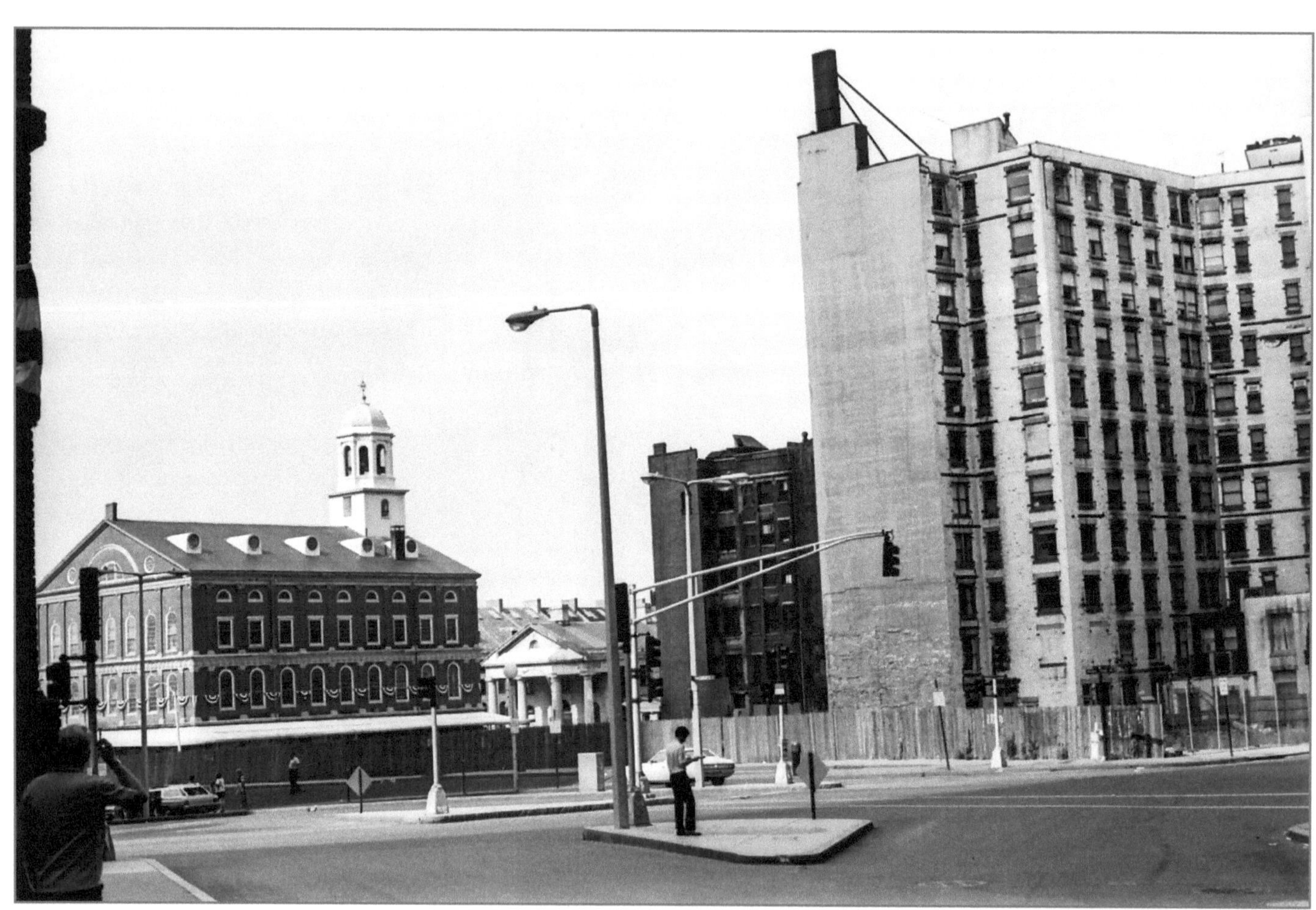

Faneuil Hall

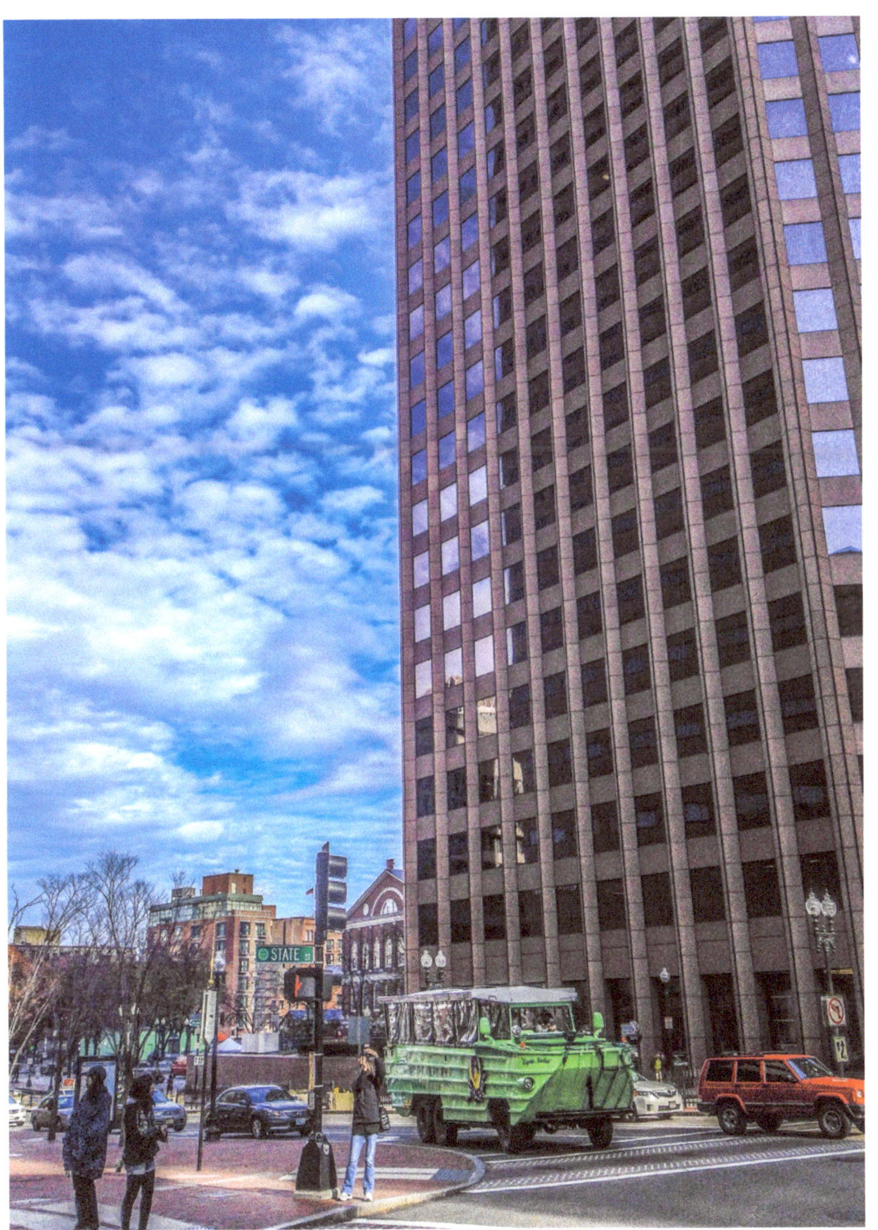

Computers were coming out of the closet, literally. Early computers, such as the Univac, took up entire rooms. And "minicomputers" needed the space of a very large closet. Hewlett Packard delivered the first fully programmable desktop computer in the early 1970's. These devises were labeled "programmable calculators".

A patent was granted for the computer mouse in 1970. Two years later, Intel introduced the microprosessor, the cd was invented and Atari released the first successful commercial video game called "Pong". Larry Page and Segey Brin, the founders of Google, were born in 1973 and Microsoft was founded in 1975. It was the beginning of the beginning.

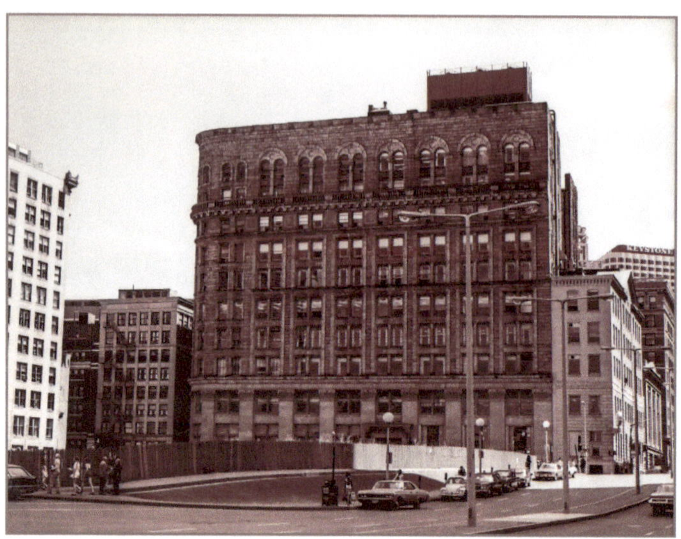

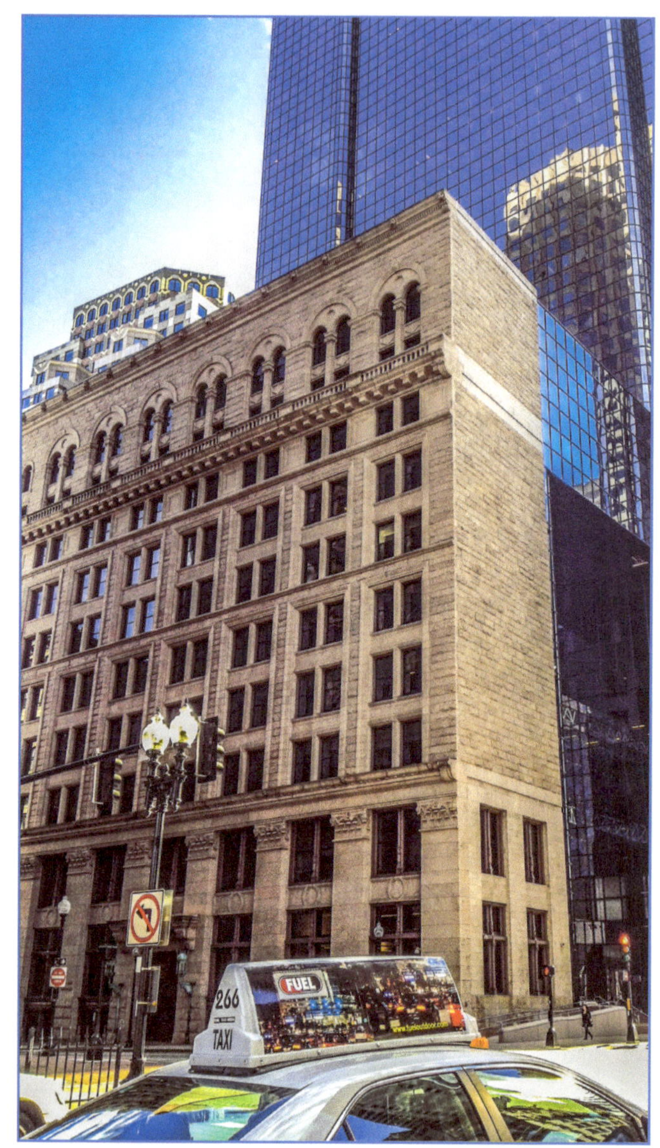

The Exchange Building at 53 State Street housed the Boston Stock Exchange. As the 1970's began, the floor of the Exchange had literally been raised and false ceilings were constructed to accommodate new electronics that were bringing the markets into the future. Young, eager traders on the Exchange worked diligently around the construction as business continued.

Older specialists, men in their 60's and 70's, did their business at a different pace. Early lunch and a late return followed by a silent stretch amid the din on one of the old leather couches. Tensions mounted and grumbling occasionally ensued when construction workers had to move or realign a couch. A new guard was coming.

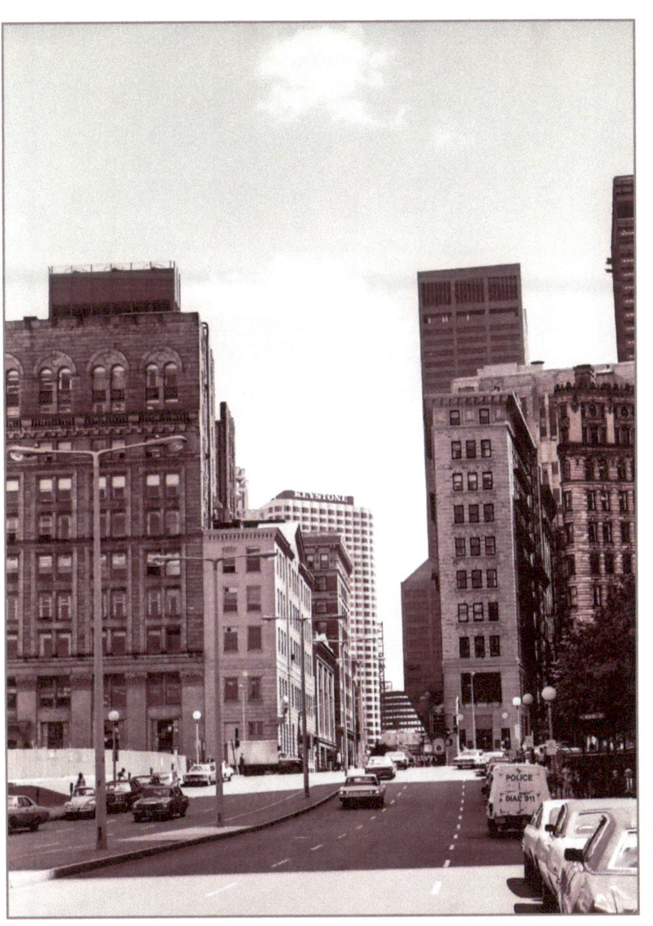

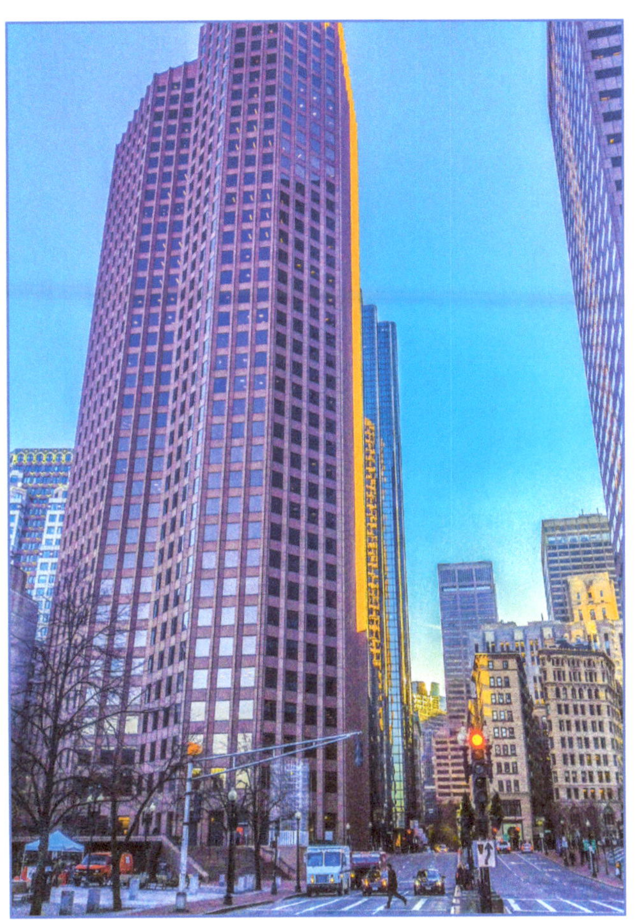

Congress Street

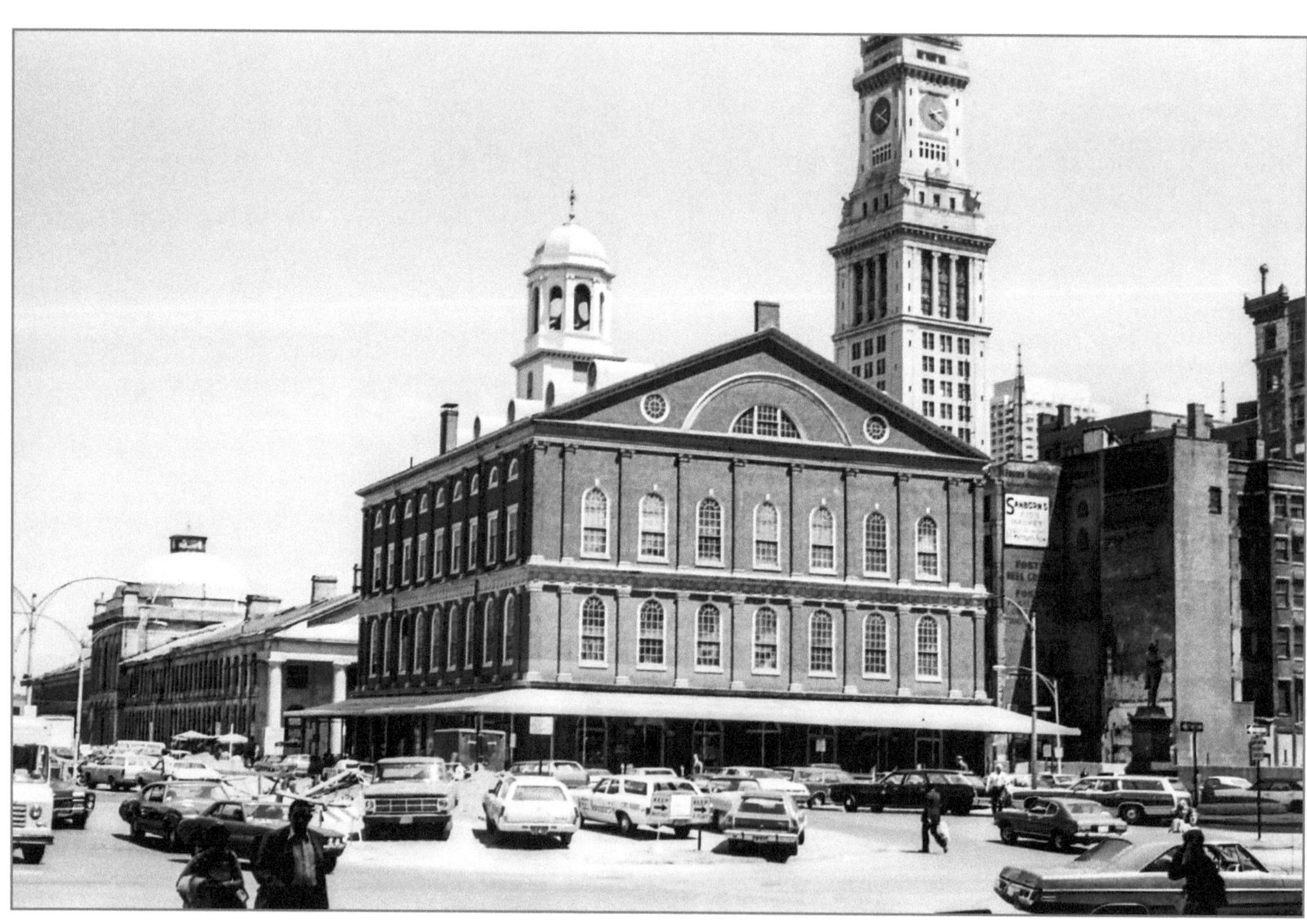

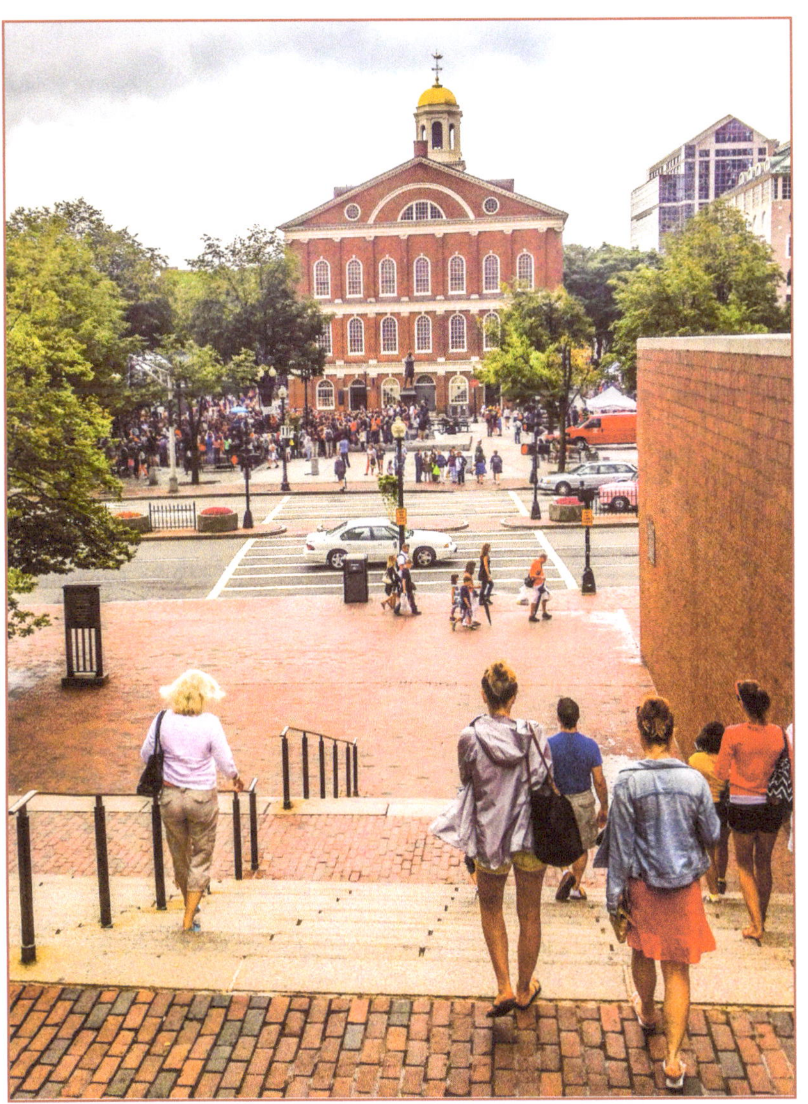

The renovation project at Faneuil Hall and Quincy Market was the signature renewal effort in Boston in the early 1970's. Butchers and restaurant suppliers had occupied Quincy Market and the cellars of Faneuil Hall. The buildings needed major restorations.

Before leaving for the day, the butcher threw a few pieces of lousy meat into a large wood barrel and moved it next to the chopping block. In the morning, the barrel was packed with rats that got in from the table but couldn't get out. The first job of the day was to get rid of the rats.

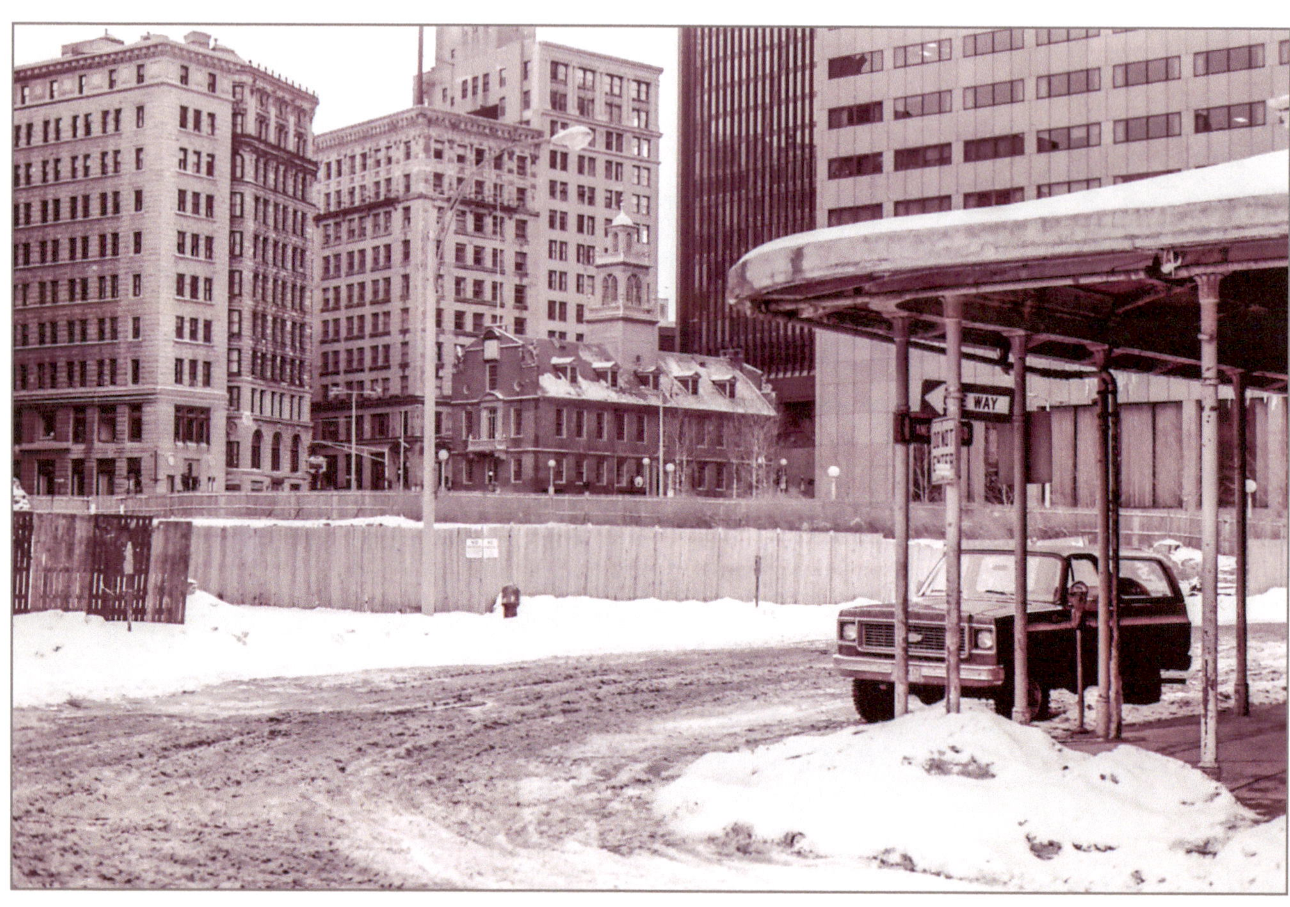
WAY
DO NOT ENTER

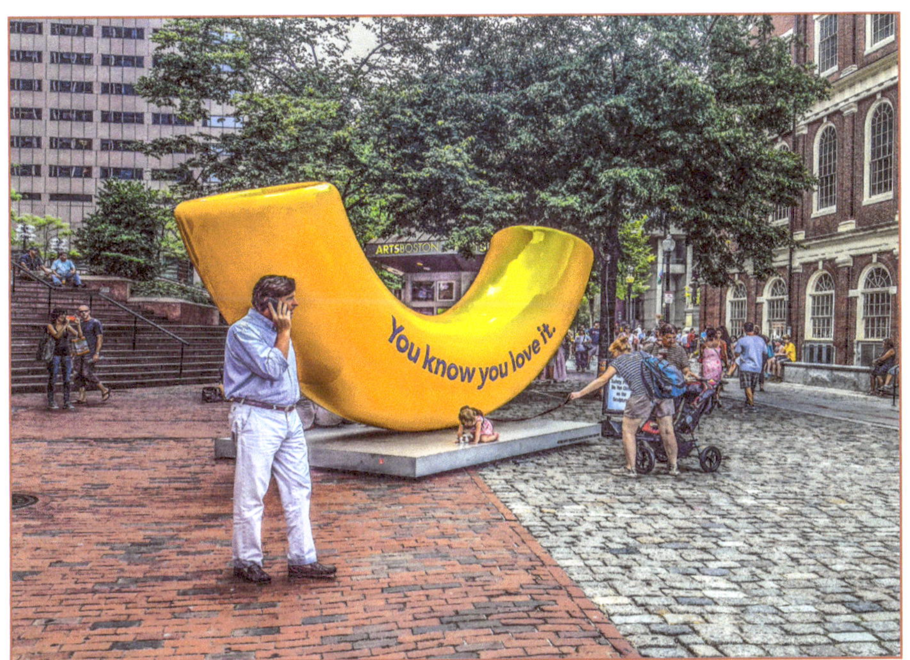

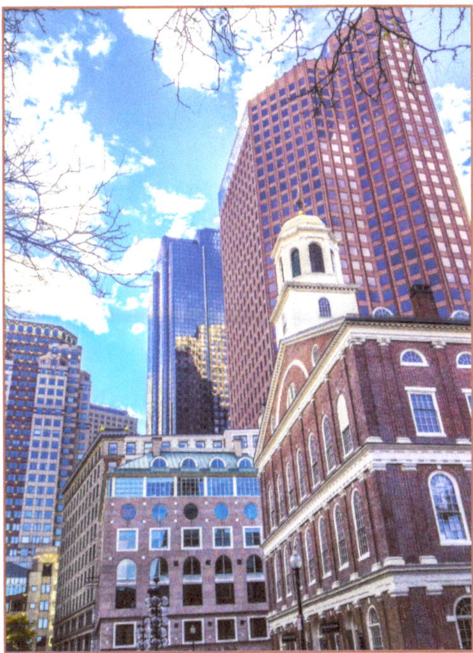

The car on the left is about eight feet to the right of where the yellow macaroni is in the photo above. Step back a few feet, and looking up, shows 60 State Street which occupies the former hole in the ground.

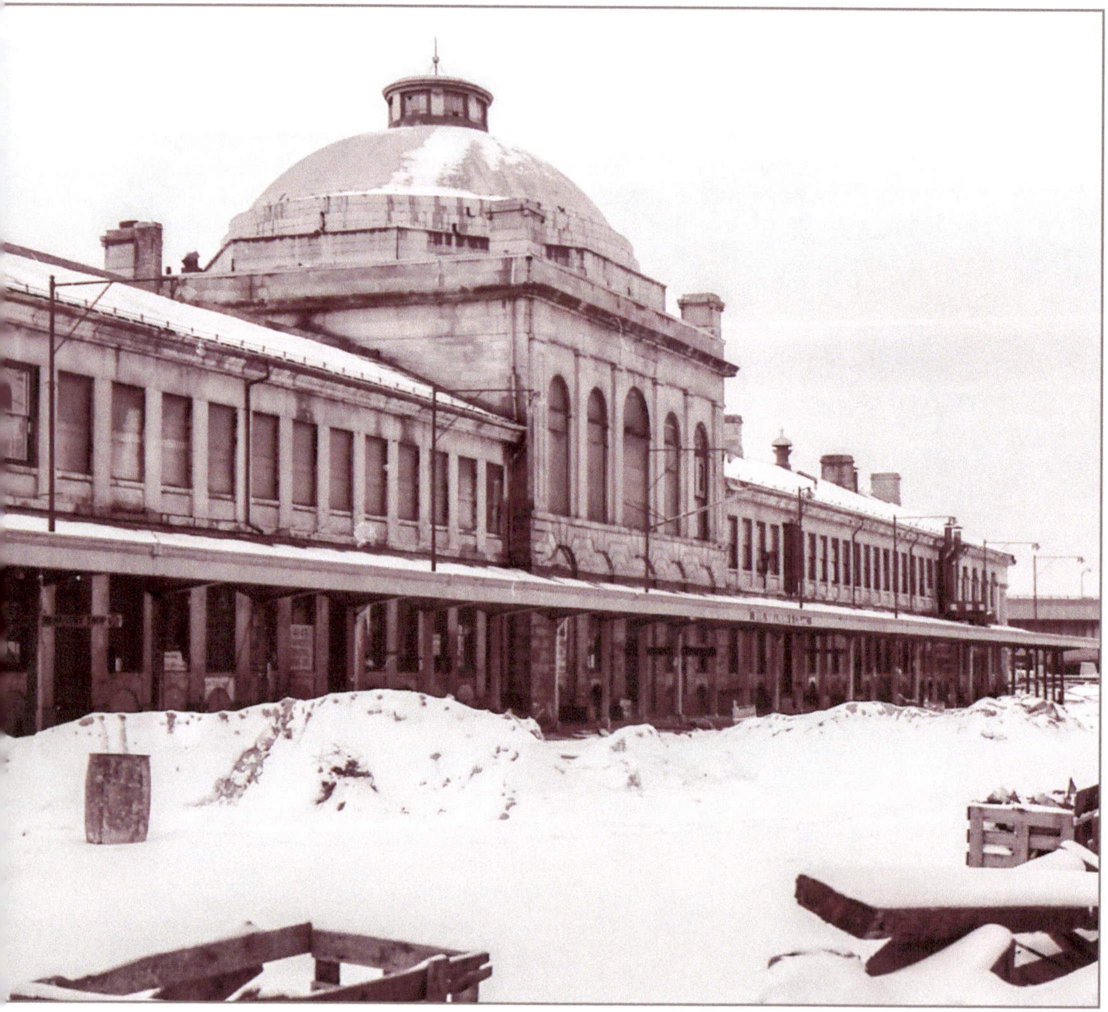

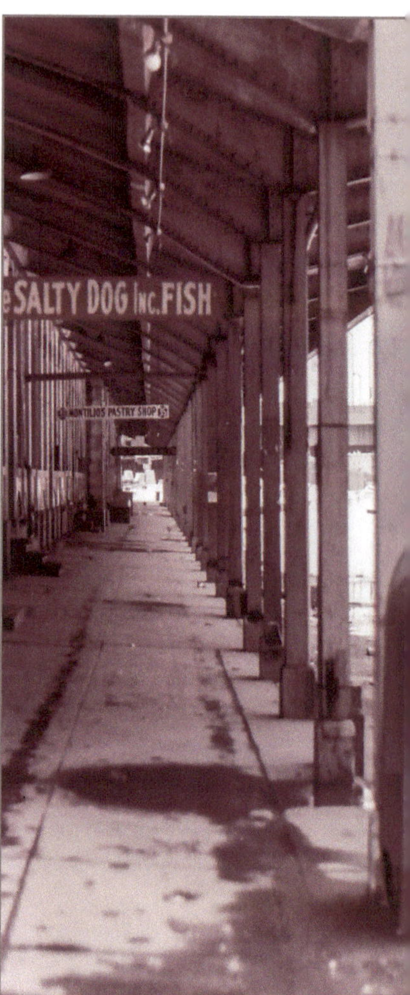
SALTY DOG Inc. FISH
MONTILIOS PASTRY SHOP

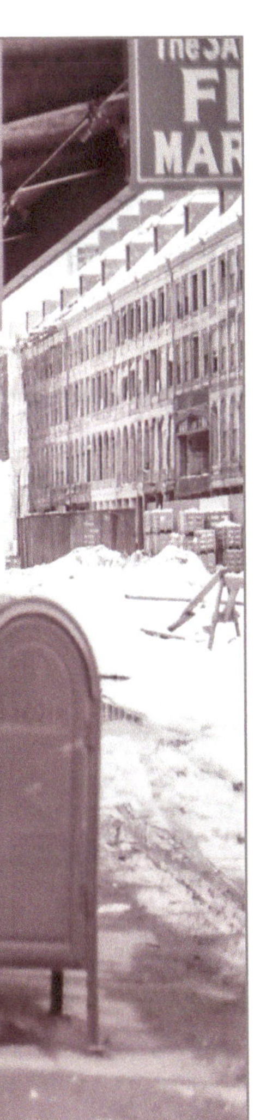

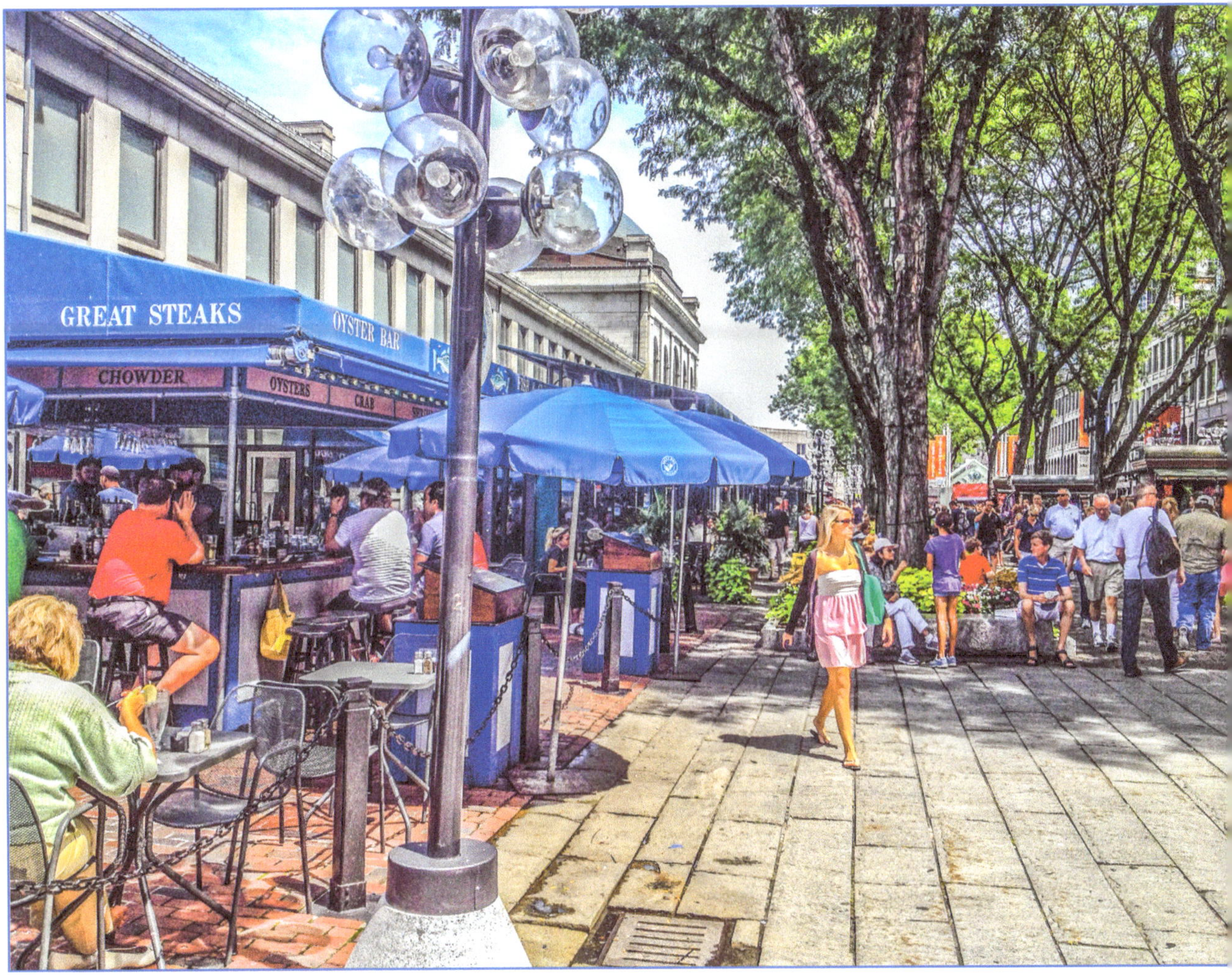

The sense of touch has become the sense of the future. The world is at our fingertips. Touch screens have taken the place of keyboards. Books and newspapers have become second best to tablets and electronic news sources. The Amazon Kindle and the Nook by Barnes and Noble can store hundreds of books within their light weight, sleek bodies.

The Apple iPad was first introduced to us in 2010. Now, in it's fourth generation, it is at the top of the tablet food chain. Other contenders on the tablet scene include Android, Windows, Google and Samsung.

Apps, thousands and thousands of them, allow tablets to do some of the same things as a desktop or laptop computer, from sending emails to watching movies.

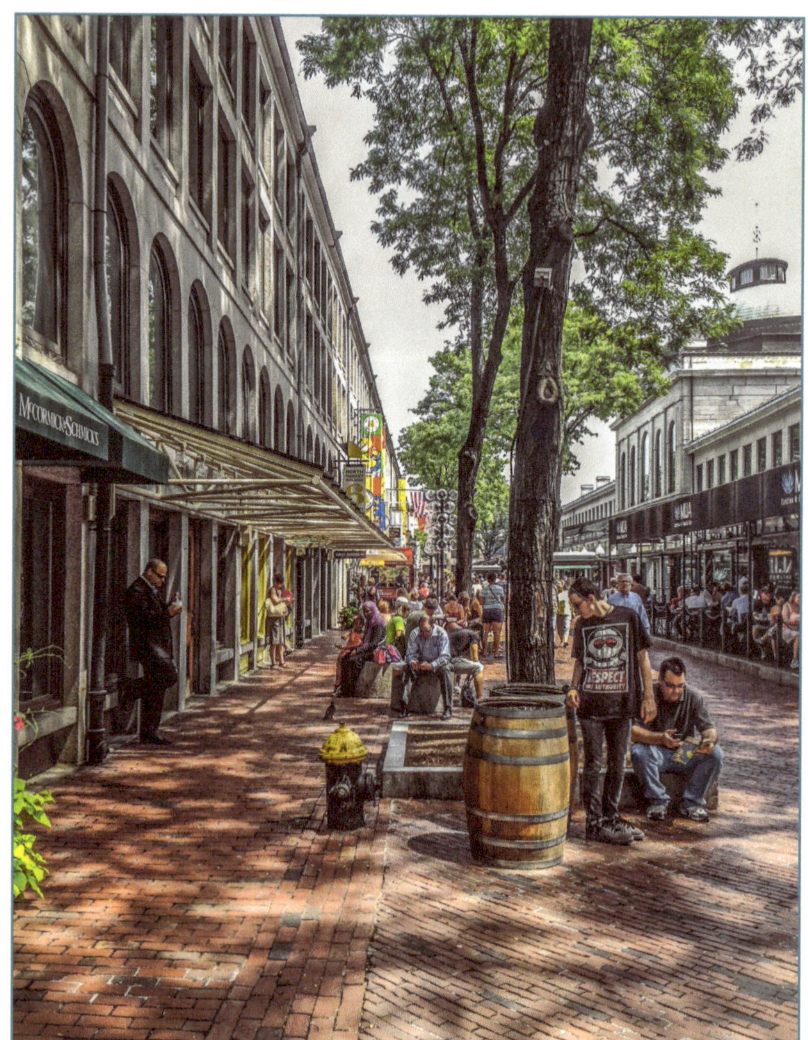

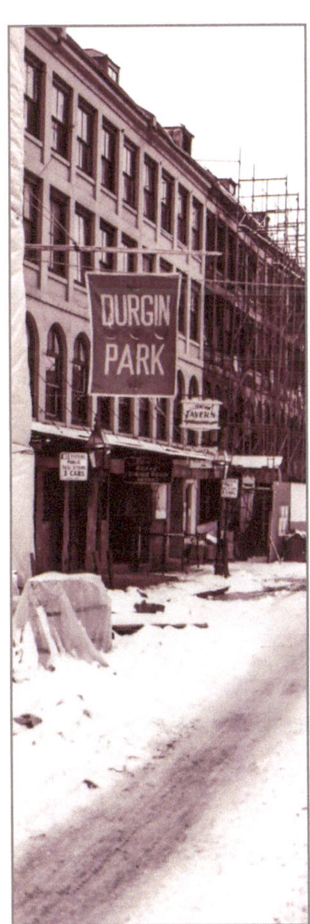
DURGIN
PARK
TAVERN

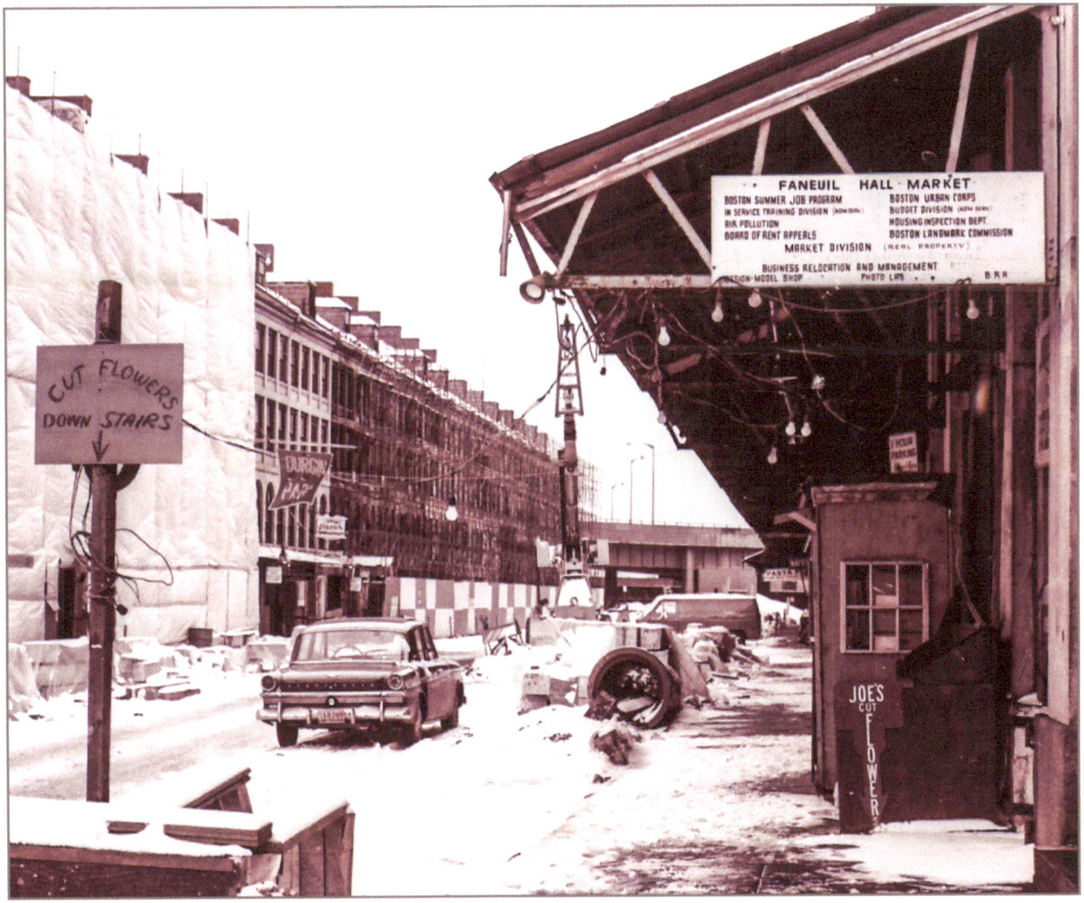

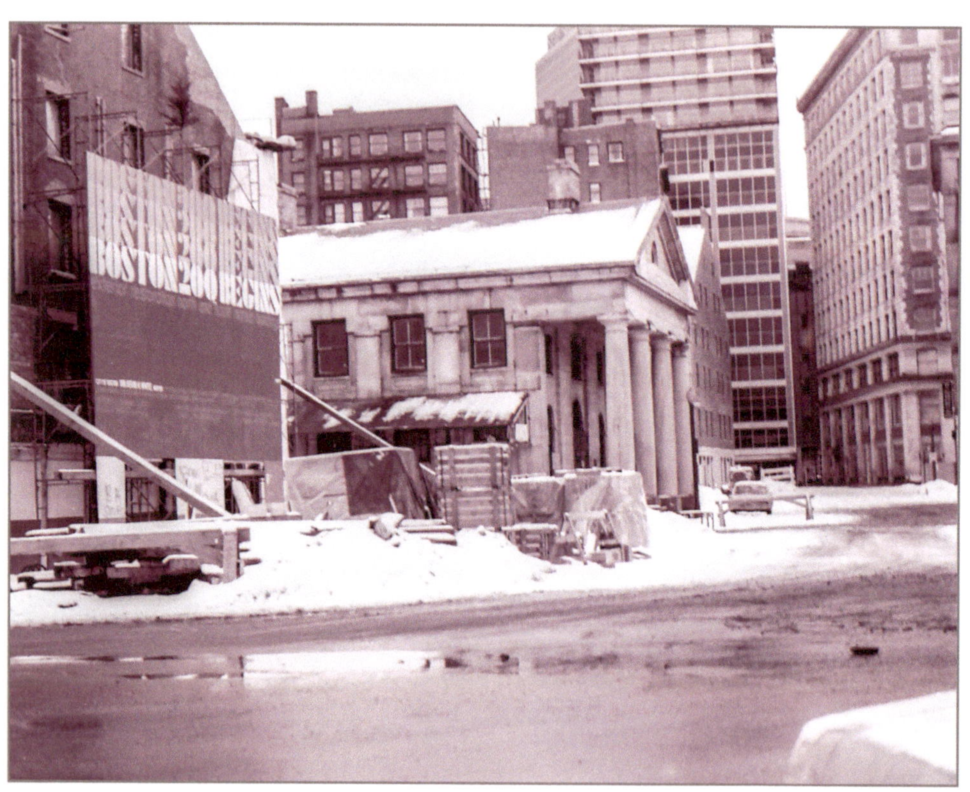
BOSTON 200 BEGINS

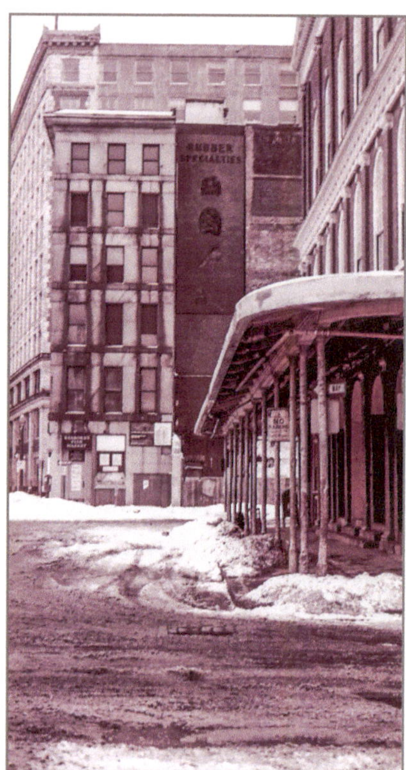
RUBBER SPECIALTIES

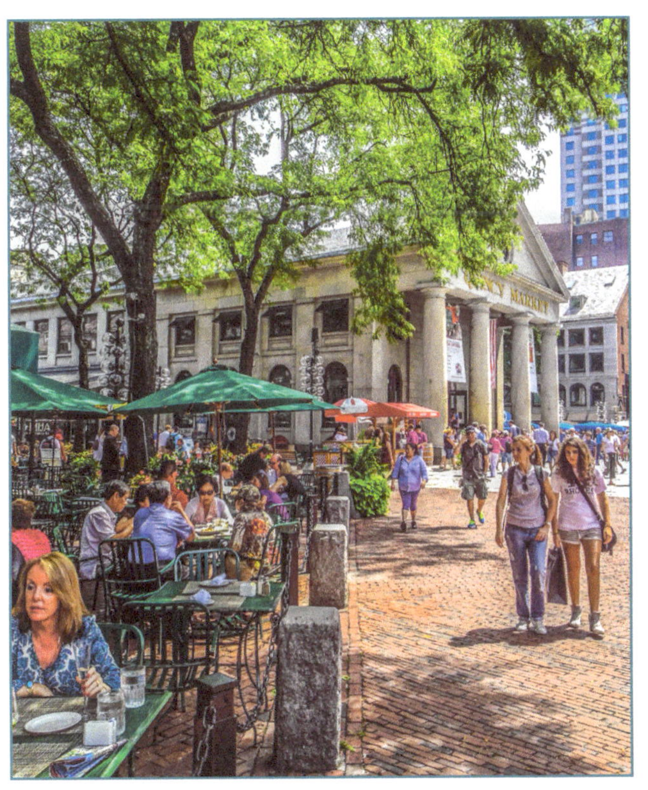

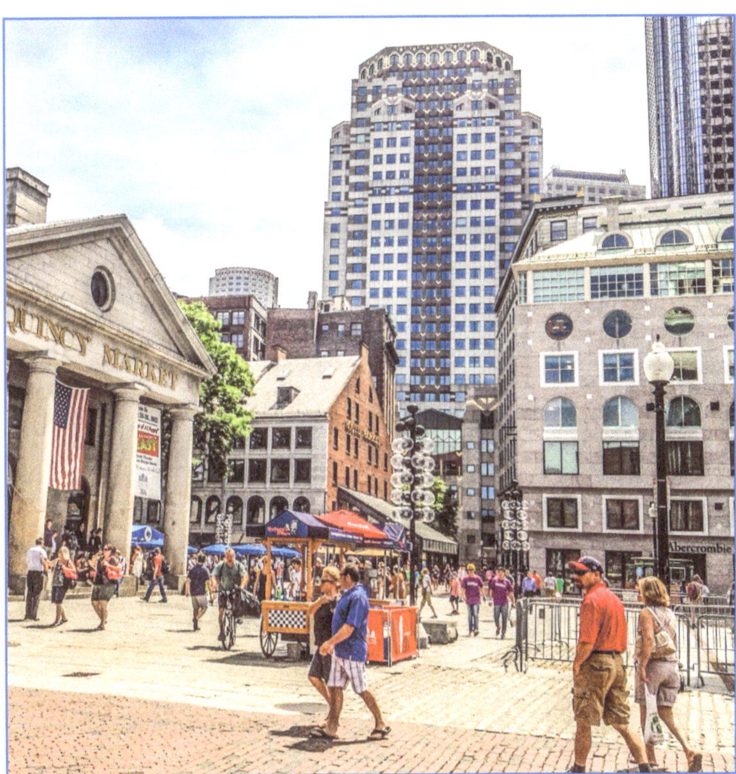
QUINCY MARKET
Abercrombie

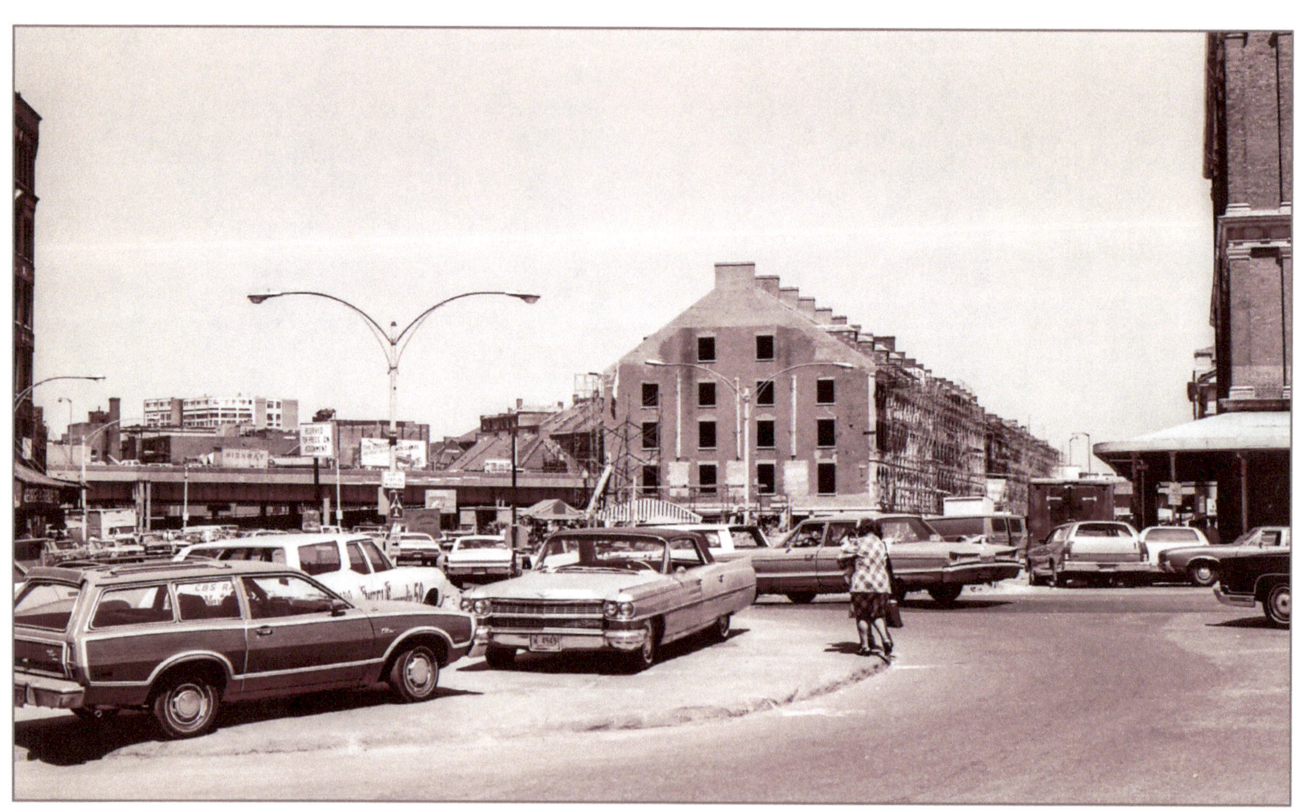

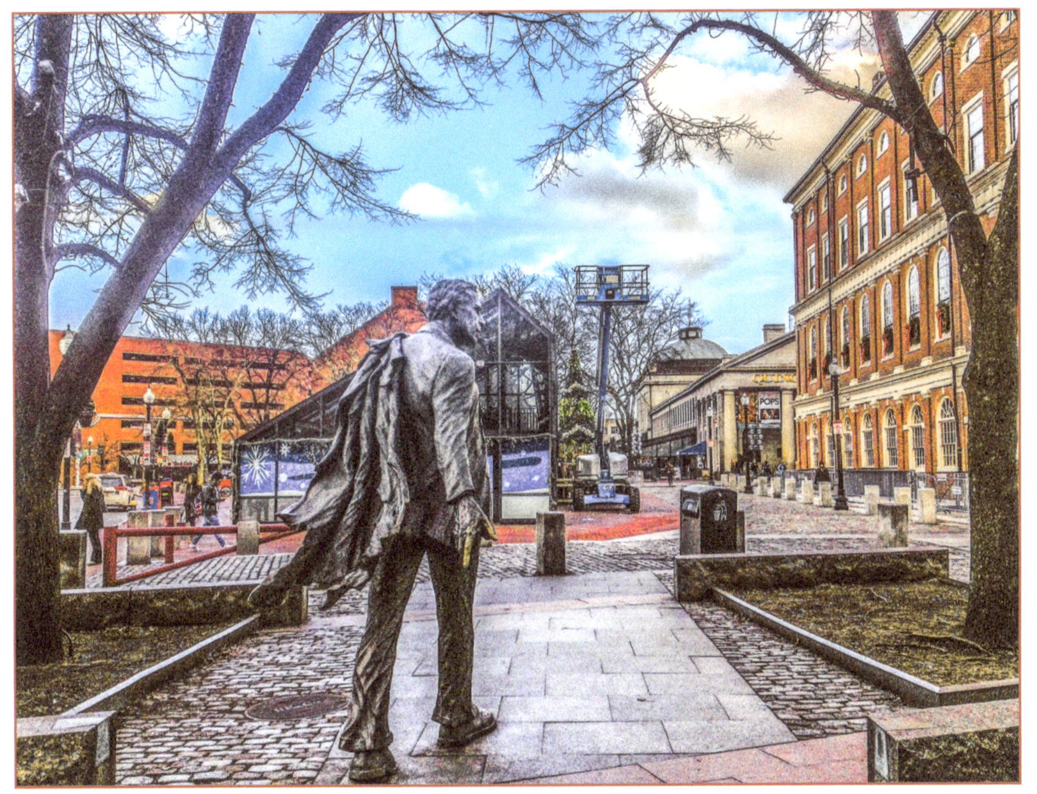

Mayor Kevin White strides with prideful nonchalance towards Faneuil Hall.

He personified a resurgence. He was young, handsome and vibrant. The new Boston City Hall had just opened across the street and his office overlooked the renovation project. He was Master of his Domain and might have been Prince of the City, but Bobby Orr lived at the Pru.

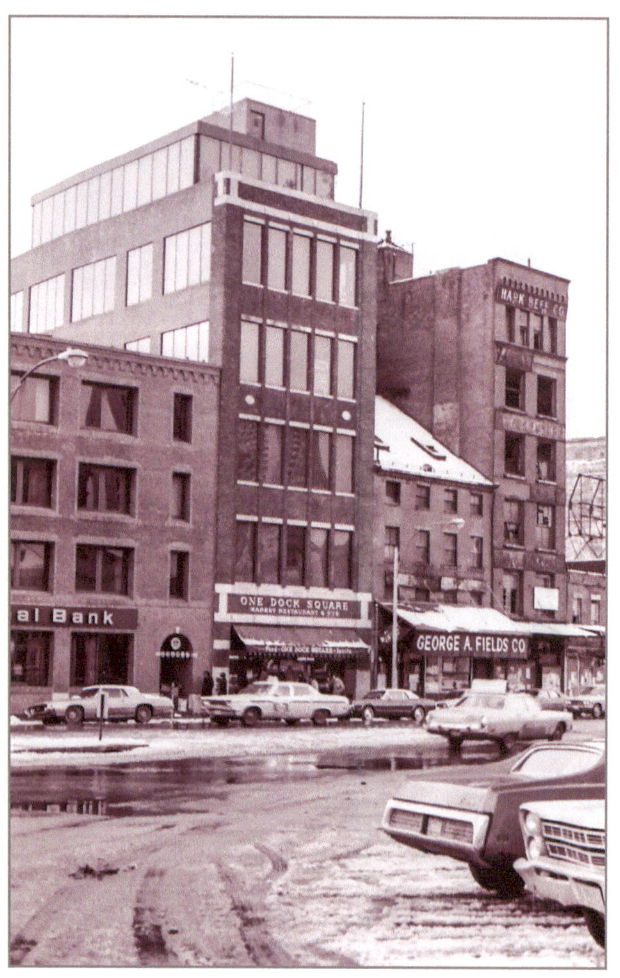
al Bank
ONE DOCK SQUARE
GEORGE A. FIELDS CO

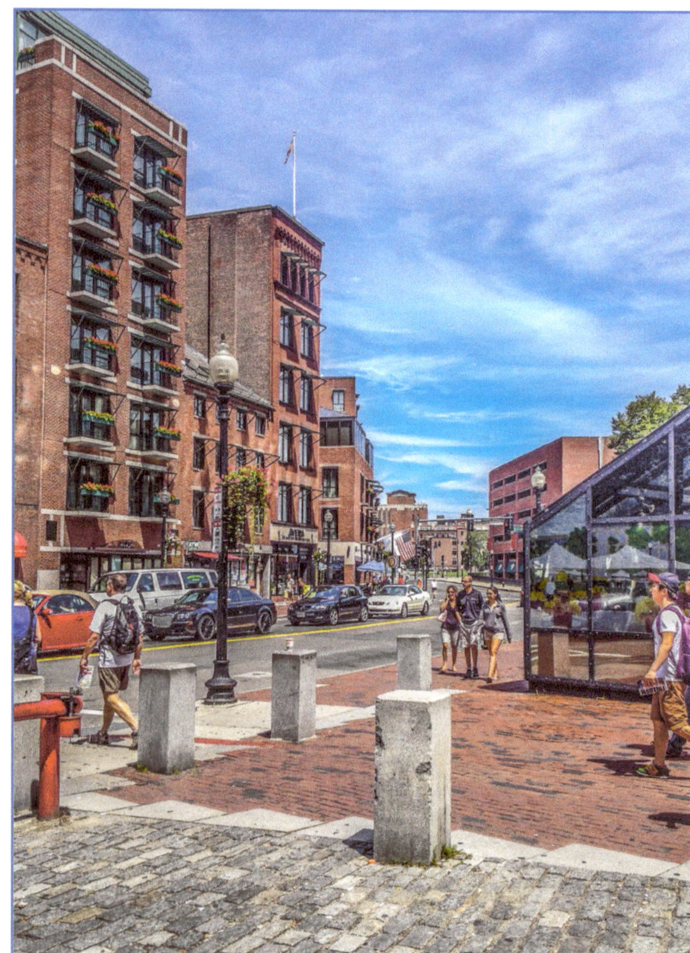

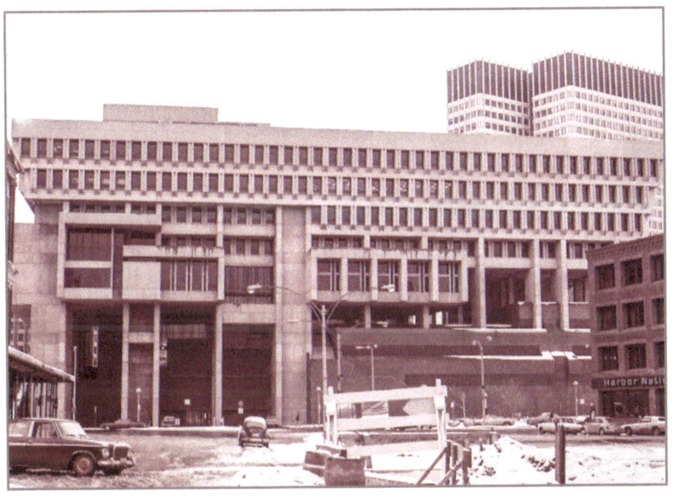

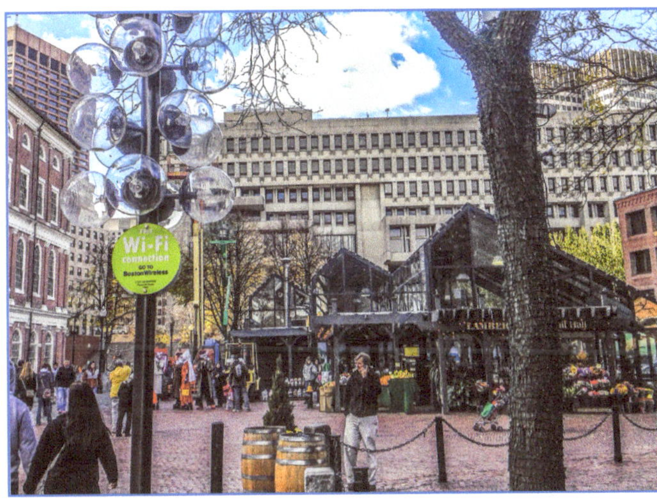

There are over one million public wifi hotspots around the world. Boston is no exception. From commuter rail trains, to the Green Monster, people are surfing the web by connecting to wifi.

The majority of people are connecting to wifi as a means of data connectivity. While 3G and 4G connectivity allow for internet access anywhere at any time, it comes at a cost. Wifi is free.

The future sales of smartphones and tablets means an increase in wireless data traffic. In order to keep up with demand it is estimated that there will be a 350 percent increase in the number of wifi hotspots as of 2015, meaning over five and a half million public hotspots worldwide.

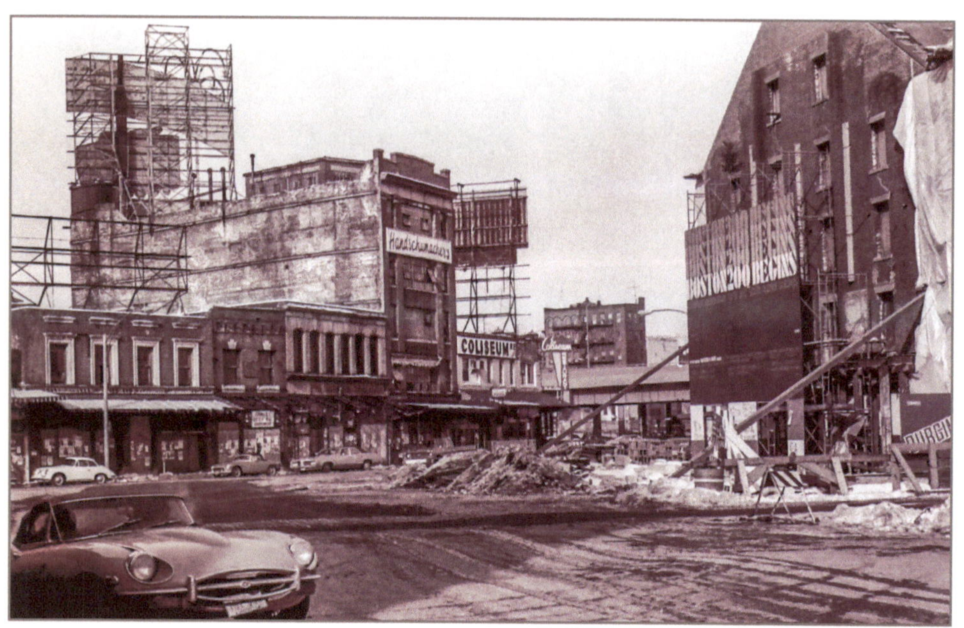

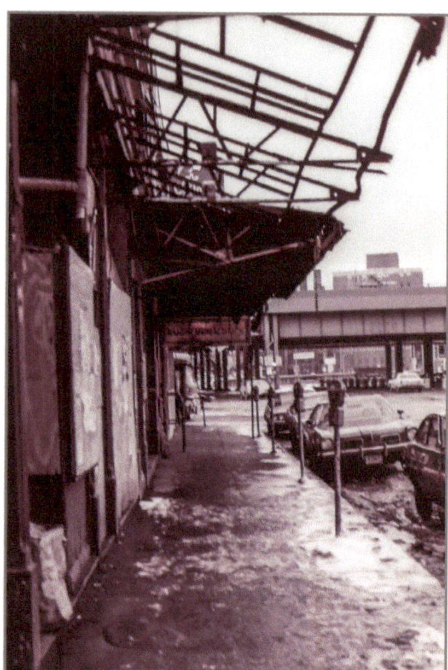

The Central Artery choked the city by dividing the North End and the waterfront from downtown.

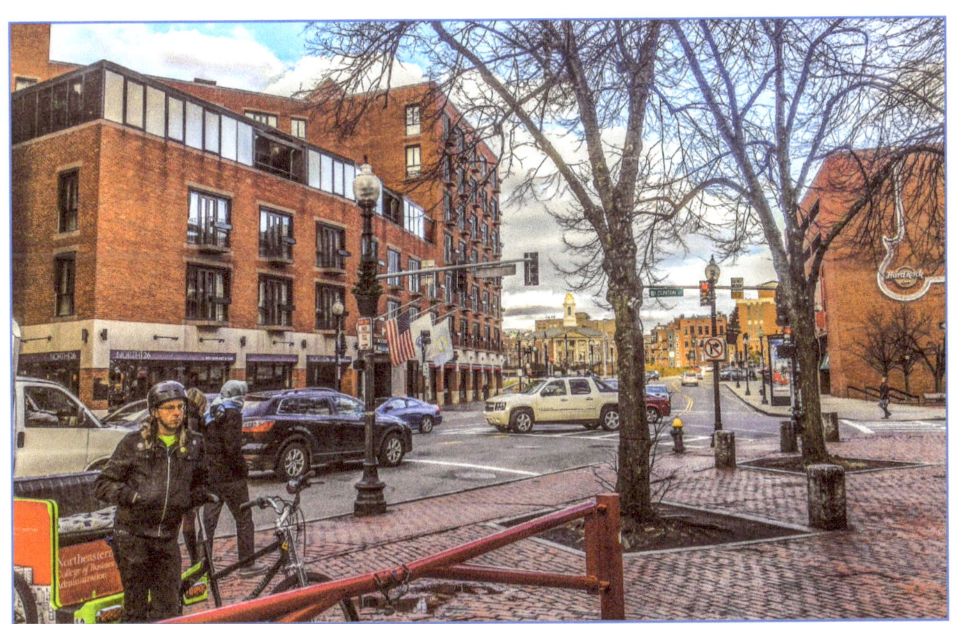

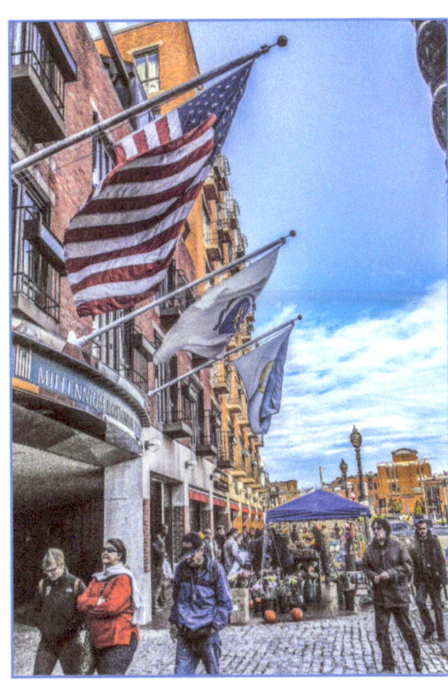

A bicycle rickshaw has replaced an XKE and the Hard Rock Cafe has made the scene. The Bostonian Hotel stands handsomely where a ramshackle row of derelict buildings had been.

The smell of raw fish still fills the air at Haymarket Square. Every Friday and Saturday open-air vendors hustle fresh fruit and vegetables, along with meats and fish.

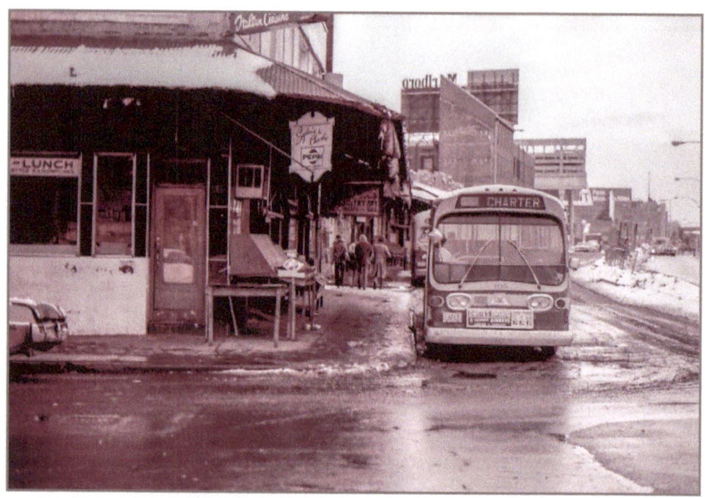

Fisheries have always been a significant source of income for New Englanders. However, years of pursuing groundfish have led to a serious decline in local stocks like cod and halibut.

In order to rebuild the number of fish that swim through our oceans, strict government quotas have been installed. But, with health awareness constantly growing, fish are in higher demand than ever before.

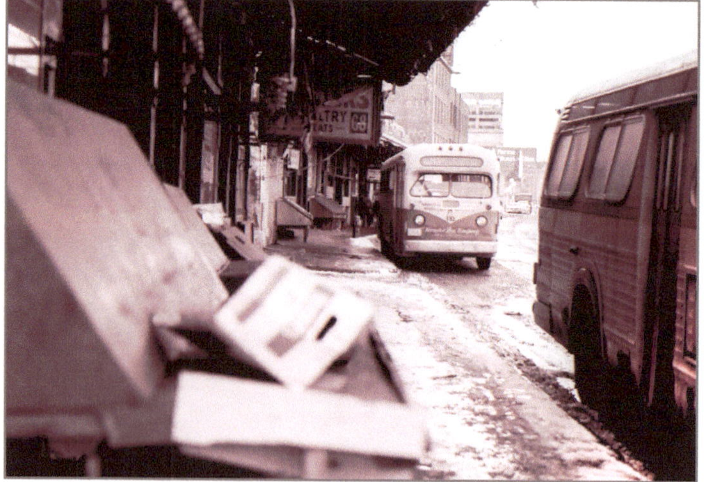

The effort to protect the fish as well as the incomes of the fishermen is of dire importance for communities across the area. By catching under utilized species and following fishing regulations, fishermen's jobs can be saved and New England's fisheries can hope for a brighter future.

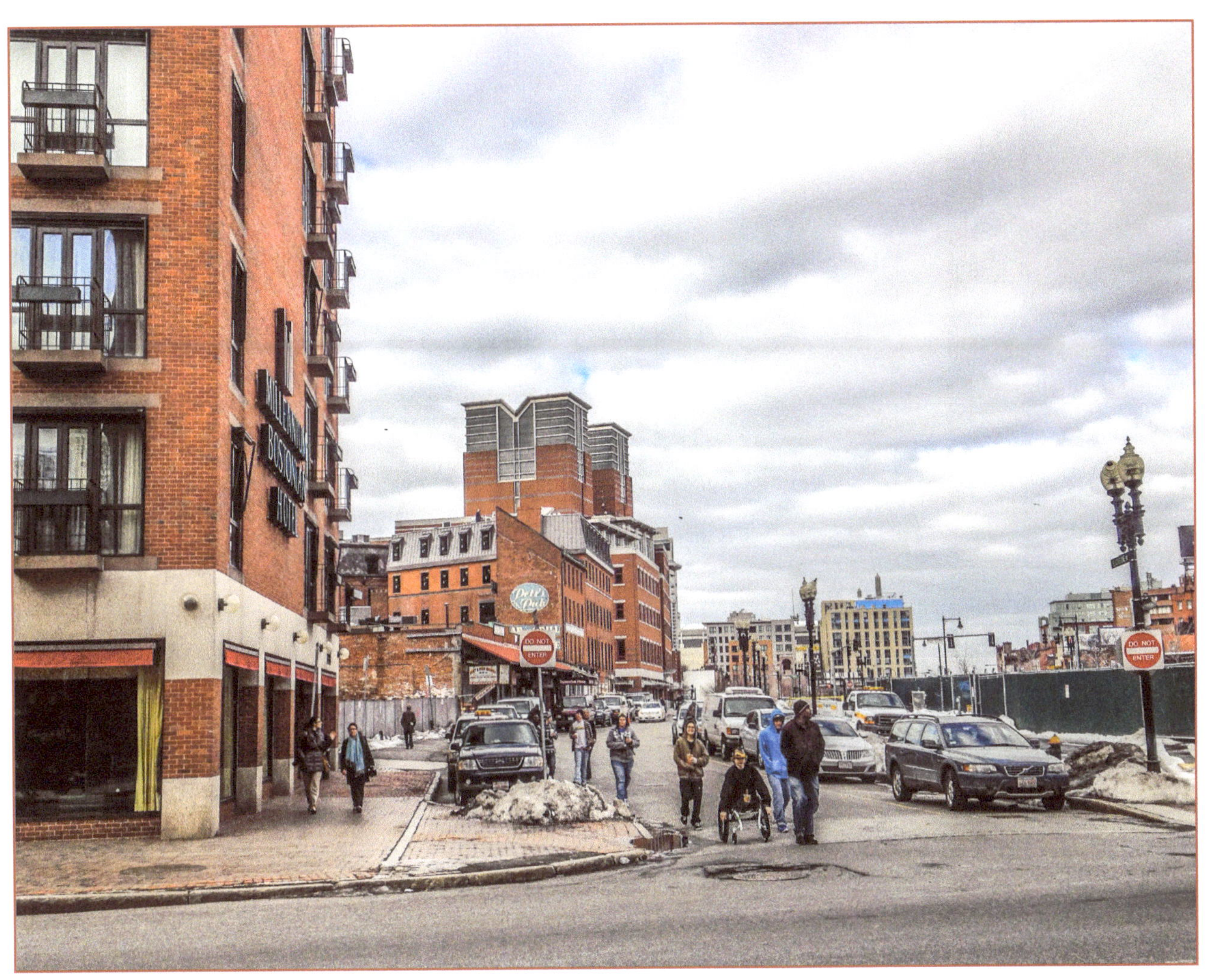
DO NOT ENTER
DO NOT ENTER

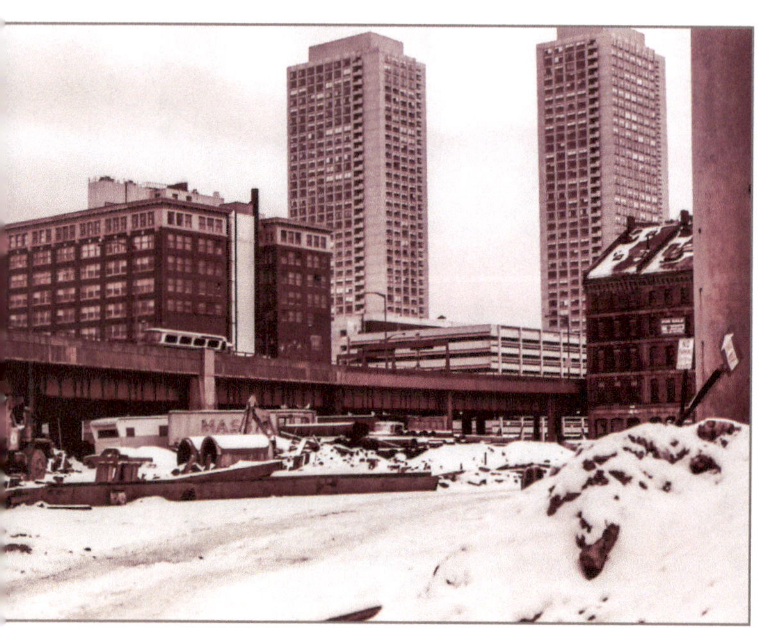

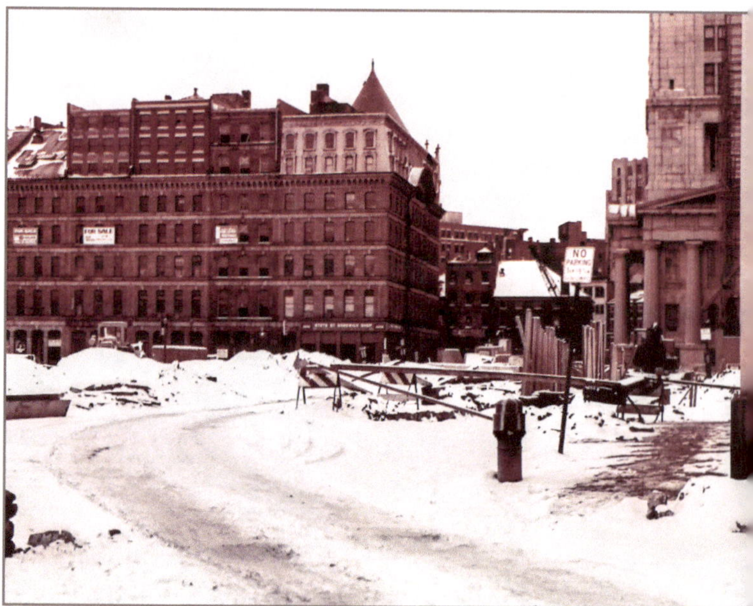

The Central Artery divides Harbor Towers from lower State Street. That view is now occupied by a plaza and the building at 200 State Street.

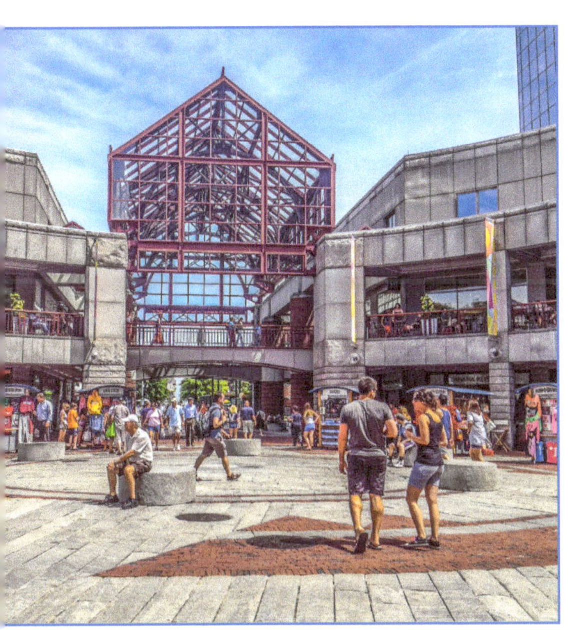

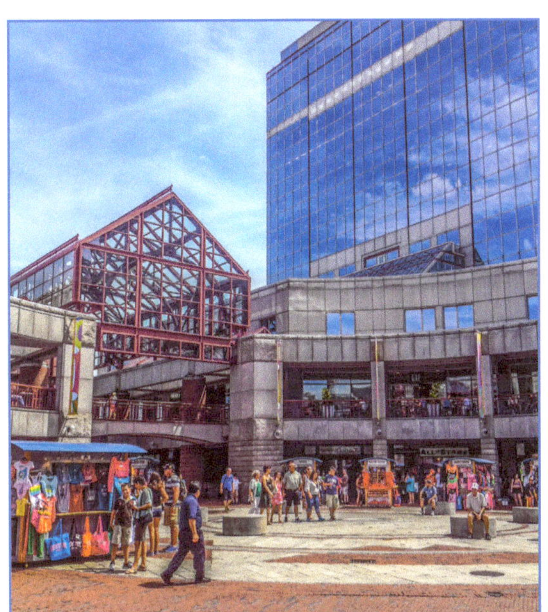

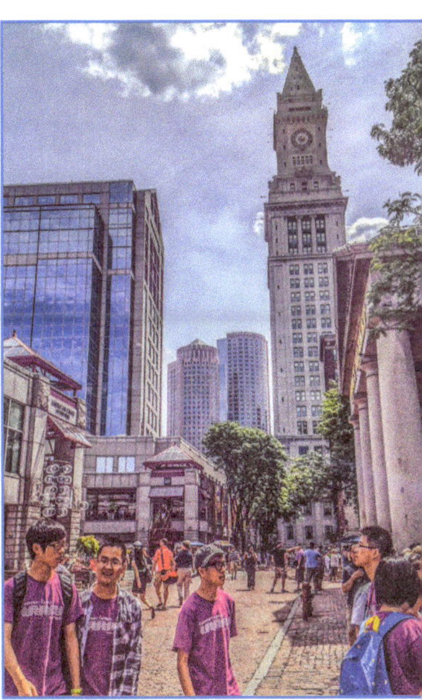

The country was not diverse. And the word *multicultural* was not part of the political jargon. The 1972 Statistical Abstract of the United States divides the population into three groups: White, Negro and other.

The abstract also informs that nationwide there were 68,864 active "Reported Narcotics Addicts". 96% of these addicts were heroin dependent. Cocaine was not on the list of abused drugs.

Right, Commercial Street looking toward the Customs House.

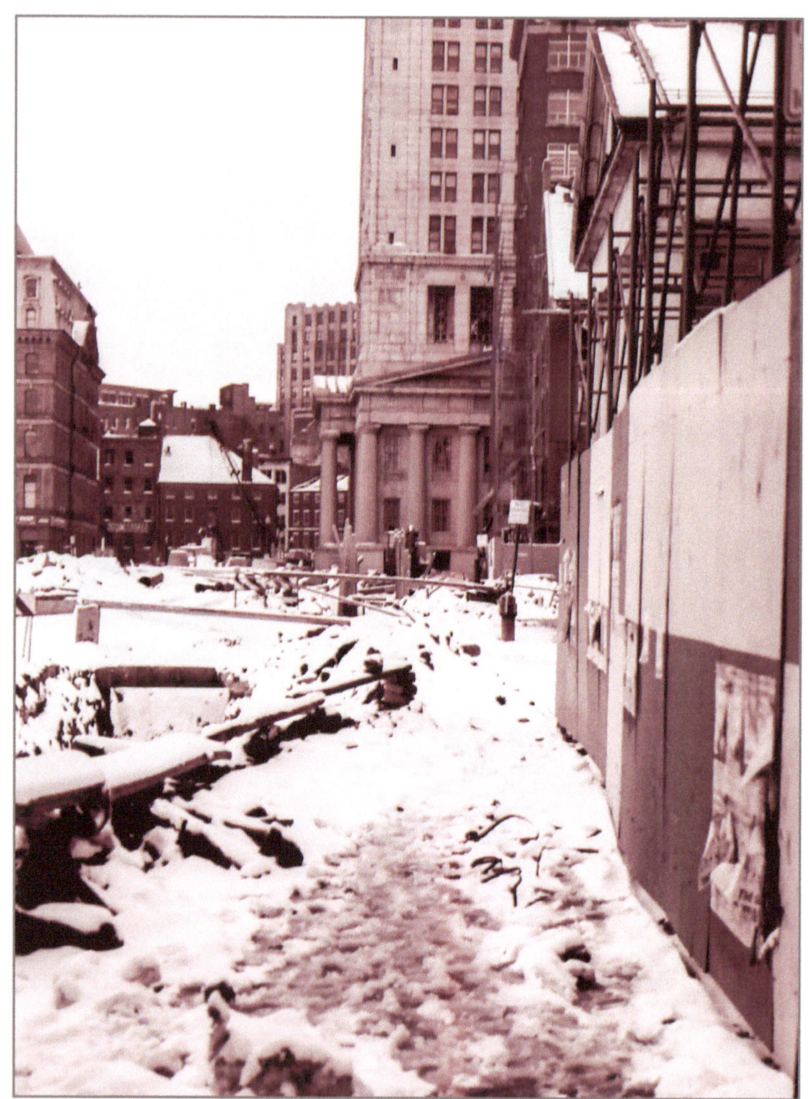

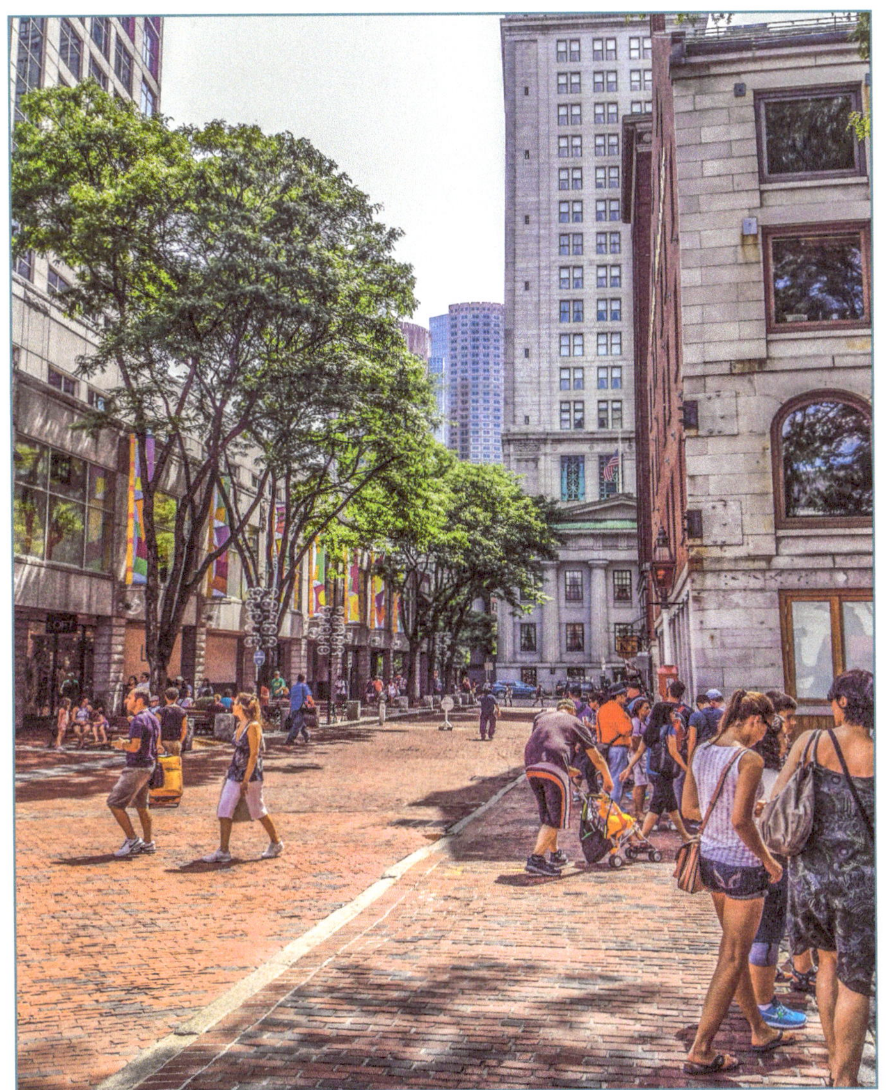

Marijuana decriminalization has been an ongoing battle since the 1970's when California reduced the penalty for possession of under an ounce to a misdemeanor.

Robert Randall sued the federal government, in 1978, when he was arrested for using marijuana to help treat his glaucoma. Randall won his case and was the first to receive government issued cannabis cigarettes, as many as 30 per month.

Massachusetts' citizens voted to legalize medicinal marijuana in 2012. At the same time, Colorado and Washington became the first states to legalize marijuana for recreational sale and use.

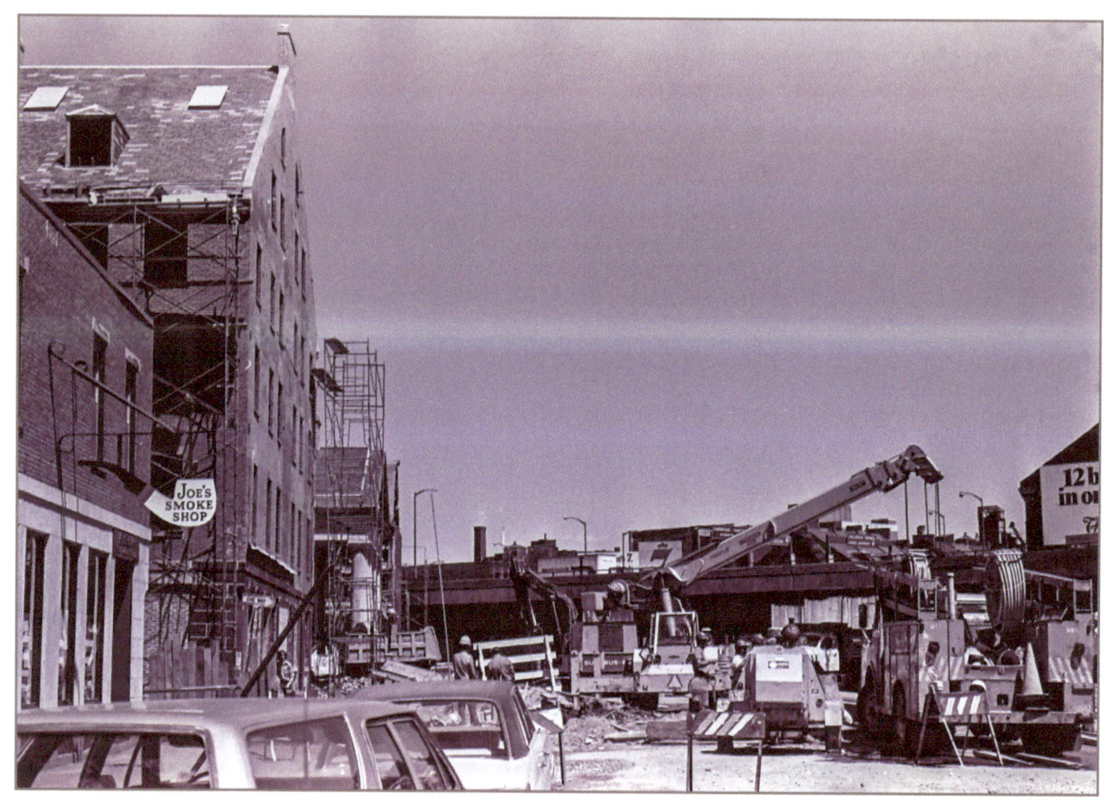

The beginning of
Commercial Street
looking toward
Quincy Market.

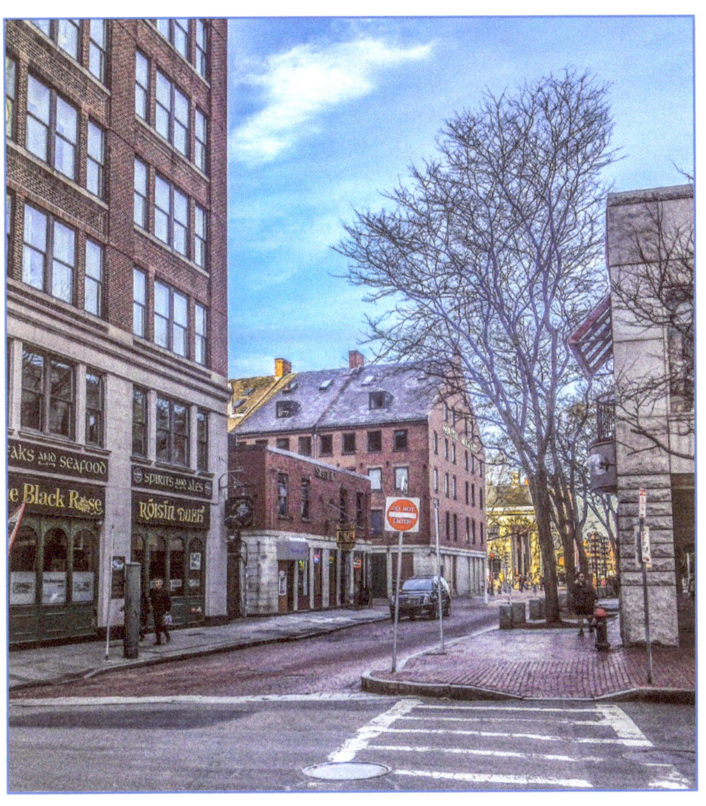
SPIRITS AND ALES
RÓISÍN DUBH
DO NOT ENTER

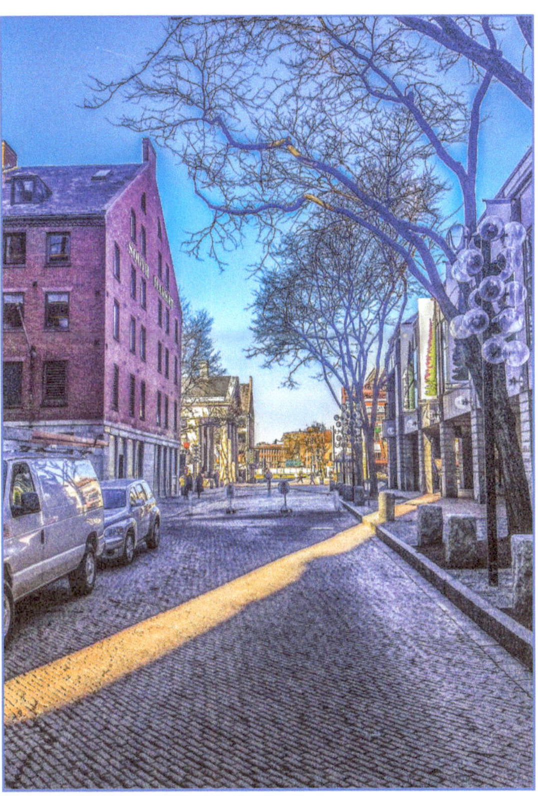

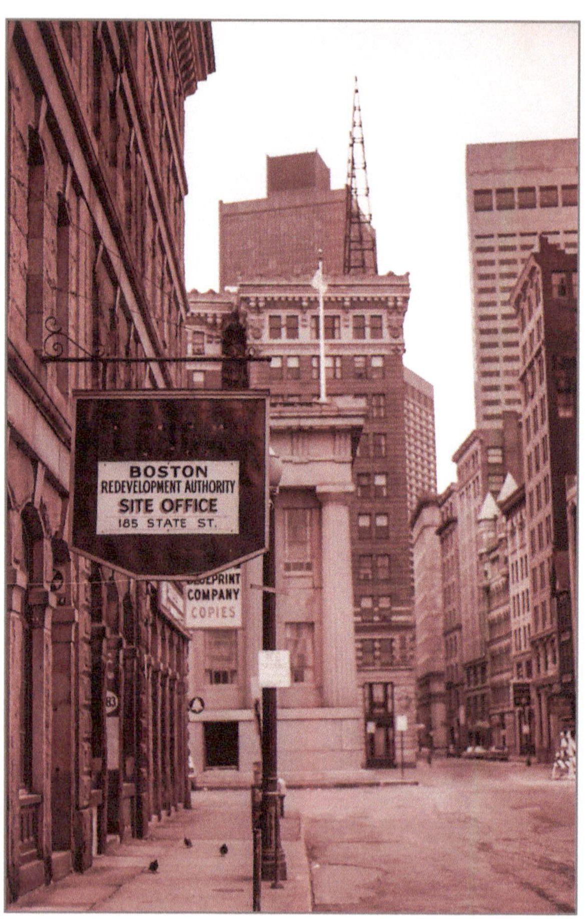
BOSTON
REDEVELOPMENT AUTHORITY
SITE OFFICE
185 STATE ST.
COMPANY
COPIES

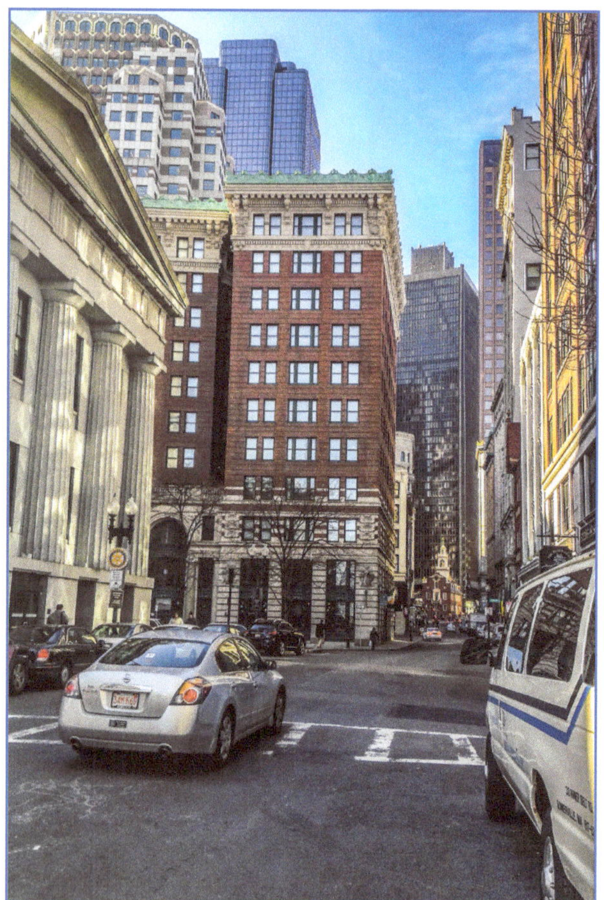

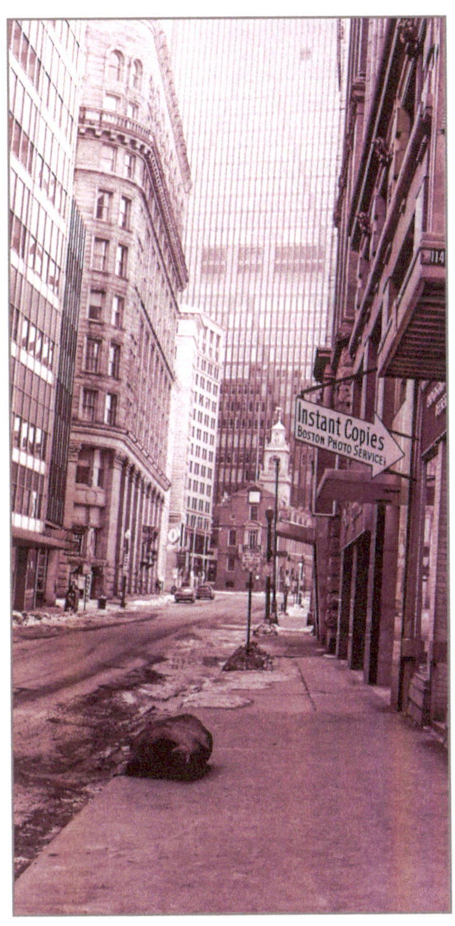

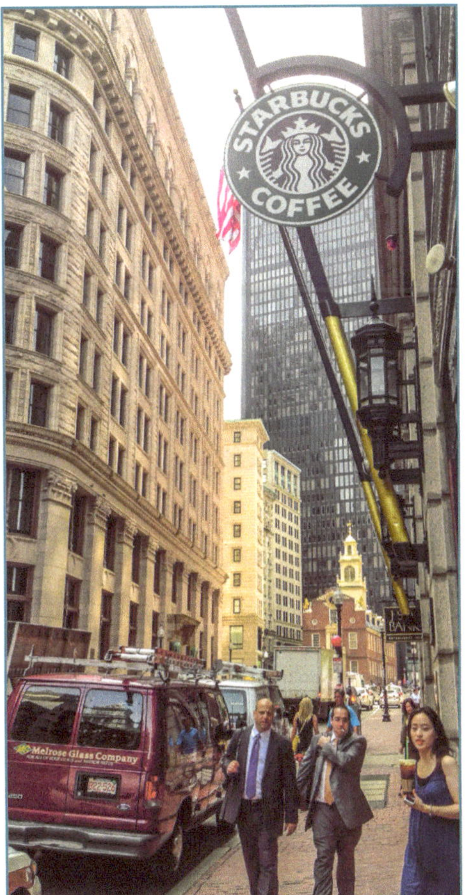

Copy shops were more common than coffee shoppes before people toted their laptops to the internet cafes.

The first email was sent in 1971 by Ray Tomlinson, a computer engineer, who sent himself a test message between two computers on the floor in his Cambridge, MA lab; he also introduced the "@" symbol in email.

Still, in the mid-nineties, a business with an email address was very unusual. Online shopping was nonexistent.

Look, up in the sky. Is that a bird? A plane? No. it's a drone.

Video surveillance will reach new heights when police departments and other agencies begin to deploy drones. Hi-res cameras coupled with face-recognition software will enhance law enforcement's ability to identify bad guys. But, at the expense of everyone's privacy.

The Federal Aviation Administration estimates that there could be 30,000 drones hovering over the US in 2020.

At right, 200 State Street fills the empty lot in front of Quincy Market.

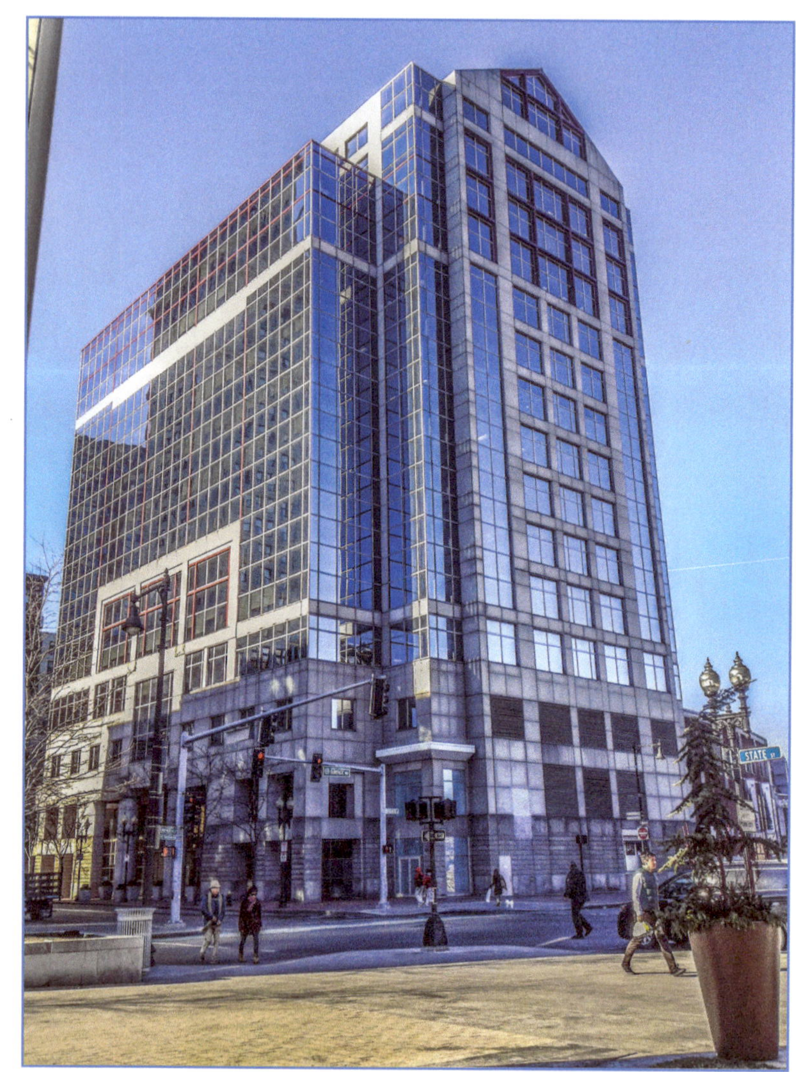

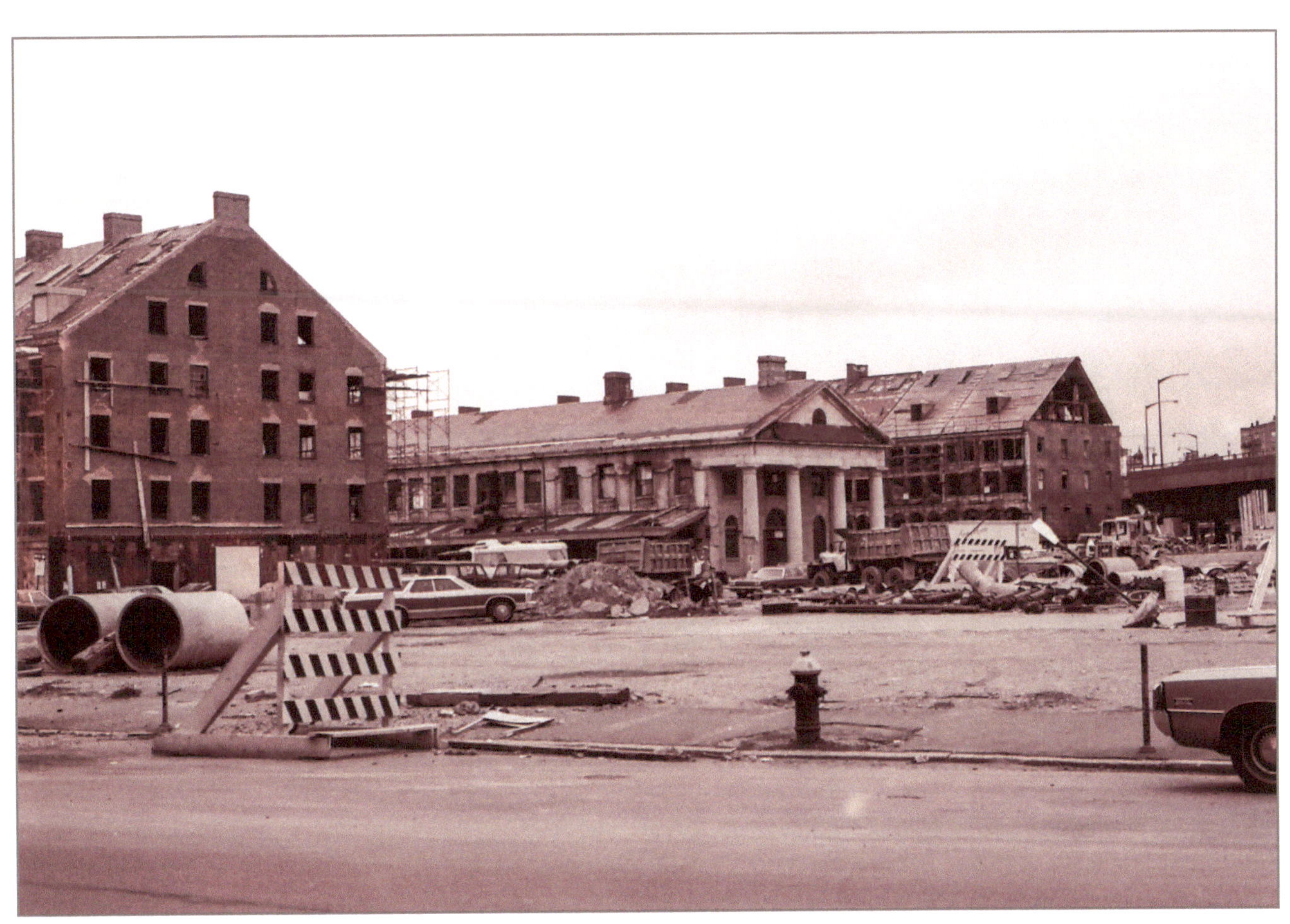

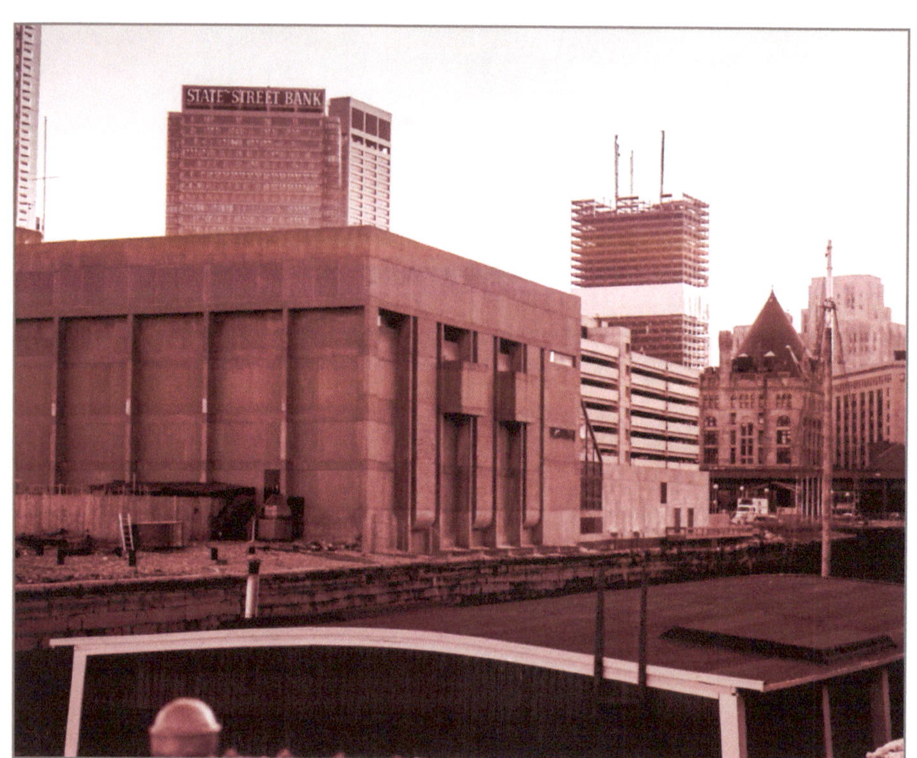

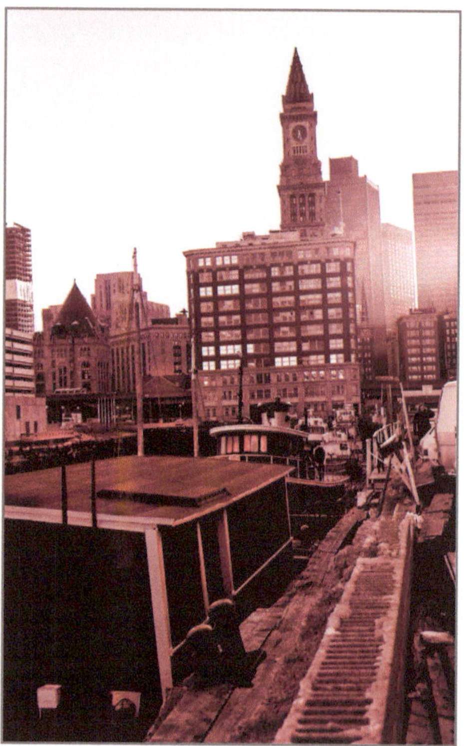

Looking towards State Street from Long Wharf.

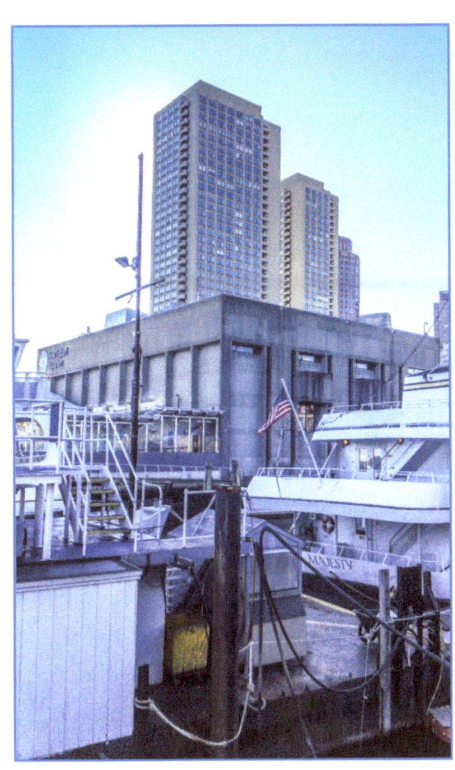

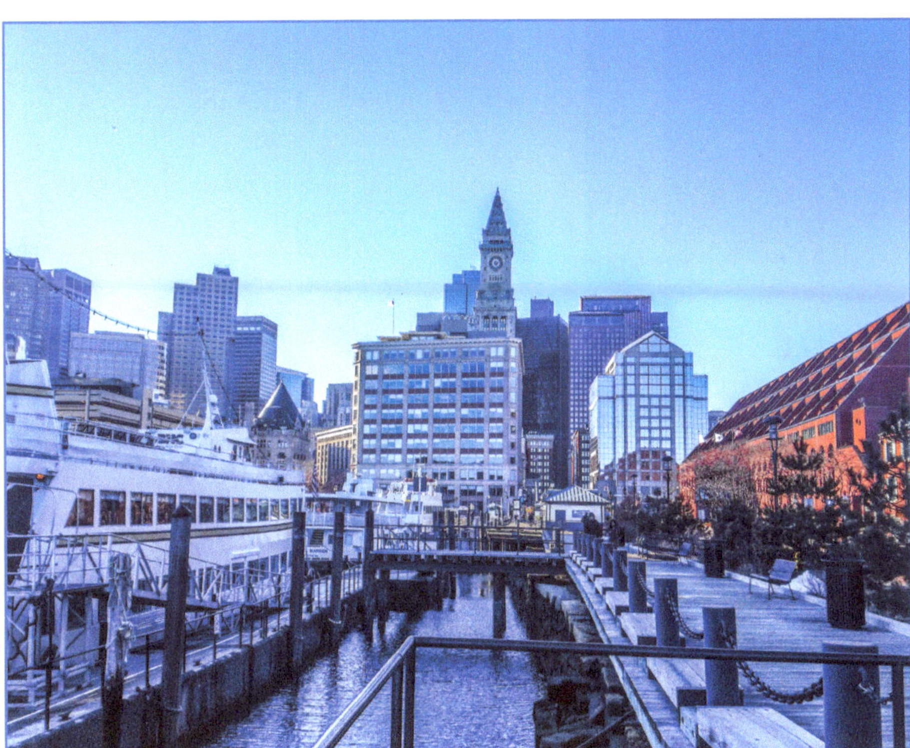

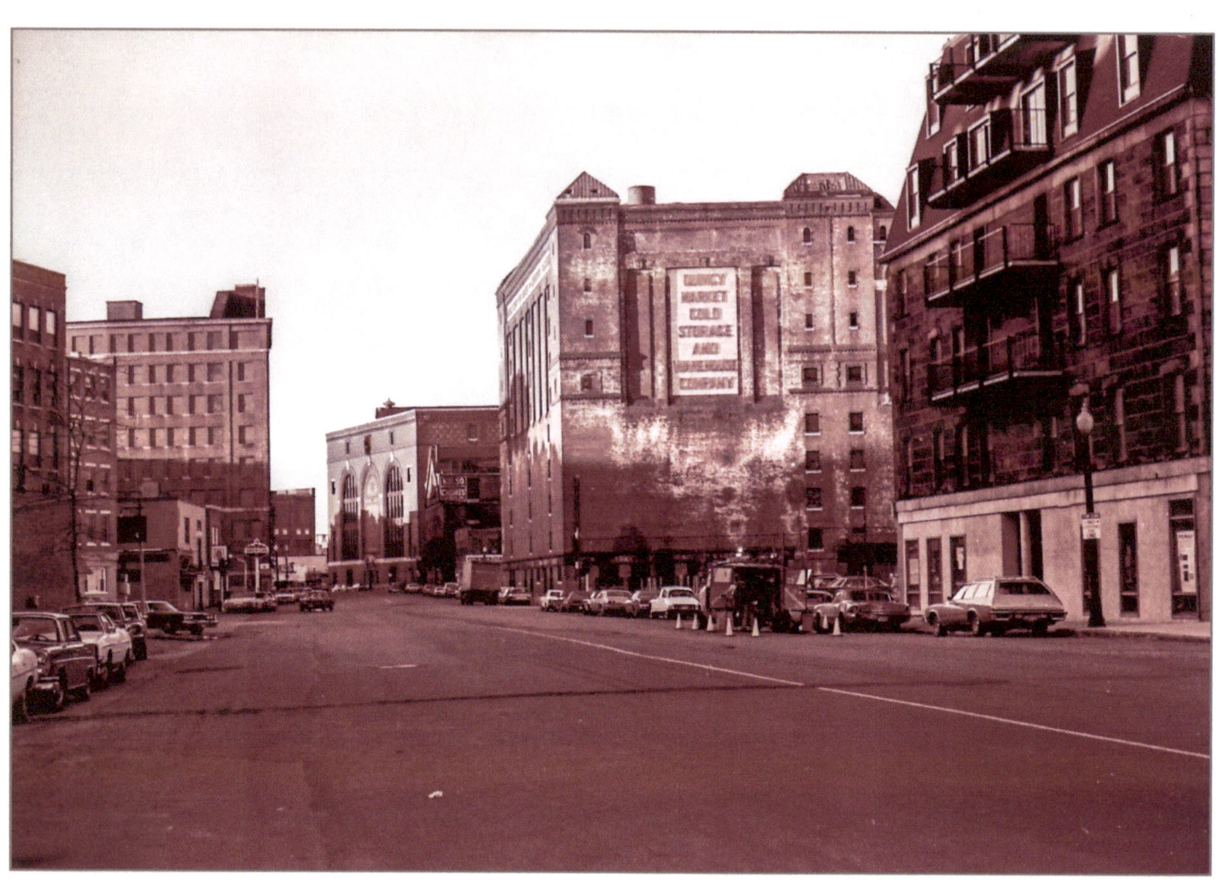
COLD
STORAGE
AND
COMPANY

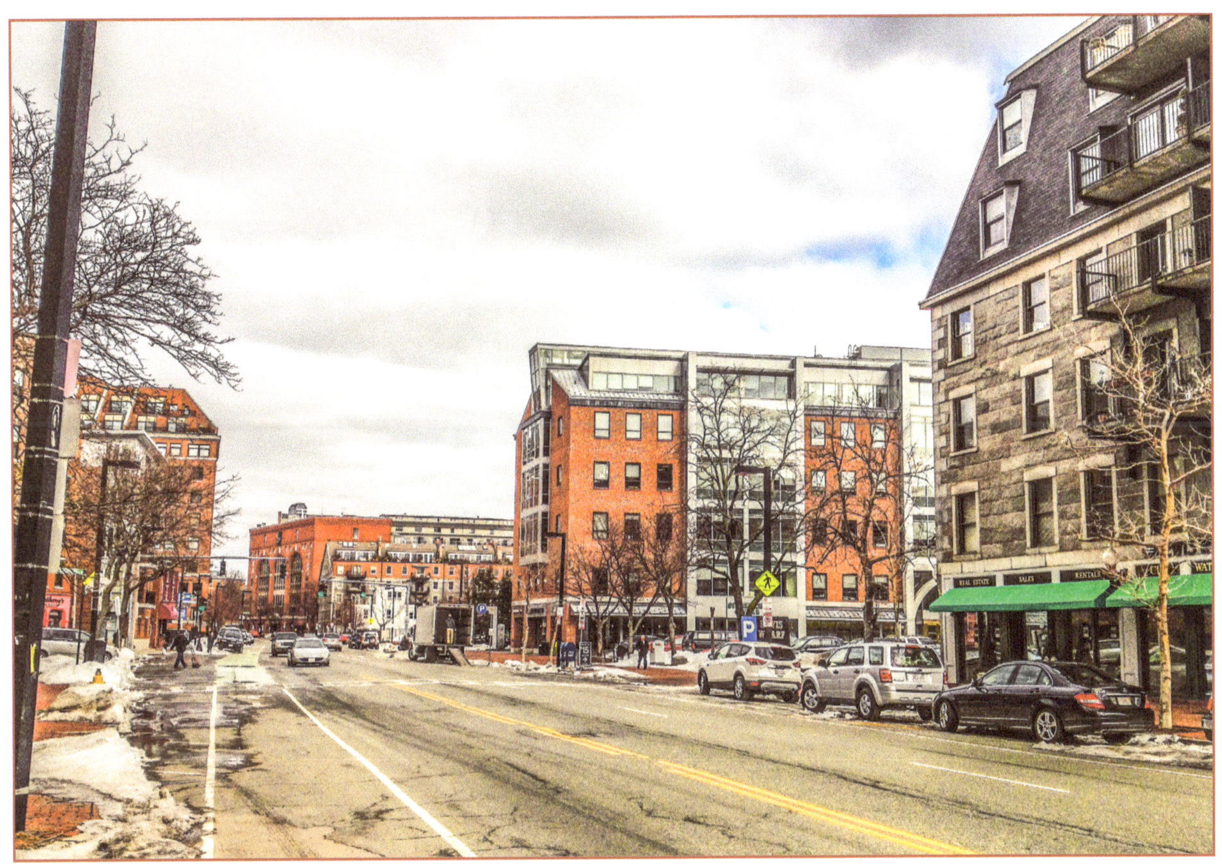

Atlantic Avenue merges into Commercial Street at the epicenter of the luxury waterfront condo market. The expensive condos replaced crumbling warehouses and a power plant.

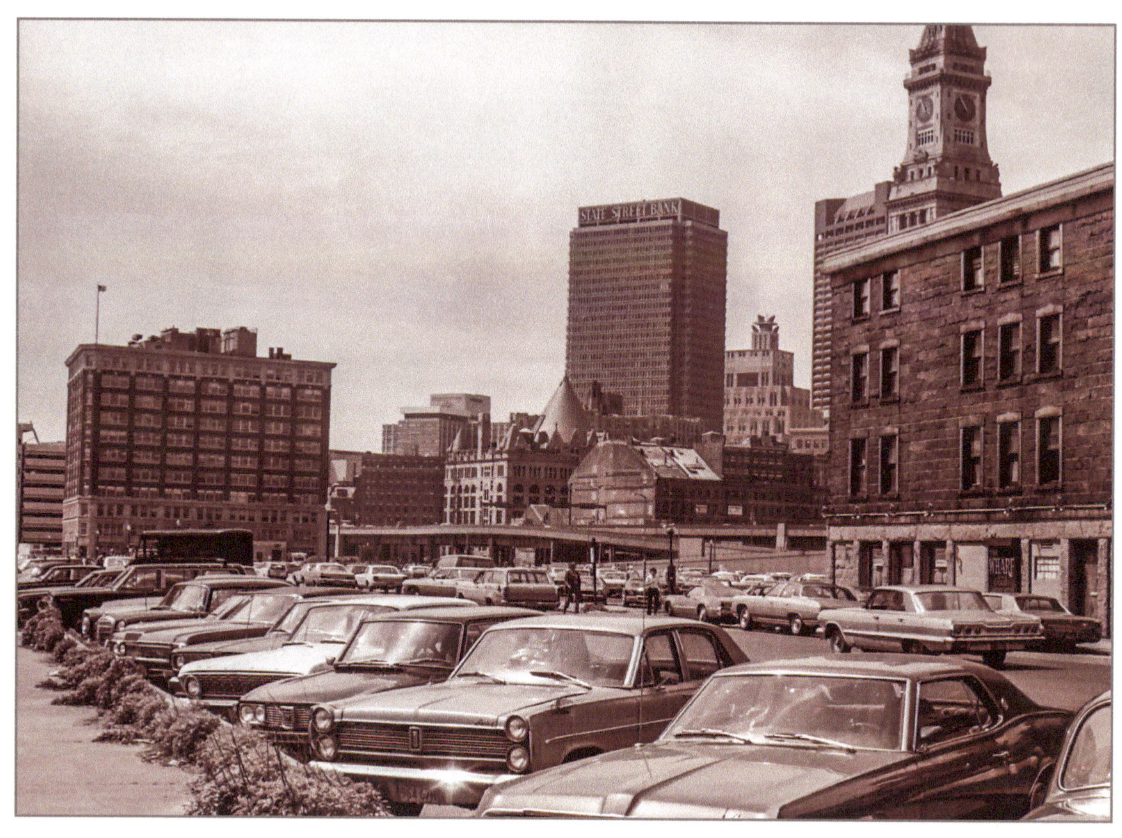

Boston is serious about bicycles. Green painted asphalt corridors course through the city and provide cyclists separation from traffic.

The Hubway bike program rents bikes from more than a hundred solar-powered, self-operated stations in the area.

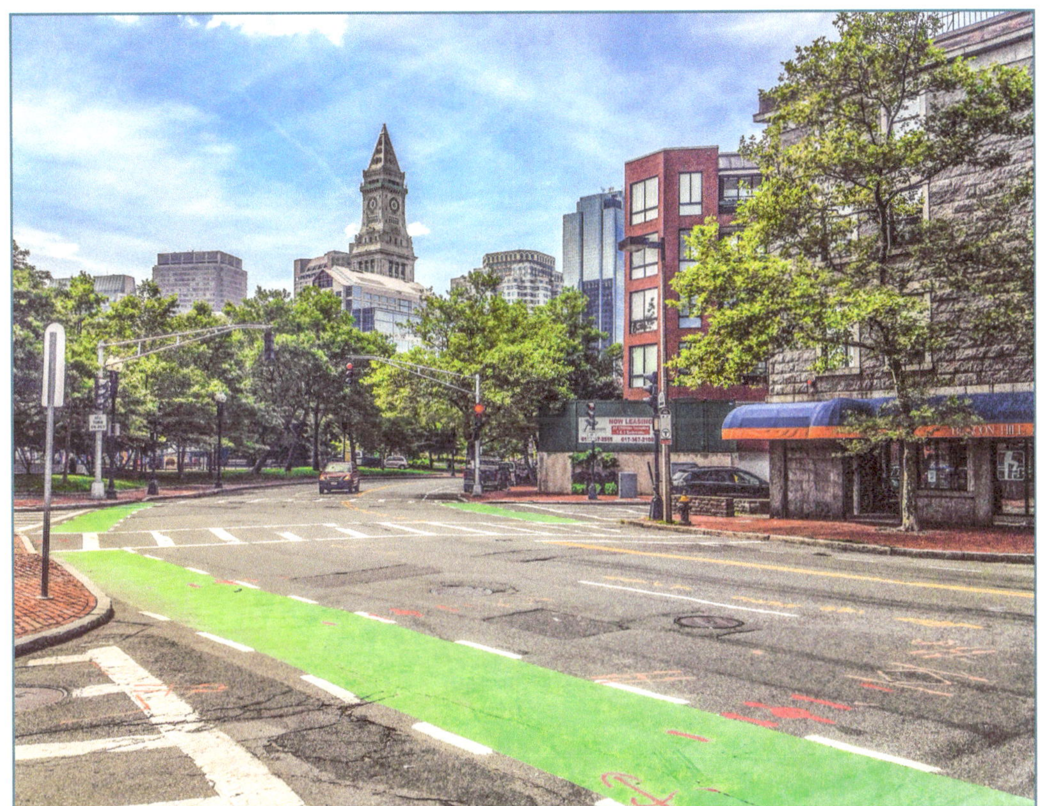
NOW LEASING

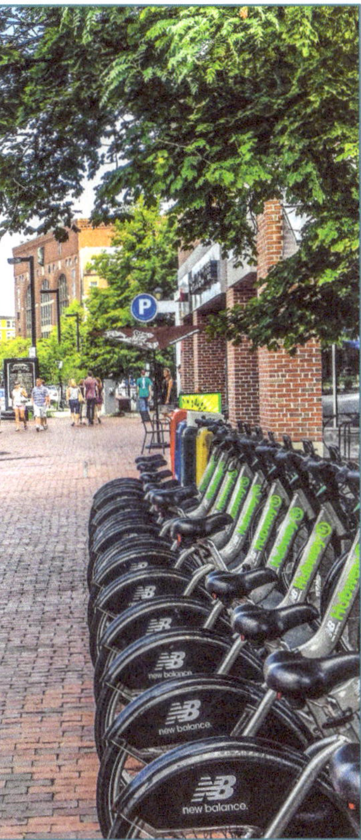
new balance

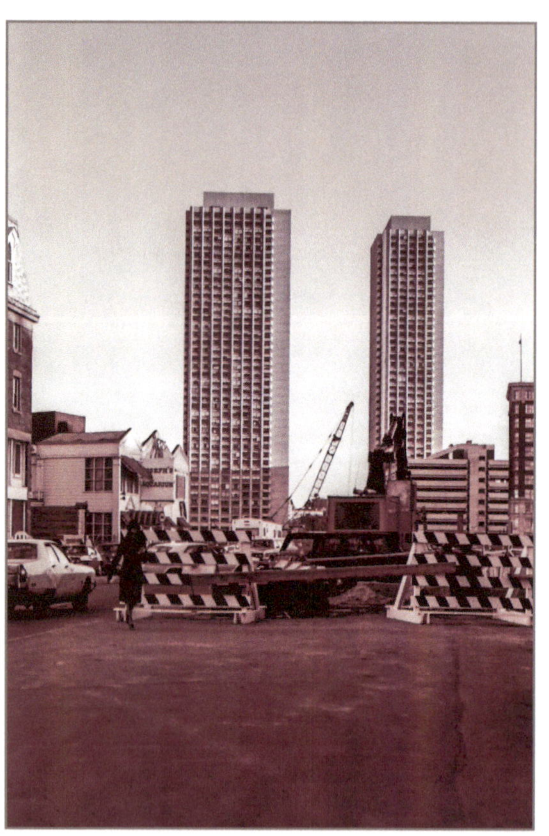

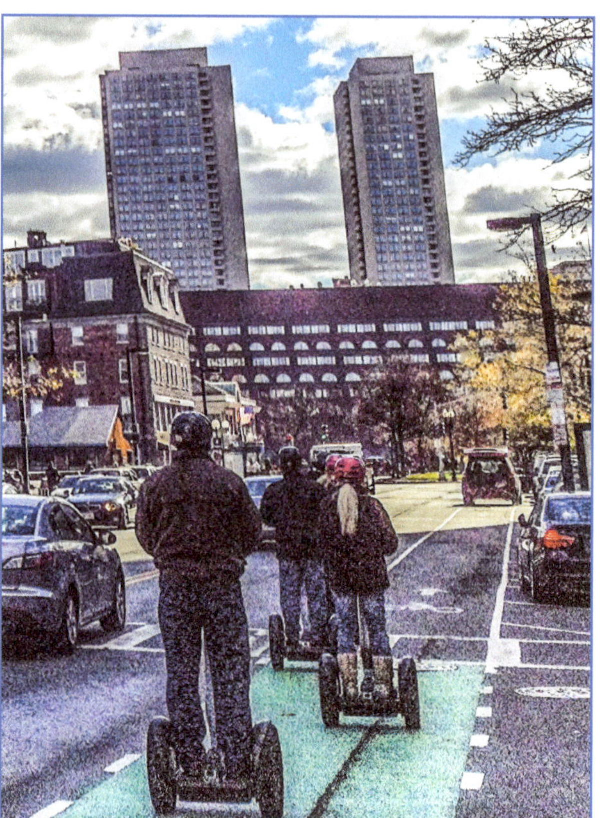

Atlantic Avenue

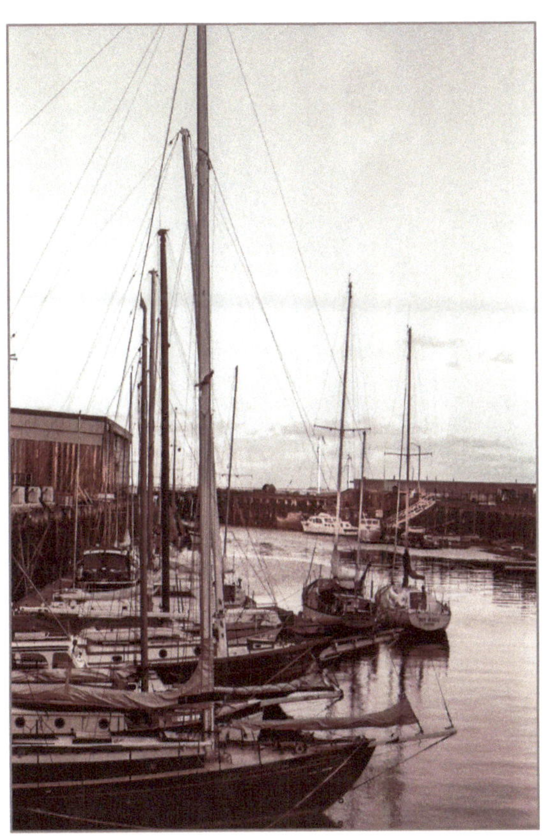

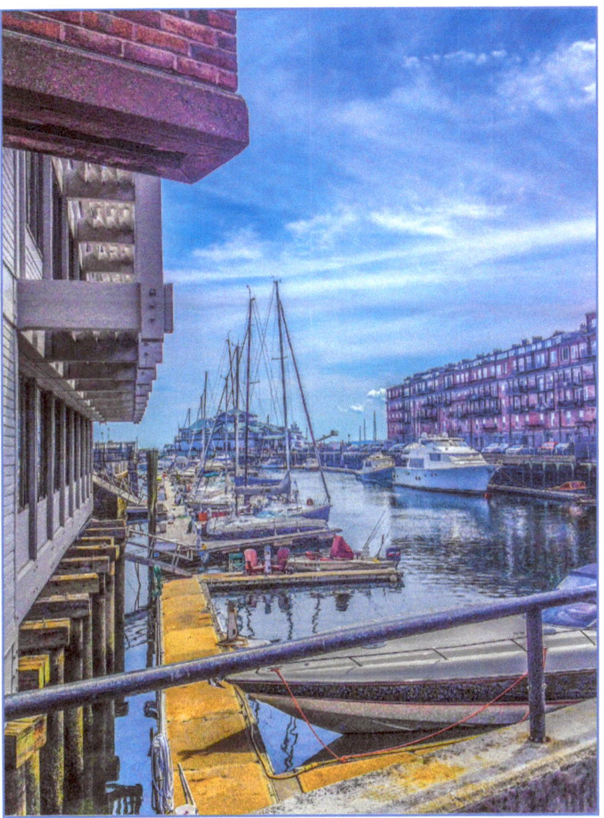

Lewis Wharf

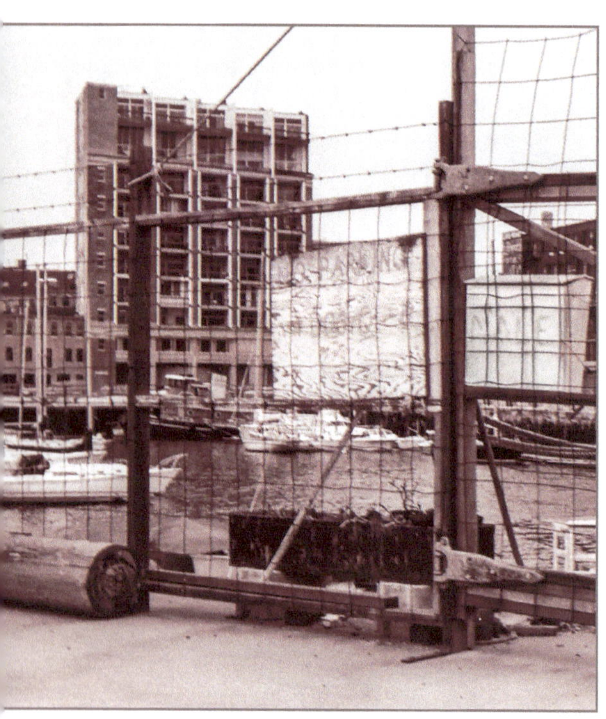

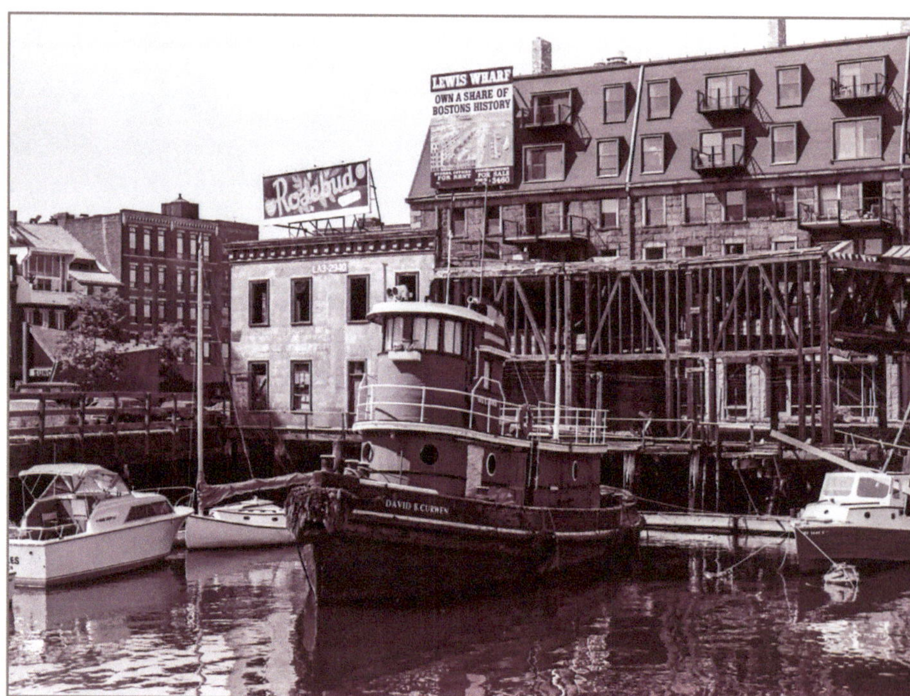

The Prince Spaghetti Building is across from Lewis Wharf on Atlantic Avenue.

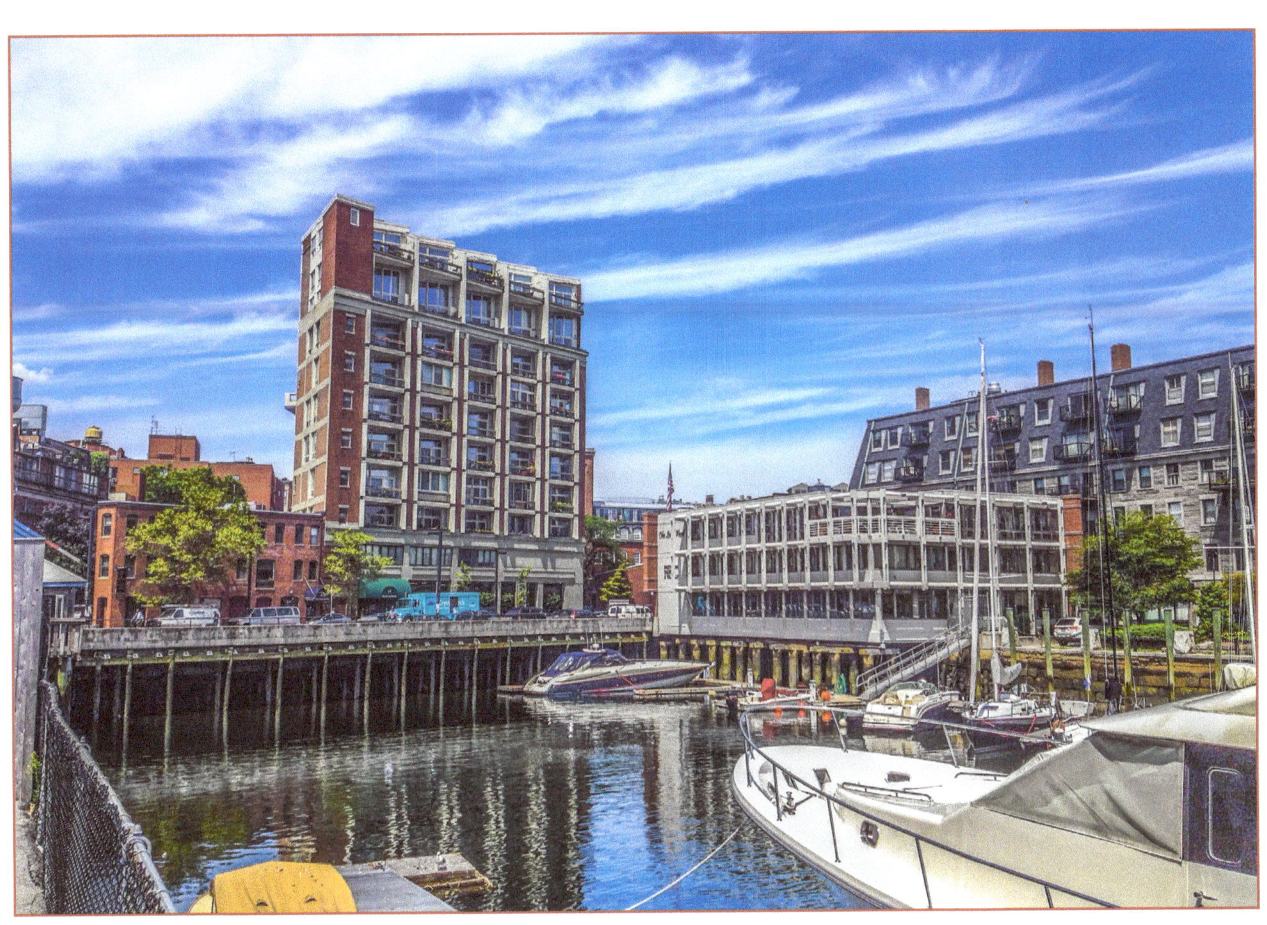

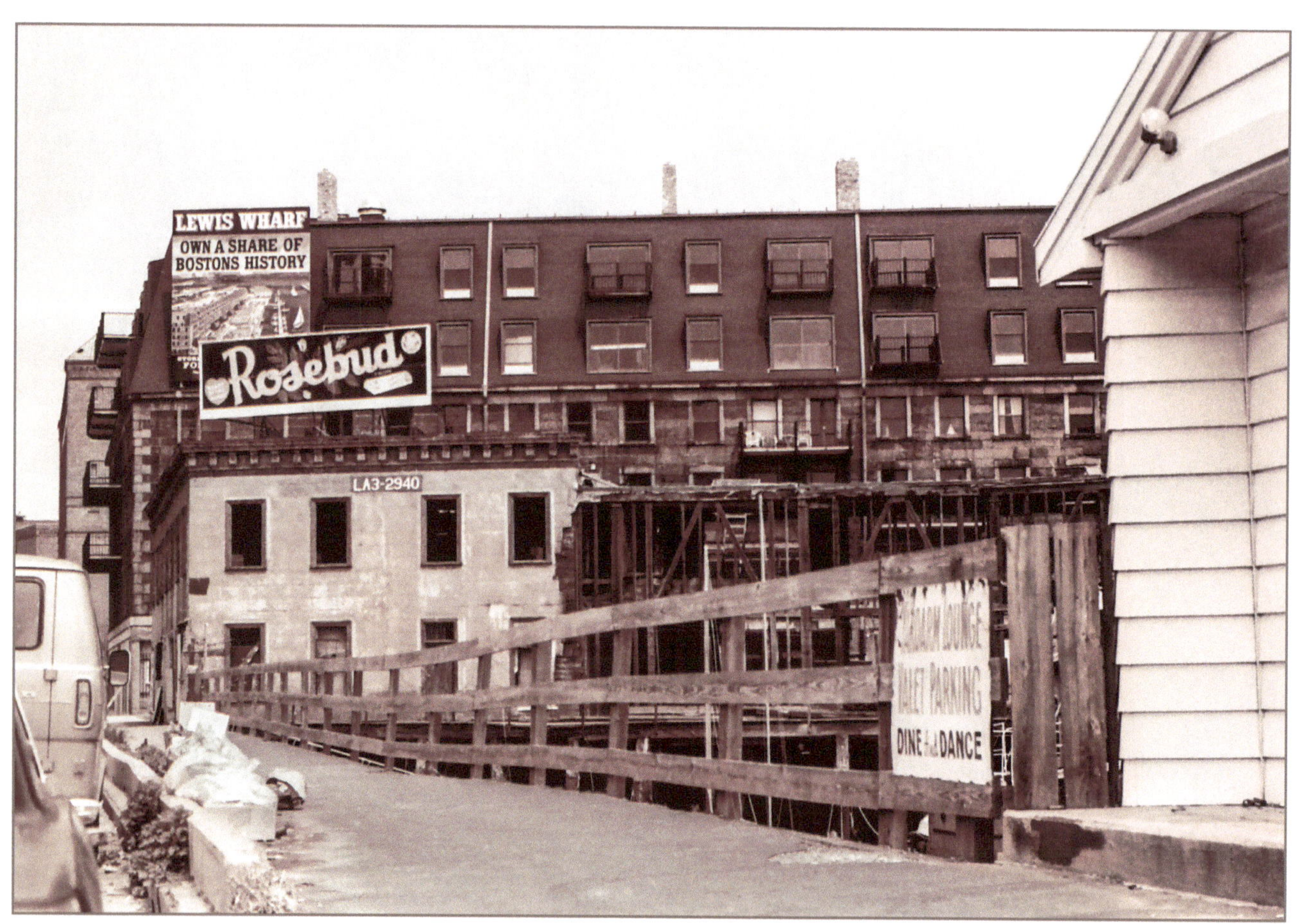
LEWIS WHARF
OWN A SHARE OF
BOSTONS HISTORY
Rosebud
LA3-2940
VALET PARKING
DINE
DANCE

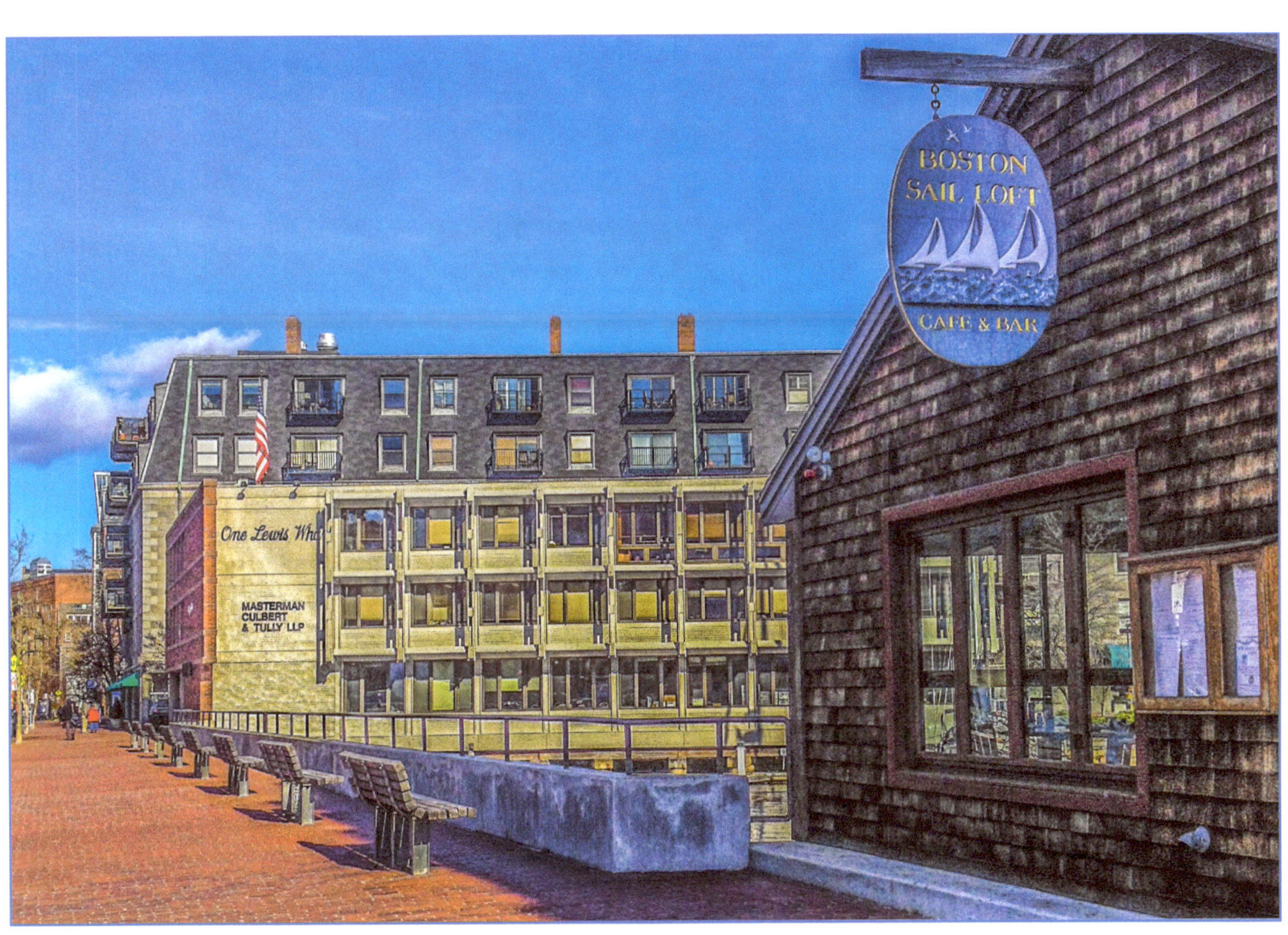
BOSTON
SAIL LOFT
CAFE & BAR
MASTERMAN
CULBERT
& TULLY LLP

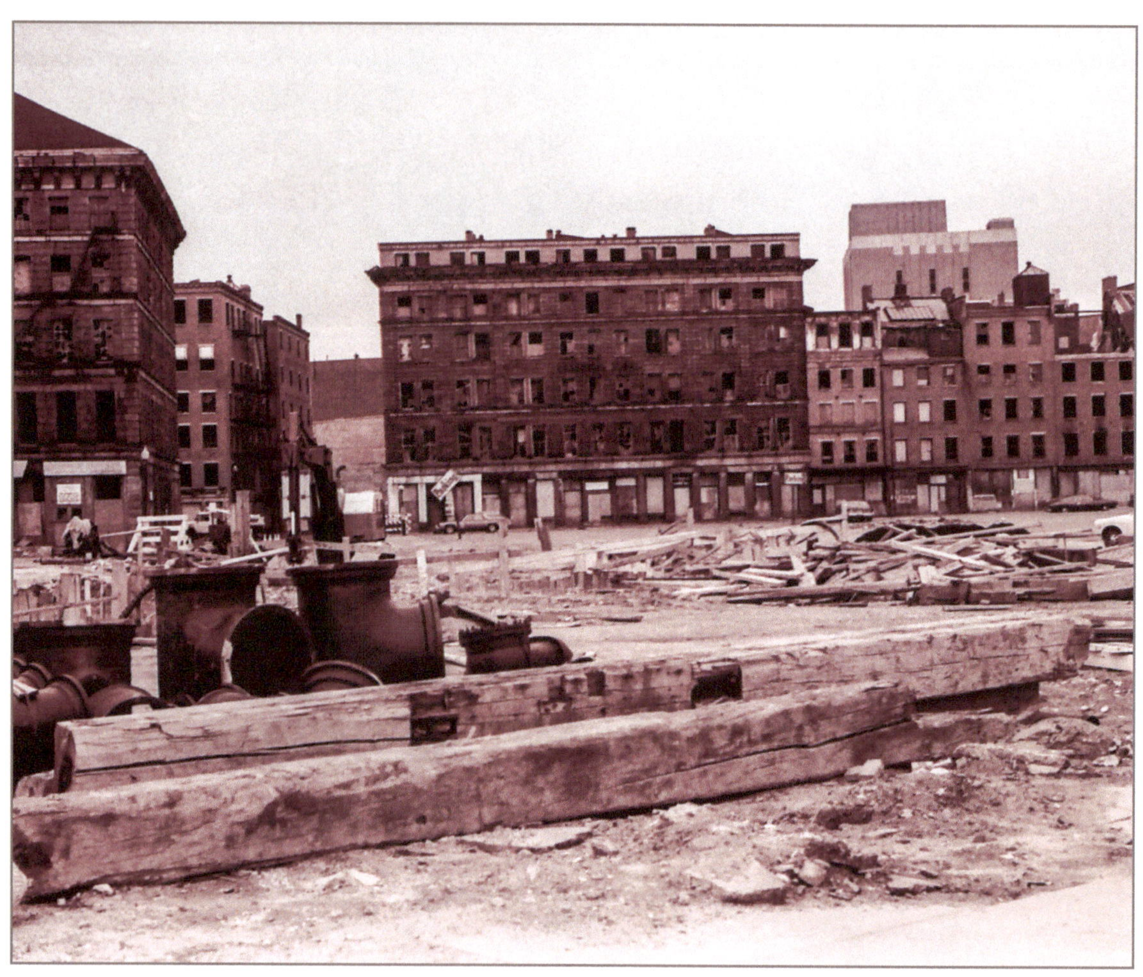

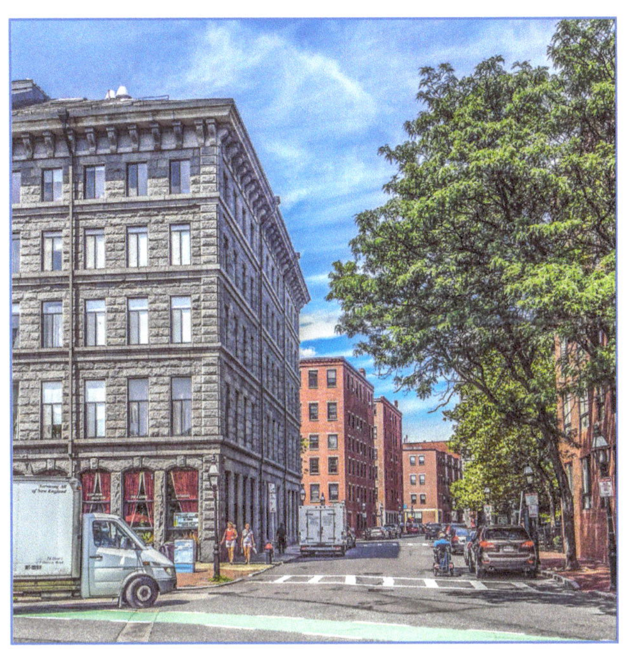

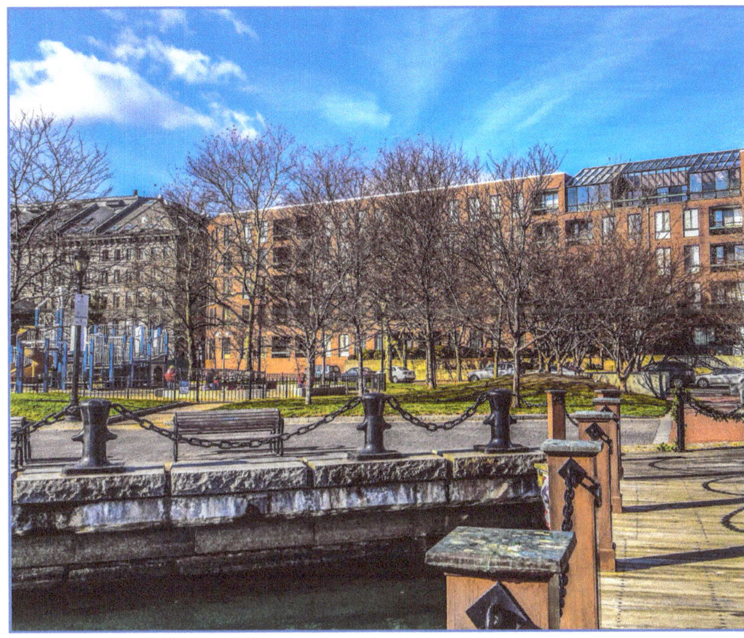

Left, looking from Atlantic Avenue across empty lots to Commercial Street.

Above right, a park and new apartments block the view to Commercial Street.

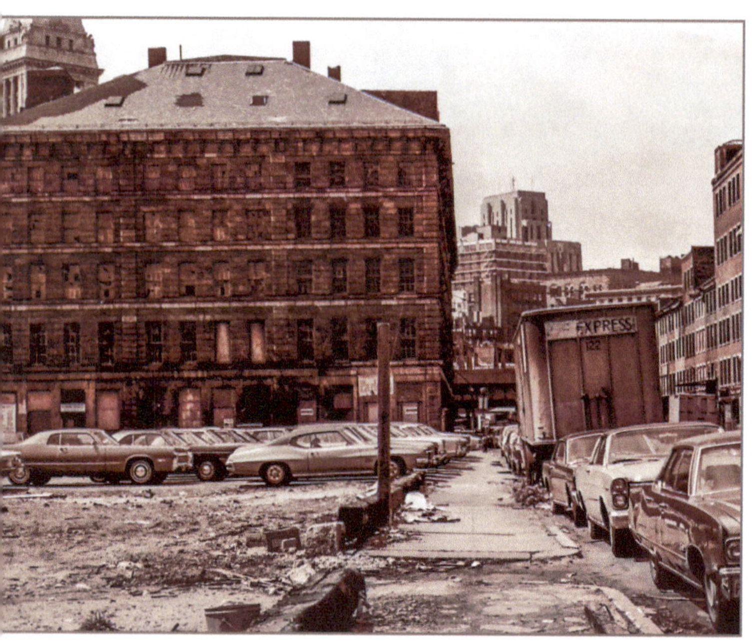

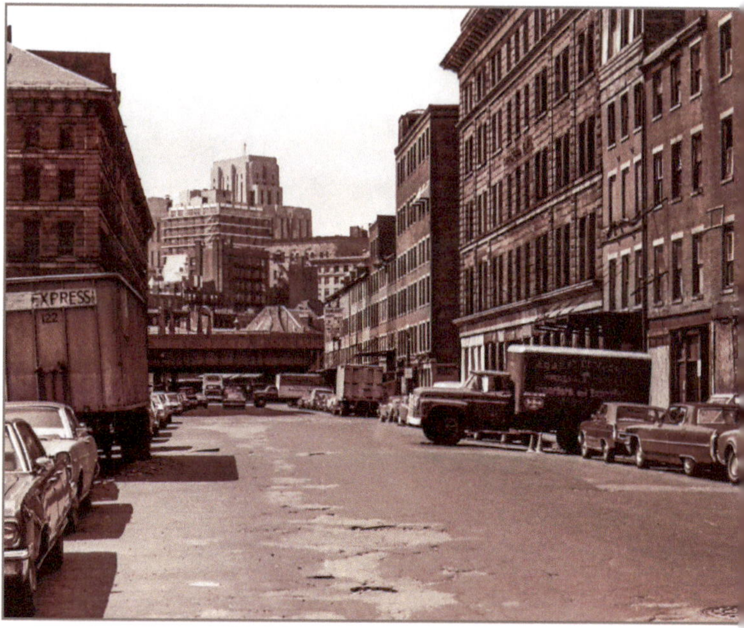

Commercial Street has been remade and it is now a residential neighborhood.

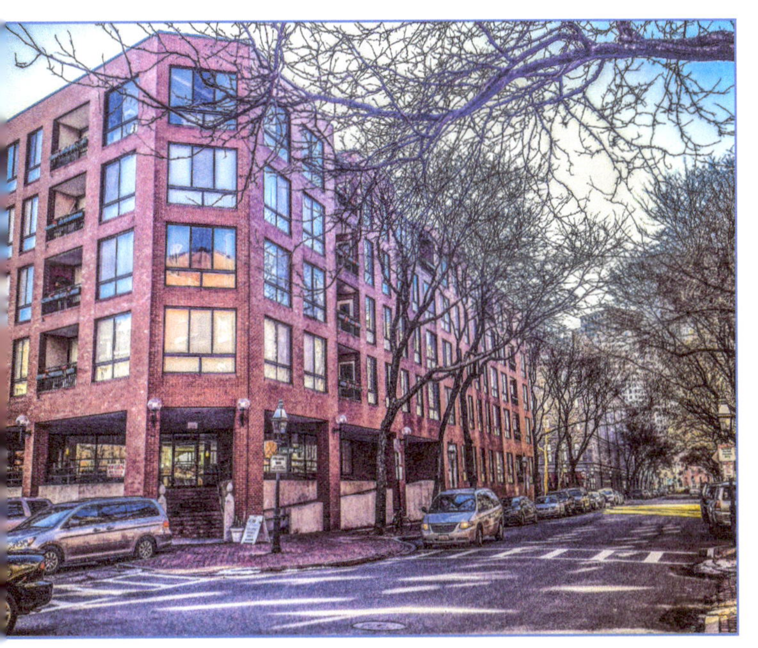

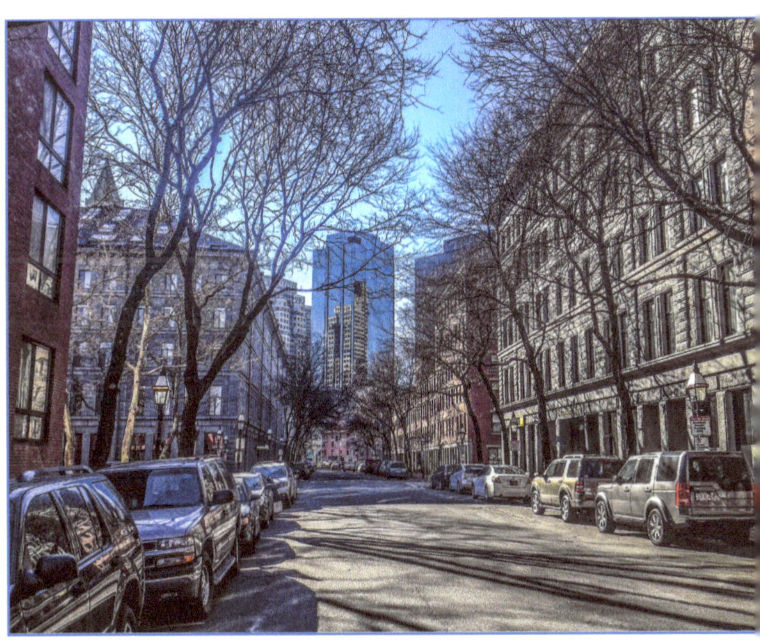

Apollo 17 was the final mission of the American lunar landing program, in December, 1972. It was the sixth time the United States had sent men to the moon.

On January 5, 1972, President Richard Nixon determined a new direction in space exploration when he said: "I have decided today that the United States should proceed at once with the development of an entirely new type of space transportation system ... that can shuttle repeatedly from Earth to orbit and back."

The last space shuttle flight, STS-135, ended July 21, 2011, when Atlantis rolled to a stop at its home port, NASA's Kennedy Space Center in Florida.

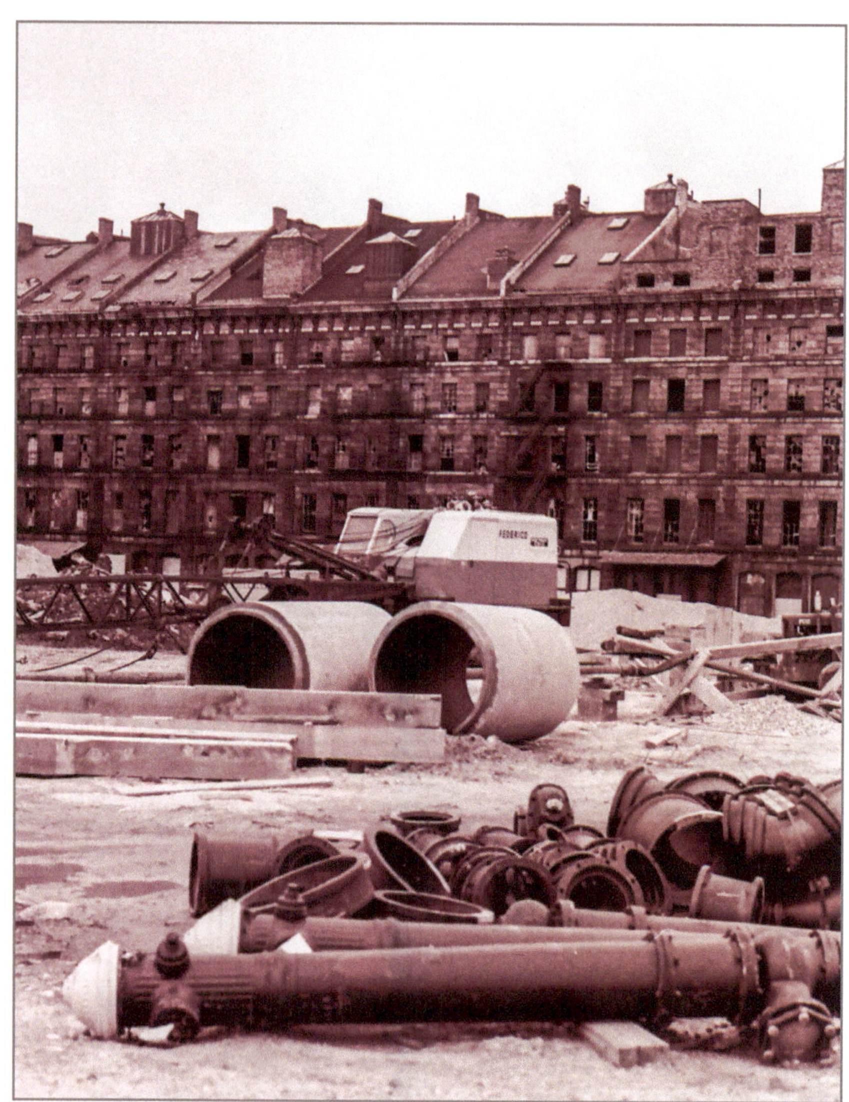

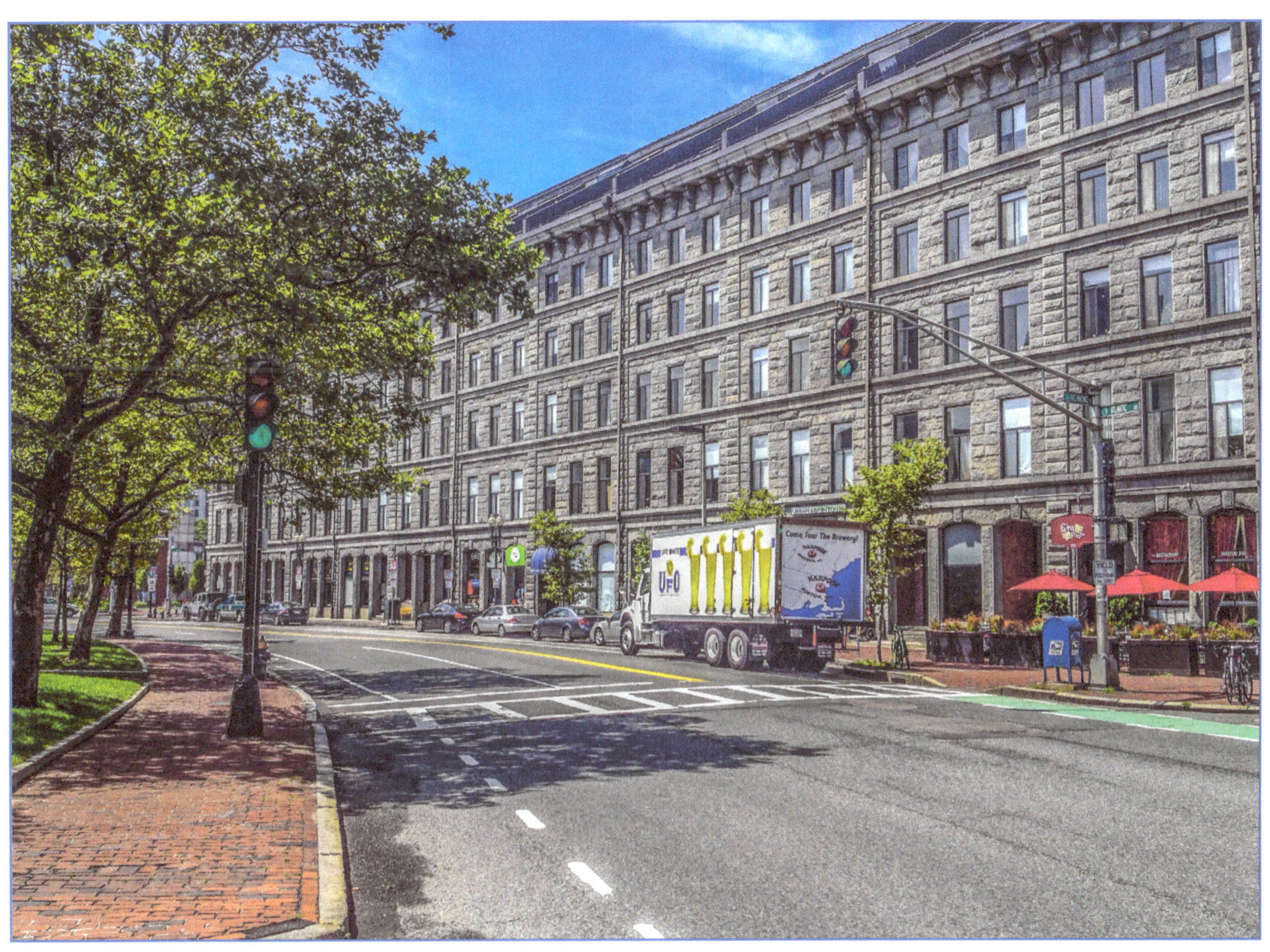

The Mercantile Building on Atlantic Avenue.

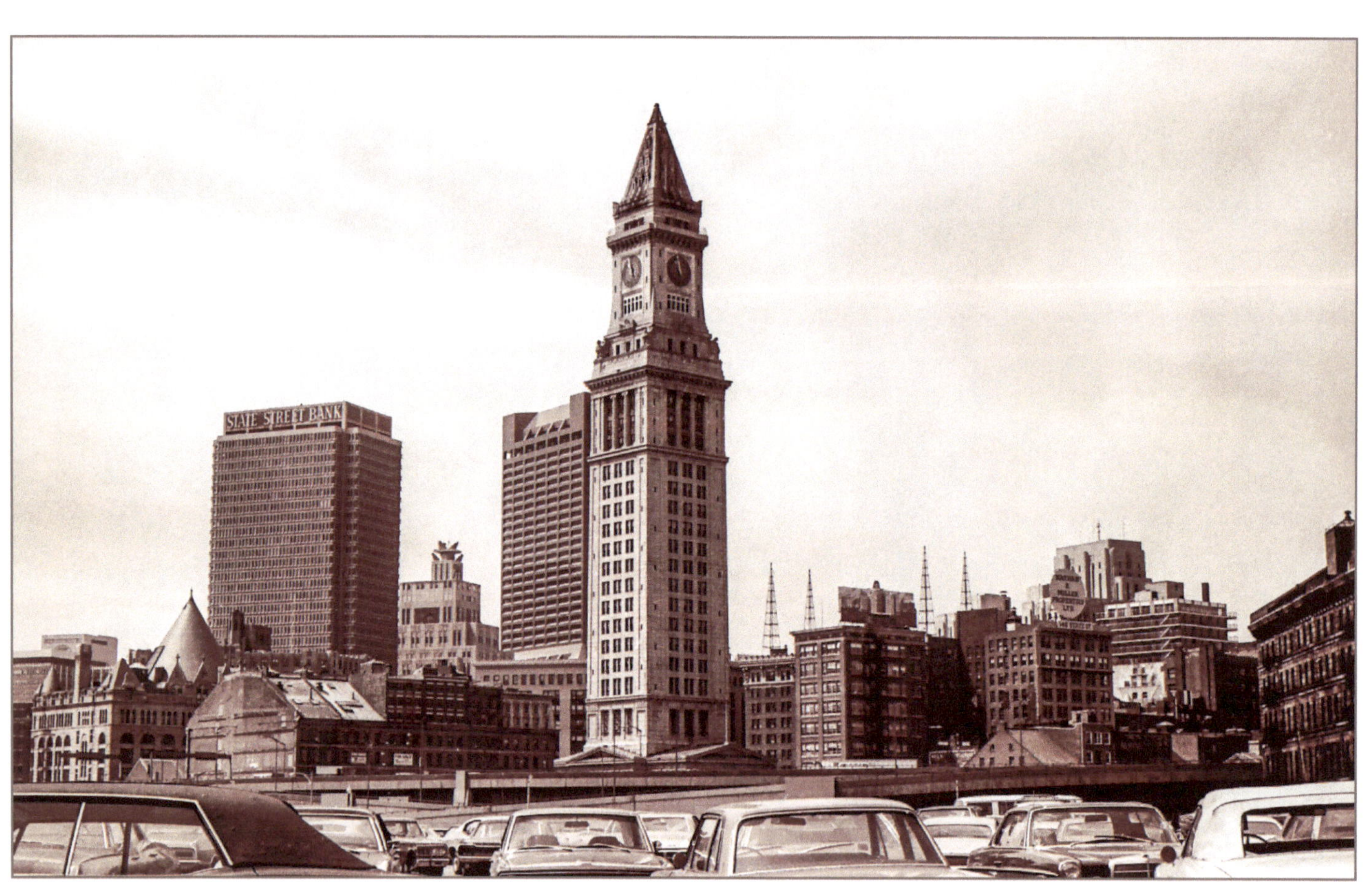
STATE STREET BANK

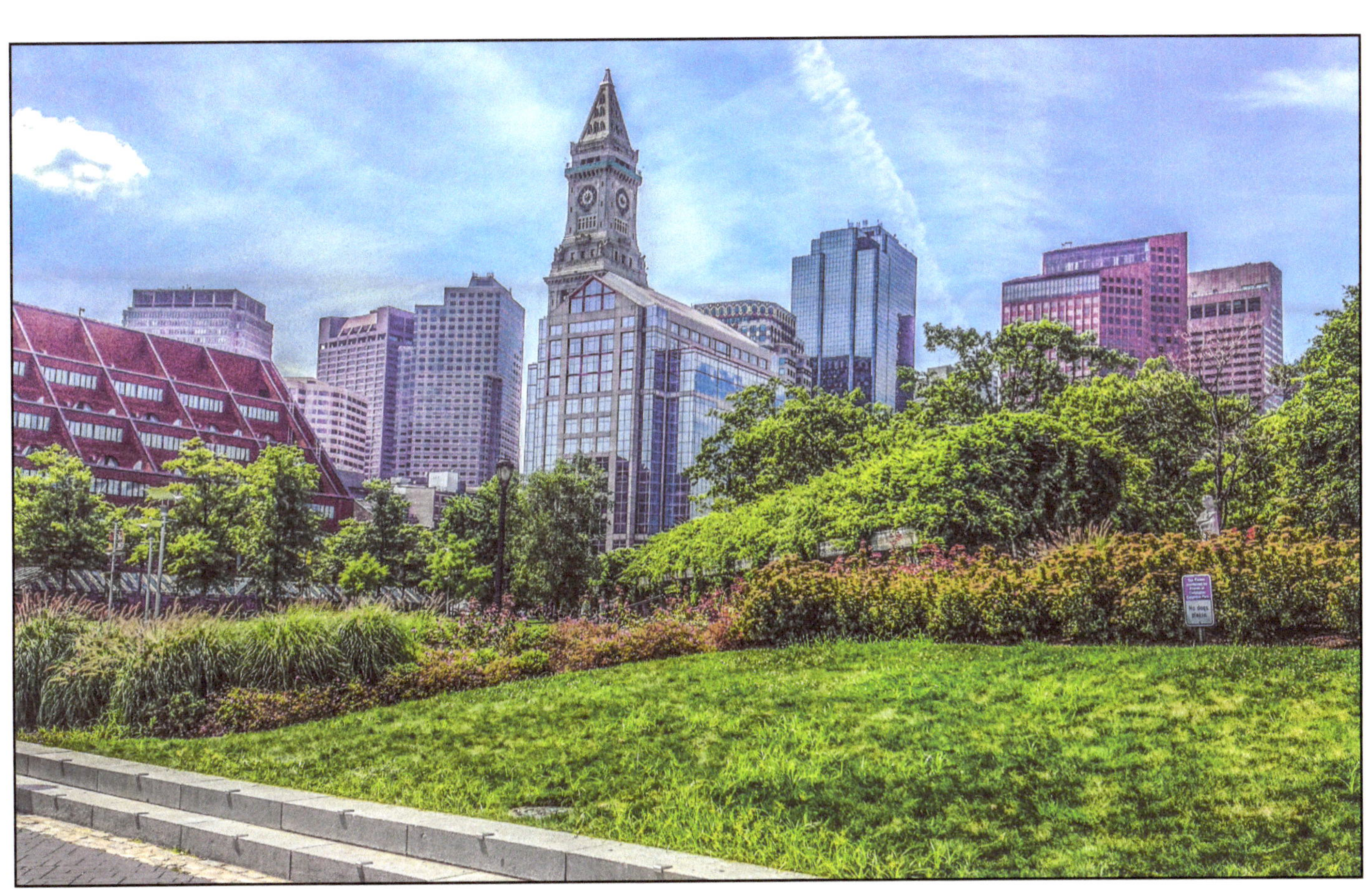

Environment was a seldom used word which referred to one's immediate surroundings, not something of planetary dimensions. It did not become a global crusade and international issue until after the first Earth Day in 1970 and the following efforts by groups with broader political agendas. Environmentalism became a cause.

That first Earth Day was attended by millions of hippies and flower children across the country at public events. But this was not a major issue of the day. The war in Vietnam garnered the headlines.

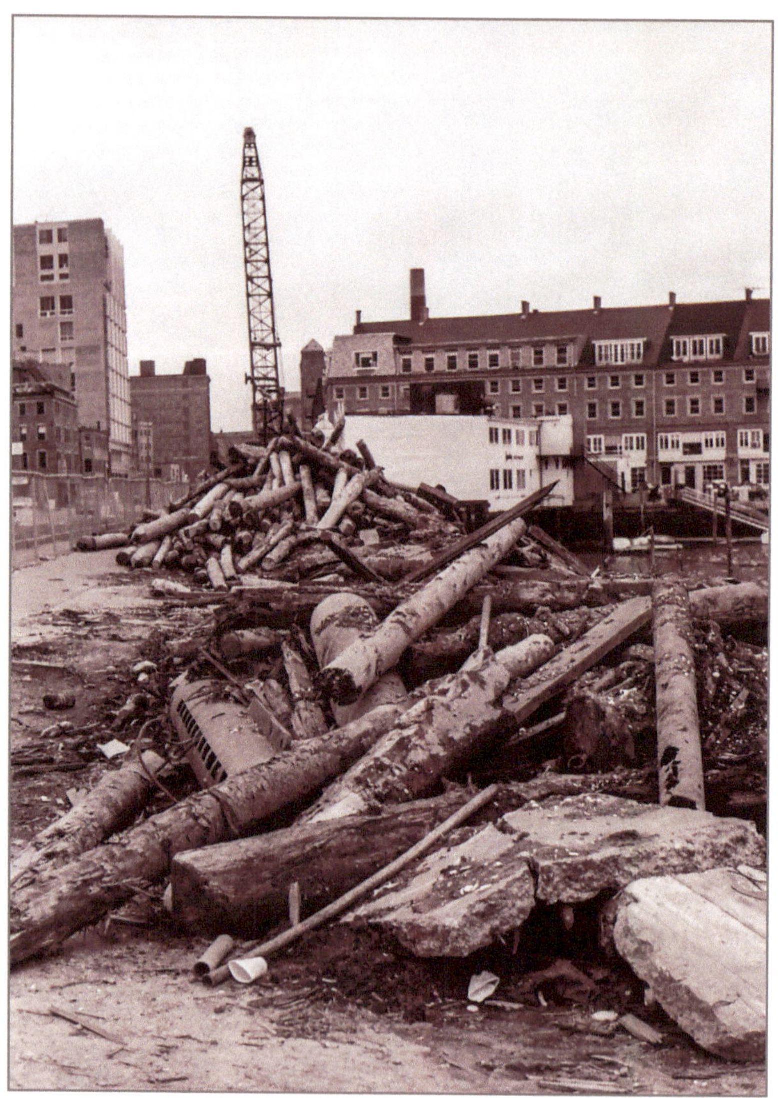

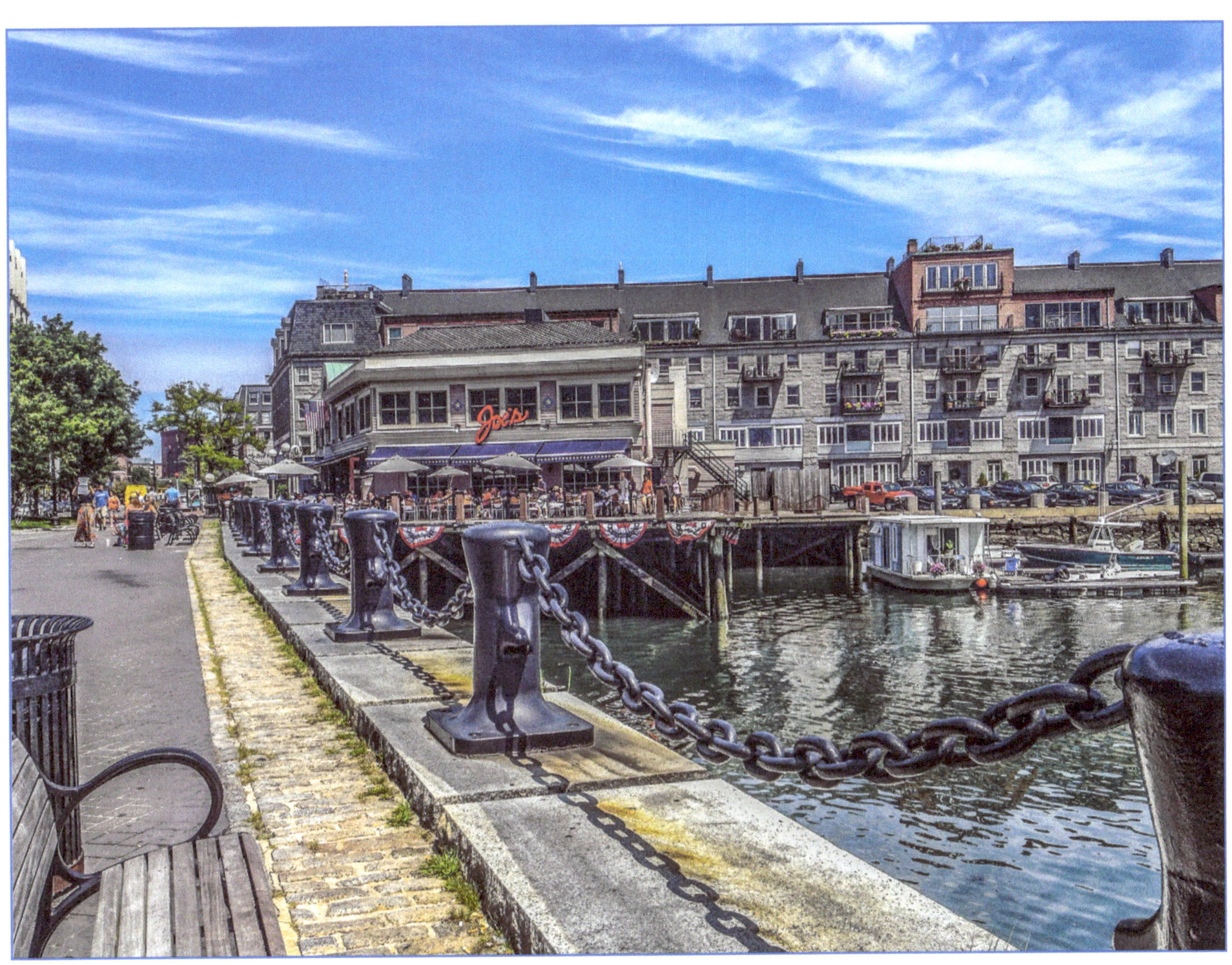

Commercial Wharf

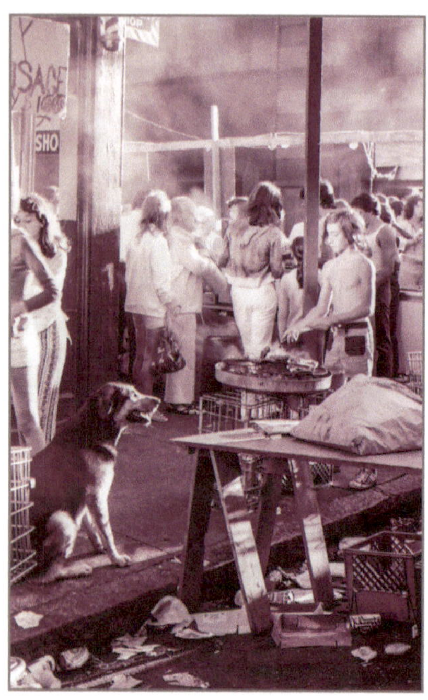

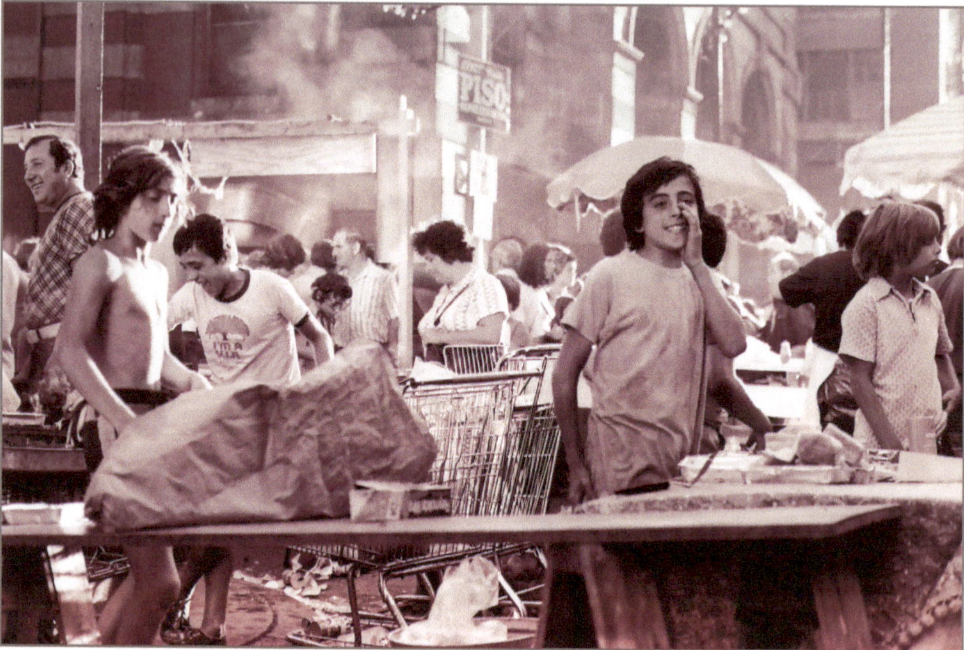

Digital imaging is unconstrained by the physical limitations of film, the financial realities of its cost, or, the time it takes to develop and print. It's about battery life, storage capacity and the data plan.

A person can take hundreds of pictures in a couple of hours and post them online immediately, but just loading film in a camera could ruin a 12 shot roll. And digital images are stored on a cloud while b&w negatives are kept in a musty trunk with contact sheets.

These scenes in the North End are a couple of blocks and forty years apart.

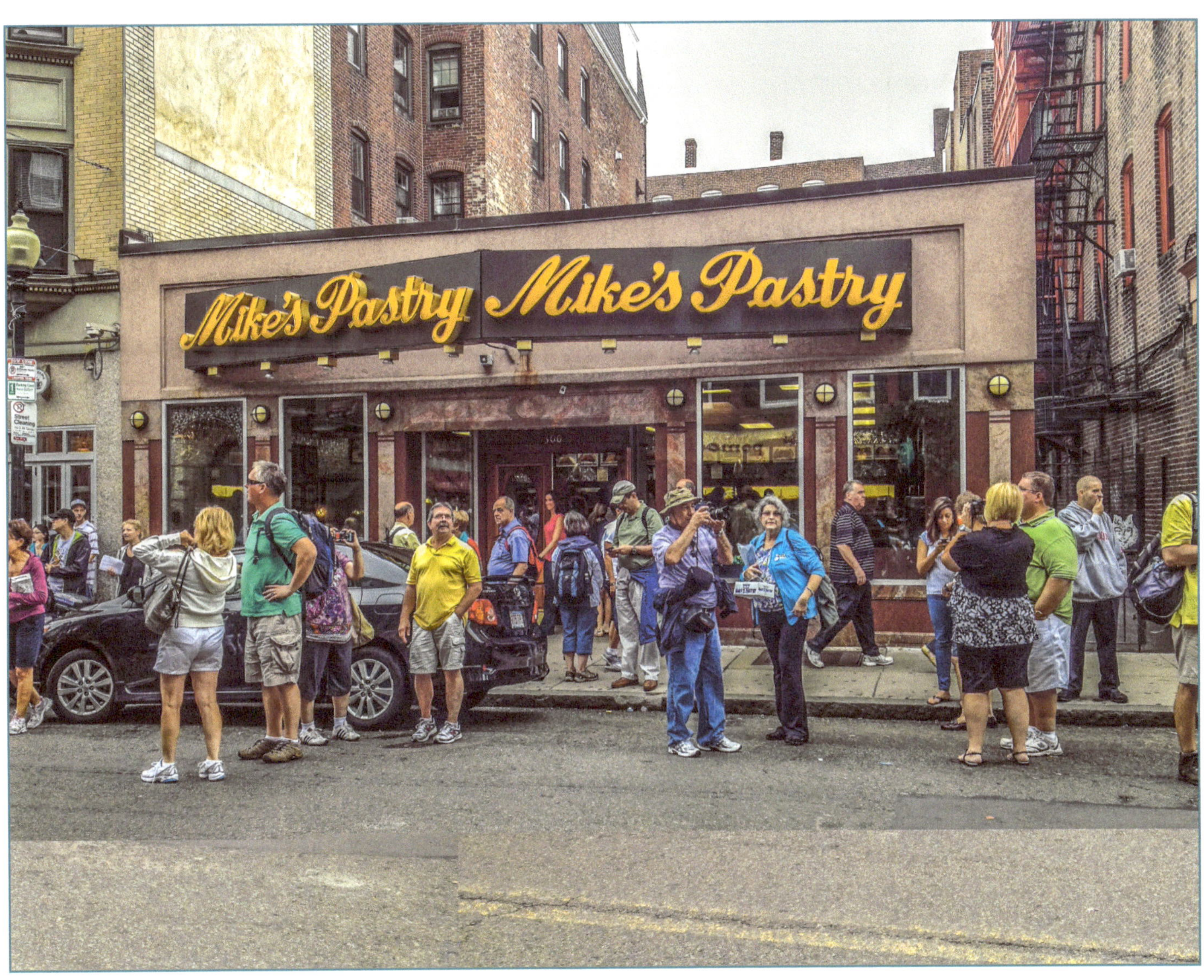
Mike's Pastry
Mike's Pastry

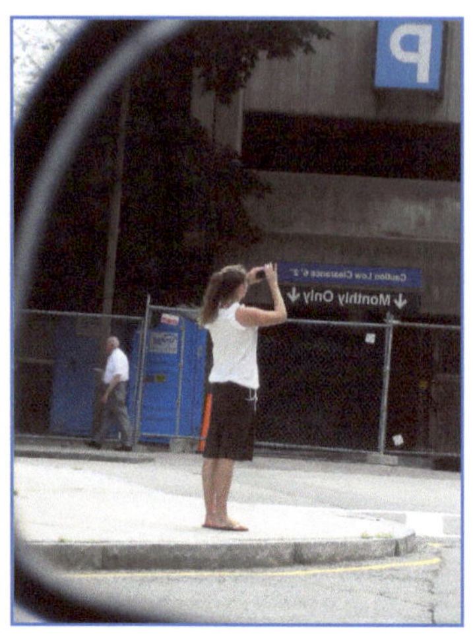

Alanna Reilly was born at St. Elizabeth's Hospital in the Brighton section of Boston. She graduated from Emmanuel College, in the Fens, in 2012.

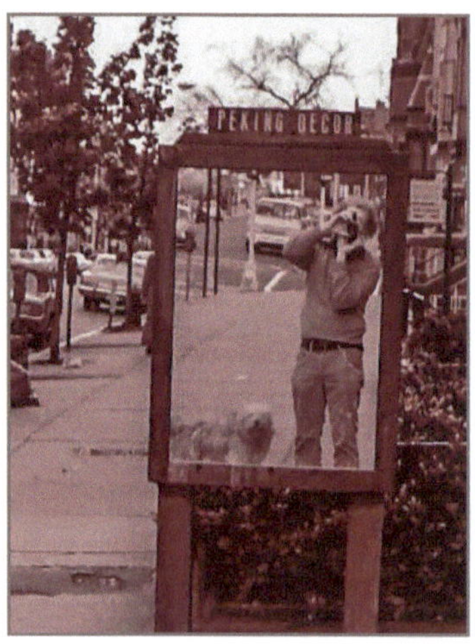

Gerald Reilly was born at St. Margaret's Hospital in the Dorchester section of Boston. He has enjoyed a life long affinity for the City.

www.ingramcontent.com/pod-product-compliance
Lightning Source LLC
LaVergne TN
LVHW070123110826
845147LV00002B/176